Intercultural Ethos Mediation
with the Mass Media

FORUM INTERDISZIPLINÄRE ETHIK

Herausgegeben von Gerfried W. Hunold

Band 27

PETER LANG
Frankfurt am Main · Berlin · Bern · Bruxelles · New York · Oxford · Wien

Jong Bom Lee

Intercultural Ethos Mediation with the Mass Media

Sympathy as the Means for the Mediation
of the Christian Ethos in the Modern
Confucian Society

PETER LANG
Frankfurt am Main · Berlin · Bern · Bruxelles · New York · Oxford · Wien

Die Deutsche Bibliothek - CIP-Einheitsaufnahme

Lee, Jong Bom:

Intercultural ethos mediation with the mass media : sympathy as the means for the mediation of the Christian ethos in the modern Confucian society / Jong Bom Lee. - Frankfurt am Main ; Berlin ; Bern ; Bruxelles ; New York ; Oxford ; Wien : Lang, 2001
  (Forum Interdisziplinäre Ethik ; Bd. 27)
  Zugl.: Tübingen, Univ., Diss., 2000
  ISBN 3-631-37197-7

BJ
1475
.L44
2001

D21
ISSN 0937-3861
ISBN 3-631-37197-7
US-ISBN 0-8204-4382-4

© Peter Lang GmbH
Europäischer Verlag der Wissenschaften
Frankfurt am Main 2001
All rights reserved.

All parts of this publication are protected by copyright. Any utilisation outside the strict limits of the copyright law, without the permission of the publisher, is forbidden and liable to prosecution. This applies in particular to reproductions, translations, microfilming, and storage and processing in electronic retrieval systems.

Printed in Germany 1 2 3 4 6 7

To my parents

Acknowledgement

With the great help of many persons with the heart of gold, I could have this work done. Some of them deserve my special thanks. Prof. Dr. Gerfried Werner Hunold, my Doktorvater, has given me every possible good advice, with which I could improve both my work and myself. Prof. Dr. Kyo-Hun Chin has been a long lasting guide for me wherever I was. Rev. Sung-Pal Park, whom I admire much, has been my personal role model. Prof. Dr. Albert Biesinger has given me encouragement to keep go on when I was down. Prof. Dr. Michael Eckert has showed me an interest in my work. Dr. Meinrad Limbeck, a good teacher of my life, has done his best for me in every possible situation. He will be always remembered. Dr. Thomas Weißer, a wonderful person whom I owe many things in various ways. Peter, a great friend of mine who is not only helpful but also thoughtful. They are all my great help.

Carina and Hyacinta are wonderful persons who have taught me the positive point of view and "Mut zum Leben".

My parents are just the best in this world. My sisters and brother are to be mentioned for their amazing and sacrificing support for me. It is not just for my work but also for my life itself. They know very well what I mean with it.

June 13, 2000, at Wilhelmstift in Tübingen

Contents

1. Prologue : An Attempt to the Intercultural Understanding --------------- 11

2. Aim and Method of the Study -- 16
   2.1 Intercultural Understanding with the Interactive Mass Media ------------- 16
   2.2 Phenomenological Approach to the Theme --------------------------------- 18

3. Preliminary Concepts Related to the Theme -------------------------------- 19
   3.1 The Modern Confucian Society --- 19
      3.1.1 General Concept -- 19
      3.1.2 The Chinese Model: Patriarchal Society --------------------------------- 20
      3.1.3 The Japanese Model: Feudal Society ------------------------------------ 22
      3.1.4 The Colonial Model: Incessant Search for Identity -------------------- 25
      3.1.5 The New Approach of Mutual Understanding in the Globalized
           World --- 27
   3.2 The Christian Ethos: Phenomenologically Understood --------------------- 29
   3.3 Sympathy as the Mediating Concept for Intercultural Understanding ---- 31
   3.4 The Merit of the Phenomenological Method ------------------------------- 32
   3.5 Mass Media as the Appropriate Medium ----------------------------------- 33

4. The Loci of Sympathy in Its Religious Origin ------------------------------ 36
   4.1 The Confucian Jen as the Sympathy of Humanism ----------------------- 36
      4.1.1 Whose Jen is It? - Confucius versus Mencius -------------------------- 36
         4.1.1.1 The Etymological Meaning of Jen --------------------------------- 36
         4.1.1.2 Confucian Jen as the Ideal Concept of Perfection ---------------- 38
         4.1.1.3 Mencian Jen as the Human Concept of Virtue -------------------- 40
      4.1.2 Jen and the "Ideal Man of Virtue" -------------------------------------- 43
      4.1.3 The Anthropological Aspect of Jen ------------------------------------- 44
      4.1.4 The Sociological Aspect of Jen --- 47
      4.1.5 The Moral Aspect of Jen -- 47
   4.2 Christian Love as the Sympathy of Social Justice -------------------------- 50
      4.2.1 The Pauline Interpretation of Christian Love -------------------------- 50
      4.2.2 The Theological Aspect of Christian Love ---------------------------- 52
      4.2.3 The Anthropological Aspect of Christian Love ------------------------ 54
      4.2.4 The Sociological Aspect of Christian Love --------------------------- 56
      4.2.5 The Moral Aspect of Christian Love ---------------------------------- 57

5. Sympathy in Its Phenomenological Context --- 61
5.1 The Etymological Exposition of Sympathy --- 61
5.1.1 συμπάθεια: The Western Understanding of Sympathy --- 61
5.1.2 Tong Qing: The Asian Understanding of Sympathy --- 63
5.1.3 συμ and πάθος: The Synthesis of Emotion and Will --- 64
5.2 Person as the Subject of Sympathy --- 65
5.2.1 The Dynamic Relation of Mind and Body --- 65
5.2.2 "I" and "Me": The Complexity of Identity with Mead's Theory --- 68
5.2.3 The Transcendental Ego as the Center of Identity --- 71
5.2.4 The Intersubjectivity as the Prerequisite of Mutual Understanding --- 75
5.2.5 The Life World as the "Common Sense" for Sympathy --- 76

6. Sympathy in its Mode and Phenomena --- 81
6.1 The Mode of Sympathy --- 81
6.1.1 Positive and Negative - Scheler versus Schopenhauer --- 81
6.1.2 The Genetic Development of Sympathy --- 84
6.1.3 The Extension of Sympathy in the Society from Individual --- 85
6.2 The Phenomena of Sympathy --- 87
6.2.1 Sympathy with Other as the Reactive Concern for Fellow Human Beings --- 87
6.2.1.1 Empathy as the Primary Phase of Passive Sympathy --- 87
6.2.1.2 Mitgefühl as the Social Prerequisite for Sympathy --- 89
6.2.1.3 Ce Yin: The Confucian Understanding of Sympathy --- 91
6.2.2 Sympathy for Other with the Sense of Responsibility --- 94
6.2.2.1 Condolence as the Primary Phase of Active Sympathy --- 94
6.2.2.2 Compassion: The Action with the Sense of Responsibility --- 98
6.2.2.3 Benevolence: The Ideal State of Sympathy --- 103

7. Sympathy in the Modern Confucian Society --- 105
7.1 New Challenges in Understanding the Confucian Society --- 105
7.1.1 The Disruption of the Traditional Concept of Time and Space --- 105
7.1.2 The Wreckage of the Traditional Intellectualism through the Technological Development --- 107
7.1.3 The Limits of Adopted Myth of Perpetual Progress --- 109
7.2 Sympathy Lost as the Results of Misfitted Modernity in the Confucian Society --- 111
7.2.1 The Collapse of the Traditional Confucian Humanism --- 111
7.2.2 The Broken Bondage of Family Relation --- 114
7.2.3 The Partial Understanding of Christianism as Meta-Physical Idea --- 115
7.2.4 The Bad Case of Capitalism Lacking the Spirit of Christian Morality --- 118

8. Limited Sympathy Mediation with the Traditional Mass Media ------- 122
8.1 The Unilaterality of the Traditional Mass Media -------------------------- 122
8.1.1 The Communication of One to Many: A Condition for Manipulation --- 122
8.1.2 Monopolized Information as Commodity ----------------------------- 124
8.1.3 Manipulated Consensus for Special Group-Interest ------------------- 127
8.2 The Distorted Sympathy: The Abuse of the Unilateral Mass Media ------------------------------------ 131
8.2.1 Manipulated Sympathy for the Biased Group-Interest ---------------- 131
8.2.2 Closed Sympathy as the Result of the Disintegration of Society --- 133
8.3 Problematic Ethos Mediation Based on the Unilateral Understanding - 134

9. Sympathy Diffusion through the Interactive Mass Media ---------------- 137
9.1 Interactivity: The New Dimension of Mass Media ------------------------ 137
9.1.1 Multi-Reciprocity: The Condition of Just Communication --------- 137
9.1.2 Open Information as the Basic Terms of Open Society -------------- 140
9.1.3 The Democratic Structure of Reciprocal Communication ----------- 142
9.2 The Open Mass Media as the Appropriate Medium for Mutual Understanding -- 145
9.2.1 Formal Prerequisites -- 145
9.2.1.1 The Institutionalization of Interactivity -------------------------- 145
9.2.1.2 The Multiplexing of the Mass Media ----------------------------- 148
9.2.1.3 The Reciprocal Control of the Mass Media --------------------- 149
9.2.2 The Betterment of Contents -- 151
9.2.2.1 The Limitation of Sex and Violence for the Just Mass Media 151
9.2.2.2 Advertisement Management ----------------------------------- 153
9.2.2.3 Sympathetic Role Model as Preferred Mediator ---------------- 155
9.3 Interactive Ethos Mediation in the Information Age ------------------- 157

10. The Initiation of Modern Confucian Society with Sympathy ---------- 159
10.1 Mutual Understanding under the Environment of Open Information - 159
10.1.1 Intersubjective Understanding: Escape from the Special Group-Interest to the "Enlightened Self-Interest" -------------------------- 159
10.1.2 Intercultural Understanding in the Globalized World ------------- 161
10.2 Sympathy for the Accommodative Society ------------------------------ 164
10.2.1 The Symbiosis of the Monadic Identities --------------------------- 164
10.2.2 The Harmonious Society as the Extended Confucian Family ---- 168
10.3 "Symbiotic Society" with the Interactive Communication of Masses 169
10.3.1 Communicable Identity Building as Prerequisite for Mutual Understanding -- 169
10.3.2 The Open Consensus Built for the Just Mutual Understanding -- 171

11. Epilogue: Love in Jen and Jen in Love ------------------------------------ 176

Bibliography -- 182

Appendix -- 189

1. Prologue: An Attempt to the Intercultural Understanding

For many people in the West the tantalizing fragrance of hot coffee and the softly melting butter on a slice of bread in the morning are irresistible temptations, but for many people in Asia they cause not seldom just a stomachache. For many people in the West the ringing bells of the church on Sunday are heavenly music, but for many people in Asia it is an annoying infringement upon the peaceful rest on a sunny Sunday morning.

There are still many cases of unbridgeable abysses between different cultures, but many people of younger generation in the world, regardless of their cultural differences, not only know who Michael Jackson is but also like his song even if sometimes many of them do not quite understand the text of the song. As Coca-Cola, Michael Jackson would not become so famous in the whole world if it were not for the mass media. What would have happened if the followers of Jesus Christ had had radio, TV, and even the Internet, besides their wonderful belief and enthusiasm? It is for everybody's guess.

Man tends to believe what he wants to believe as much as what he must believe. That is the main reason why there have been so many zealots not only with the matter of religion but also even with that of natural science. It has little changed in our age. Our era is called "Information Age" in comparison to the Industrial Age of the 18th century. We cannot exactly pinpoint the beginning of this age, but we may say that it has begun with the invention of telephone by Alexander Graham Bell in 1876. Forty-nine years later, John Logie Baird made a machine called "Television" which has become the favorite medium of the Information Age. In 1927, the closed-circuit pictures of Herbert Hoover were sent from Washington, D.C. to New York, and an experimental TV station was built there in the Empire State Building in 1932.[1] Until recently audiovisual information can be transmitted from a point to almost all corners of the world by telephone and television, but it was not until the invention of computer, Internet and WWW (World Wide Web) that we really have begun to call our era the Information Age.[2] Only since the middle of the 1980s, computer and Internet

---

[1] Keenan, Kelvin L., "Advertising" in Handbook on Mass Media in the United States: The Industry and Its Audiences, Erwin K. Thomas and Brown H. Carpenter (Ed.) (Westport, CT: Greenwood Press, 1994), xiv

[2] The first all-purpose digital computer, ENIAC (electronic numerical integrator and computer), was invented by J. Eckert and John Mauchly at the University of Pennsylvania in 1946.

The history of Internet has begun with the Sputnik-Shock. President Dwight D. Eisenhower saw the need for the Advanced Research Projects Agency (ARPA) after the Soviet Union's 1957 launch of Sputnik. The organization united some of America's most brilliant people, who developed the United States' first successful satellite in 18 months. Several years later ARPA began to focus on computer networking and communications technology. In 1962, Dr.

have become relatively ubiquitous commodities. The new era has just begun. Therefore we may still have different opinions about the definition of the Information Age, and of the media, especially the mass media. The traditional mass media like book, newspaper, periodic, radio, and TV do still have their strongholds in the society. As the refinement of gadgets for the Information Age

---

J.C.R. Licklider was chosen to head ARPA's research in improving the military's use of computer technology. Licklider was a visionary who sought to make the government's use of computers more interactive. To quickly expand technology, Licklider saw the need to move ARPA's contracts from the private sector to universities and laid the foundations for what would become the ARPANET. (By Will Lewis and Randy Reitz)

The visible results of Licklider's fruitful approach came short after... 1969: The first LOGs: UCLA – Stanford. (According to Vinton Cerf:) The UCLA people proposed to DARPA to organize and run a Network Measurement Center for the ARPANET project... Around Labor Day in 1969, BBN delivered an Interface Message Processor (IMP) to UCLA that was based on a Honeywell DDP 516, and when they turned it on, it just started running. It was hooked by 50 Kbps circuits to two other sites (SRI and UCSB) in the four-node network: UCLA, Stanford Research Institute (SRI), UC Santa Barbara (UCSB), and the University of Utah in Salt Lake City. (According to Knight-Ridder Newspapers:)

The plan was unprecedented: Kleinrock, a pioneering computer science professor at LCLA, and his small group of graduate students hoped to log onto the Stanford computer and try to send it some data. They would start by typing "logwin," and seeing if the letters appeared on the far-off monitor. "We set up a telephone connection between us and the guys at SRI...," Kleinrock, now 62, said in an interview. "We typed the L and we asked on the phone, 'Do you see the L?' 'Yes, we see the L,' came the response. We typed the O, and we asked, 'Do you see the O.' 'Yes, we see the O.' Then we typed the G, and the system crashed...Yet a revolution had began"...(Source: Sacramento Bee, May 1, 1996, p.D1)

The history of WWW has begun in CERN (even though the name for this laboratory is now Laboratorie Europeen pour la Physique des Particules, European Laboratory for Particle Physics, it was originally called Conseil Europeen pour la Recherche Nucleaire, European Council for Nuclear Research, and its initial has not changed since). While consulting for CERN June-December of 1980, **Tim Berners-Lee** writes a notebook program, "Enquire-Within-Upon-Everything", which allows links to be made between arbitrary nodes. Each node had a title, a type, and a list of bi-directional typed links. "ENQUIRE" run on Norsk Data machines under SINTRAN-III. In March 1989, "Information Management: A Proposal" written by Tim BL and circulated for comments at CERN (TBL). Paper "HyperText and CERN" produced as background (text or WriteNow format). In May 1990, same proposal recirculated. In October project proposal reformulated with encouragement from CN and ECP divisional management. Robert Cailliau (ECP) is co-author. **Tim picks World Wide Web as a name for the project** (over Information Mesh, Mine of Information, and Information Mine). **In November initial WorldWideWeb program developed on the NeXT (TBL)** . This was a wysiwyg browser/editor with direct inline creation of links. In November technical student Nicola Pellow (CN) joins and starts work on the line-mode browser. Bernd Pollermann (CN) helps get interface to CERNVM "FIND" index running. TBL gives a colloquium on hypertext in general. In Christmas line mode browser and NeXTStep browser/editor demonstrable. Access is possible to hypertext files, CERNVM "FIND", and Internet news articles. --- Main sources from the Web Site of www.internetvally.com

advances, the renovation of our way of thought is forcefully demanded whether we like it or not. There are many people who have an intention to merge computer, TV and Internet into a machine called "Interactive TV" or "Internet TV" which would work for multi-purposes in the future. It is not only hardware, i.e., computer, TV and Internet, that goes under change, but also software, i.e., computer programs and the way of human thought.

Intangible knowledge and information are becoming the prime driving forces of the society in the coming centuries, as the traditional tangible goods have been so until now. The wired or globalized world means a world of communication and mutual understanding where isolation and the lack of information just have to mean under-development.

The mass media of our age still does not have their ideal form, if any, but we cannot live without them, not even a single moment. How the world of technology of the day can be defined is not a simple matter, but one thing is clear that we cannot imagine other than the mass media where technology shows its triumphal advancement. One of the newest technologies for the mass media is the interactive TV. We cannot only choose what we want to watch but also react instantly to the program of any broadcasting station. This reciprocal relation between the masses and the mass media is new. There has been just a unilateral relation between them until now. A viewer has had just two chances until now: either to stay tuned or to keep changing TV program channels until he finds what must be the most suitable for his need. The viewers could hardly influence the mass media. Only the passive audience rating is counted for the commercial purpose of the mass media. With the interactive TV, a viewer can react directly to the program he is watching, and he can even change the contents of it.

Neither hardware nor software alone guarantees the full interactivity of the interactive TV itself. The mass media cannot change themselves radically before their position as the main providers of information is challenged and become just partners of the whole information management processes. The danger of information monopoly by some big broadcasting companies still lingers in our Information Age. Only the building of the interactive mass media could prevent this.

If information cannot be shared among people democratically, it is much worse than the Middle Ages when the small army of intellectuals and rulers monopolized it. In the Middle Ages, the illiteracy of the masses was not a great social problem because the main economic basis of the society was agriculture, which needed not the speculative knowledge written in Latin, but the practical knowledge, which could be learned and handed down mainly through bare experiences. The total social productivity then was not hurt by the monopoly of information, but promoted somehow by the ignorance of the multitude because it contributed, if passively, the sociopolitical stability in the Middle Ages.

In the Information Age, information monopoly means distortion of the social structure because information is the basic resource of the social wealth. When not enough wealth is produced or unjustly distributed among the people, there is always the social unrest. The democratic mass media, which are called the sympathetic mass media here, play here an important role not only for the stable and harmonious society, but also for the true mutual understanding among the people in the globalized world.

Multicultural ethos mediation is a good example of mutual understanding in the globalized Information Age. When we want to understand other cultures, which cannot help having local characters, we need an interpreter, or rather, a mediator. Before our age, there have been many attempts of individuals to understand other cultures, but individual effort has had always its limit in scope and universality because every individual must have his personal biography influencing greatly his way of thought and point of view. Even a society, in which an individual has grown and is assimilated, has also its own character and point of view, which can be interpreted not seldom as prejudice. Spatio-temporal distance has made it much difficult for the people of the world to understand each other before our age.

In our globalized Information Age, there are still many difficulties in mutual understanding among different cultures, not only because the information revolution is still under way, but also because mutual prejudices still linger. It is always a problem as long as the correct point of view for a society can be, more or less, a prejudice for the other society, especially when it goes about the matter of norm and consensus building. That is why we need a mediator. Consensus cannot be made unless all affected can freely accept the consequences and the side effects that the general observance of a controversial norm can be expected to have for the satisfaction of the interests of each individual.[3] As real experiences in the life world show, accepting a foreign proposal, let alone a foreign norm, is extremely difficult because it means not seldom abandoning one's interest. It is much like the Christian self-sacrifice for the enemy.

It is clear that we need a universal norm for the mutual understanding among people, especially when we want to avoid relativism, both moral and philosophical, but tacitly forcing the other party to accept one's own norm unconditionally is sometimes worse than the relativism. In this case, we need a third party, which could be accepted by both concerned parties, so that it could be avoided the forced universality of a norm. We cannot guarantee that this third party has a true neutrality until another truly neutral party guarantees it. Here happens the problem of logical regression, which cannot be solved easily. That is why we need a parallel consensus building, for which it is not needed for the

---

[3] Habermas, Jürgen, Moral Consciousness and Communicative Action (Cambridge: MIT Press, 1990), p93

concerned parties to give up their respective positions, let alone their respective identities. Certainly, it presupposes tacitly the universality of human reason, but it is the human reason in the life world, i.e., on the basis of common sense. Two parties can begin to build consensus when they accept what they want to accept. When there are points, which they cannot accept, they can stow them away for a moment, i.e.; they can make a phenomenological ἐποχή upon them until they find out the acceptable common ground. Until then, they can have parallel consensus, which is partly shared but has a potential of the true consensus in the future. Parallel consensus means not partial consensus, which might be confused with compromise, but an open consensus for the future.

For this kind of consensus building, it is very important that we have the sympathetic mass media. The mass media has been already a very important means for the consensus building, but it has been mostly for the mobilization of the masses to make profit for some people who has been in the position of information manipulation. Such phenomena have been and still are very pervasive in many modern Confucian societies. The traditional Confucian hierarchical sociopolitical structure has facilitated such manipulation of the mass media by the rulers, but the rash increase of the enlightened middle class, which is the result of the economic development intended to calm the sociopolitical discontents under the dictatorial regime, has made it impossible for the rulers any more to maintain the rigid social structure as before. The sociopolitical change is under way in most of the Asian countries which have been under the strong Confucian influence of old China even if the mode and speed of the change are vary according to their different situation. Almost all kinds of the modern mass media in the Asian countries have been imported from the West only after the "Opening to the West (開 港)", therefore they are foreign to the traditional Confucian society, and have to be assimilated to the existing hierarchical social structure. Freedom of the press has had to be ceded for the harmony of society, which was the supreme priority in the Confucian tradition. Even in the mass media themselves, the hierarchical structure has been accepted as a norm. Nevertheless, the sociopolitical change in the modern Confucian society is forcing the renovation of the mass media, and the technological progress in the Information Age made it even the necessary step for the bare survival of the mass media in the next centuries.

The commercialization of the mass media and its bad influence for the society in the West have already provoked the discussion about the mass media ethics. The commercialism itself cannot be blamed because the mass media themselves have become the commercial entities as any other industries in the post-industrial society. They have to make profit to survive in the society of severe competition.

However, what the modern mass media need is the "enlightened commercialism", a commercialism with the sense of responsibility for the society. It is not clear how the mass media in the modern Confucian society can strike two birds at once, i.e., inner democratization and enlightened commercialism. The hierarchical structure of the traditional Confucian society can be truly Confucian only when it is based on the rational humanism, which cherished by all Confucian gurus. Freedom of the press is good as long as it goes with the Christian ethos of love, which shows us the way to the individual freedom in the community of fraternal and even self-sacrificing humanism. This humanism practiced in the form of interactivity is an approach to the ideal society, and at the same time, the multicultural understanding in the globalized world.

2. Aim and Method of the Study

2.1 Intercultural Understanding with the Interactive Mass Media

To understand other cultures, we need, most of all, information about them. This information must be true, i.e., there must be no distortion in the source of the information, no change by the transfer of the information, and last but not least, no prejudiced interpretation of the information. In this chain of information processing there has been tremendous progress in the part of the information transfer with the help of the telephone lines and computer networks in our age.

As the globalization goes on in rapid stride, changes happen not only in the field of commerce and finance but also in other fields and one of them is the cultural one. However, the intercultural understanding does not go as smoothly as the international monetary transaction, not only because there still lacks the gadgetry for the intercultural understanding between different cultures but also because there are still too many stereotypic pictures of the other party, which exert great negative influence in mutual understanding. It is quite strange that in our age of Internet, i.e., the "information highway" with the computerized network of information exchange, there should be such a distorted intercultural understanding. It is true that there is still quantitative limits to Internet since there are just about 100 million people in the world who has the direct access to the Internet.[4] Before Internet comes, there already has been the network of information, i.e., newspaper, radio and TV. They are called the mass media because of their relation to the public as the masses. These mass media exert still great influences upon many people who just want to know and to understand the facts of the world. As a matter of fact, most of the people in the developed

---

[4] Weltbild, N. 14, 4. Juli 1997, (Augsburg: Weltbild GmbH, 1997), p 29, In 2000 it is expected more than 200 millions are connected to the Internet.

countries have chances to have too much information to be digested every day. Even though the information inundation happens in everyday life, there are still too many problems in intercultural understanding. We can make various efforts for the better mutual understanding between different cultures. One of them could be the improvement of the mass media.

As well known, the massive information dissemination through the mass media has an enormous influence in manipulating the consensus building of the masses. Especially in a time of extreme situation, for example wartime, the intentional manipulation of the mass media by the hands of small number of rulers has been a matter of course regardless of the concerned parties. As a matter of fact, freedom of the press is meant to promote the democratic communication, and this kind of communication should be the unbiased reciprocal transmission of information. The mass media must be used only for this purpose when it should be truly for the masses, but in reality there are still the phenomena of monopoly and manipulation of the mass media regardless of the cultural differences. For example, in the U.S.A., where the maturity and saturation of the mass media have no equal in the whole world, the commercialization has made the mass media just a medium for the sales promotion. Not only commodity but also information itself has become something to be sold with every possible means. Advertisements are not limited for the sales promotion but also used for the manipulation of the mind of the masses. The rating of program and the amount of circulation play a critical role both for the publicity agency and the mass media. In the society of free competition, maximizing the profit is a matter of the survival of the fittest, so for that purpose every possible means is allowed when it helps. Here, the sense of responsibility for the society plays a minor role.

This is not a favorable environment especially for the mutual understanding between different cultures because only an unbiased field of communication can be supportive for the true intercultural understanding, but we cannot abolish the profit oriented structure of the mass media at a stroke. A gradual improvement of the mass media is the only possible way for the better environment with the fewest unwanted side effects. There are many ways to improve the mass media, one of them could be the interactivity as long as it is for the democratic communication.

This study is aimed to show how the interactive mass media can be helpful for the intercultural understanding between different cultures with the example of two ethos, i.e., the Christian ethos and the Confucian ethos. With the help of the concept of sympathy it is shown here how two different ethos can approach to each other, i.e., understand each other, and furthermore, how this process of intercultural understanding can be more plausible with the help of the interactive mass media. Before we begin to approach to this matter to get the idea, we have to first understand a few preliminary concepts used in this study. Two most important concepts are sympathy and the interactive mass media.

Not only the etymological analysis but also the phenomenological analysis of the concept of the sympathy is needed because sympathy is interpreted differently in different cultures. With the phenomenology of Edmund Husserl it is shown not only that the concept of sympathy can be understood without presupposition, but also that intercultural ethos mediation is possible.

2.2 Phenomenological Approach to the Theme

This study is oriented mainly by the phenomenological method, in relation to the phenomenology of Edmund Husserl. In this way the ethical moment of sympathy will be deciphered. This study is not aiming to make a field study. It is about the descriptive method, with which we may elude the mutual prejudice as good as possible. As a matter of fact this mutual prejudice or misunderstanding happens not seldom in the course of the intercultural communication. In the end this study is going to have as its object the mutual understanding of respective ethos, i.e., the Christian and the Confucian, without any presupposition which could lead to the misunderstanding.

In the course of the study, the main concepts of phenomenology, like transcendental ego, intersubjectivity and life world, will be adopted for the better understanding of the inner relation of the subject of behavior, the human being as a person who is simultaneously subject and object of moral action.

Especially in chapter 5 where man is understood as the subject of sympathy, his identity and its relation with others and the outer world proper are analyzed with the phenomenological methodology. In this way both metaphysical and empirical presupposition about the nature of man could be excluded temporarily for the purpose of understanding his dynamic intersubjective relation, and furthermore his relation to the world. In chapter 4 where the loci of sympathy in both religions, i.e., Christianism and Confucianism, are searched, the phenomenological ἐποχη is applied to avoid the doctrinal controversy about core concepts of respective religion. For the etymological understanding of sympathy descriptive method of phenomenology is also applied in chapter 6.

3. Preliminary Concepts Related to the Theme

3.1 The Modern Confucian Society

3.1.1 General Concept

One type of the modern Confucian society should mean a society which has become a modern, i.e., Western like industrialized, society from the traditional Confucian society without the experience of colonization by the Western countries. This society is distinguished from those of African, Middle and South American, Middle Eastern and even most of the Southeast Asian countries, which had to experience the Western colonial period. To that kind of society belong China, Japan, Korea, and some Southeast Asian countries. On the other hand, there is the other type of modern Confucian society, which had the experience of colonization by the Western countries. In spite of the colonial experience this society is strongly Confucian because of the long lasted influence of the neighboring super power, i.e., China, which lingers until now. To this type of modern Confucian society belong most of the Southeast Asian countries. In the end, we can distinguish three types of the modern Confucian society. We may name them the Chinese model, the Japanese model, and the colonial model respectively.

In the modern Confucian society there is a capitalistic economic system without strong individualism and laissez-faire as in Europe or in the U.S.A. This Asian capitalism is based more or less on the strongly centralized government, which controls almost all state matters. The strongly centralized political system and the Confucian social moral play still a great role in this society. Every individual has his obliged role for the harmony of the society, so he should willingly sacrifice his own interest for the merit of it.

The influence of Confucianism over almost all Asian countries cannot be overestimated. There were other religious and philosophical schools than Confucianism, which had indisputable influence on the life and culture of the Asians, for example, Buddhism and Taoism, but the political and social structure of the Asian countries could not help imitating the Confucian culture of the then world super-power, i.e., China.

Until the beginning of the "modernization" of the Asian countries, there was strongly hierarchical sociopolitical structure, which allowed minimal change in every corner of the society. This Confucian society had a well-developed centralized bureaucratic political system. The Chinese Emperor, who was called the "Son of Heaven", had his place in the middle of the world with all possible powers over the whole human beings of the world, and all rulers of other Asian countries had to obey his imperial commands. In the end, all people of the world were virtually his subjects. To control his subjects at his will, the Emperor needed not only myths about his ancestors, which justified his supreme power, but also an well-organized and loyal bureaucracy. For this purpose he found the fitting theory in the teaching of Confucius. Confucianism was a political theory with the purpose of building a harmonious society in the eyes of the rulers. The principle structure of Confucian society is simple: Under the rule of the Emperor, who incarnates Heavenly Virtues(德) in himself, the bureaucracy of scholars, who are chosen through the state-examinations, which test mainly the understanding of the teaching of Confucianism, administrates almost everything in the Confucian society for one purpose: a harmonious society where nobody feels sorry. Theoretically, this is a society where the Platonic philosopher-king rules. Interestingly there is always a chance for someone who has the heavenly virtues in himself to be an Emperor when the existing Emperor loses his qualification as the Son of Heaven. In this case it is not a revolt against the Emperor but a just revolution against the unjust ruler.

There is no after life in Confucianism as in Buddhism or Christianism, therefore everybody tries to make the best of his present life. The old Confucian bureaucrats were no exception. They managed political struggle in the name of right interpretation of the Confucian teaching. The various schools of the Confucianism became different political parties, and their disputes were both for scholastic discussion and for the power struggle. The winning party got everything, and the Emperor needed such a party rivalry among his subjects for his firm grip on the political power. To control all matters of the Confucian society in the real world, he needed too big a bureaucracy, and as most of the big bureaucratic organizations, it resulted in inefficiency, and corruption in the end.

3.1.2 The Chinese Model: Patriarchal Society

The first three sage kings of ancient China, Yao (堯), Shun (舜) and Yu (禹), were the most cherished rulers of China by Confucius himself. They had become almost the deities of heaven, but never religious figures. There is a single instance of the word "T'ien (天)", Heaven, used in the restricted sense of the Heaven, the abode of deities. It occurs in a prayer, patriotically offered up, in 1120 BC, to the immediate canonized ancestors of the first king of the Chow Dynasty, who was dangerously ill, and runs as follows:

"*If you three kings have charge in T'ien (天), Heaven, of your great descendant, let my life be a substitute for his.*"[5]

The good ruler, who might have come from the Heaven, must rule this world with earthly virtues and wisdom in China. This tradition was systematized and canonized by the works of Confucius and his followers. This tradition survived not only the great Western influences in the 19th century but also even the

---

[5] Giles, Herbert A., Confucianism and its Rivals (London: Williams and Norgate, 1915), p 11

"Cultural Revolution" in China under Mao Tse-Tung between 1965 and 1967.

China had already a contact with Christianism through the missionary work of the Jesuit priest, Matteo Ricci (1552-1610). He translated the Bible into Chinese, which has been the main source of Christianism not only for the Chinese but also for people in other Asian countries. However, as a whole, Christianism with the influence of the Western material culture had no significant influence on China until the forced "Opening to the West (開 港)".

Before the "Opening to the West (開 港)" there was already a great demand for the renewal of the Confucian society from the multitudes. China lost war against the then world superpower, Great Britain, in 1842 for the first time in her history, which was called "Opium War". After this war China was forced to open her ports to the Western countries according to the Nanking Treaty. This was not only a great humiliation for China as the middle of the world but also the beginning of the collapse of the strongly centralized Confucian society. China needed time to find a new virtuous leader after she lost her face against Great Britain, but China had to be in disgrace again, this time by Japan. In 1895, 52 years and 41 years after the "Opium War" and the "Opening" of Japan respectively, China lost war against Japan for the first time in her history, and had to yield Korea to Japan. In 1911 the Emperor of China was dethroned and China became the Republic of China in 1912, but China was too big to be totally mobilized for the modernization with ease. The Chinese had to wait another 37 years until Mao Tse-Tung won over Tschiang Kai-Schek in September 1949. The family oriented nepotism and political corruption of the party of Tschiang hindered the modernization of the Republic of China, and in the end, promoted the collapse of itself. Mao was not much better. Under the rule of Mao, who was de facto the Emperor of China after the "Cultural Revolution", the new People's Republic of China closed her door to the West and failed to become a modernized country even though she tried every possible method. Her self-esteem was so big that it took long time to open her door voluntarily to the world. The people of the People's Republic of China were accustomed to the political system of one-man dictatorship, so they had not so great difficulty to accept Mao as their new quasi-Emperor, as long as they had something to eat and a house to live in. The Chinese still have the tendency of strong personality cult that stems from the long history of China cherishing the Confucian harmonious society where the hierarchical social order had not only the absolute grip on the society but also a basis for the supreme virtue of Jen (仁). The Chinese communism has never been true to the Marxist theory. She has never opened herself to the world. Even if there had been no communistic regime in the People's Republic of China, it would have been almost impossible for her to open her door to the West with ease. It was not until the death of Mao in September 9. 1979, that the People's Republic of China really opened her door to the West and began the modernization. Nowadays, China tries to be a modern country without the change of political system of strongly centralized bureaucracy, which resembles the old Confucian one. In the middle of this system, there is the Chinese Communist Party, which resembles the old political system of the Emperor era. The experiment of the "socialistic market economy" with the old communistic political system is still under way so it is difficult to guess the future of China. Even though China will have many problems on the way of modernization without the democratic political system, she will make great achievement to some extent. There are some protests against the communistic political system mainly from the intellectuals but most of the people in China are so accustomed to the old Confucian political system that they have not so great difficulty under the communistic regime.

We can also see some small-scaled examples of Chinese model in other countries, for example, in Hong Kong, Singapore, and Taiwan. The Republic of China, i.e., Taiwan, has become a developed country with the economic matter. Under the firm grip of Kuomintang, which fled from the mainland China of Mao, Taiwan could mobilize the whole people for the modernization of the society. Here the old Confucian culture of hierarchy played an important role. Under the rule of the strong-willed leaders, whole people worked as an organism. Singapore is almost the same story. Hong Kong was under British colonial regime but it was never a democratic country. The British governors have never allowed a democratic multiparty system. Hong Kong was and is stringent Confucian hierarchical society.

Furthermore, there have been many Chinese family-oriented clans who fled from the People's Republic of China to many Southeast Asian countries, and eventually have made great fortune through commerce and finance. Not only in Singapore and Hong Kong but also in Thailand, where Buddhism rules, and Malaysia and Indonesia, where Islam is the state religion, the Chinese clans exert enormous influences. These all show very well how the family oriented Confucian society functions in relative small scale, but it becomes very difficult to mobilize people when the various influences of the West are not well adopted for the modern Confucian society.

3.1.3 The Japanese Model: Feudal Society

Before the contact with China and Korea, there was not much civilization in Japan. Just an indigenous kind of religion, which is later called Shinto, was there. Visitors from China and Korea brought Confucianism, Taoism, and Buddhism to Japan, as well as the Chinese system of writing. Around the fifth century, Chinese and Korean settlers acted as scribes for any writing needs. The early Japanese had no writing system of their own, and their system of government was based on clans. The Yamato clan claimed the greatest power, and its head was the Emperor of Japan. According to the Shinto myth, the Emperor was descended from the Sun Goddess, the most powerful kami of all, and was thus divine. Under the regency of Prince Shotoku Taishi (576-622), steps were taken to make the new ideas part of Japan. Educated in a Buddhist monastery, Shotoku was devoted to that religion. Having learned to read and write Chinese, he became intrigued by other forms of Chinese learning. He believed that Confucianism provided great lessons for government and society. He hoped that Confucian principles would help to modernize Japan. In 604, Prince Shotoku issued the Seventeen Articles Constitution, Japan's first written code of laws. Its general statement of principles described Buddhism as a universal truth for all living beings. However, in Article III, the nature of the nation of Japan is presented in terms of Confucianism:

"The lord is Heaven, the vassal is Earth. Heaven overspreads. Earth unbears. When this is so, the four seasons follow their due course, and the owners of Nature develop their efficacy."

Prince Shotoku wanted to learn more about Chinese culture from the source. He sent a delegation of Japanese students to China. His initial efforts were met with a rebuff because he had used an incorrect form of address in his letter to the Chinese Emperor: *"The Son of Heaven in the land where the sun rises [Japan] addresses a letter to the Son of Heaven where the sun sets [China]."*

Insulted, the Chinese court insisted that the letter be changed to one with due respect for the *only* Son of Heaven -and it was.[6] This incident shows the traditional relation between China and Japan. In contrast to the Korean, who never dared to call their leader as the Son of Heaven, the Japanese had no problem to call their supreme leader Emperor the same as the Chinese. The geopolitical position of Japan made it possible. China could never conquer Japan in her history. Until the unification of Japan by Tokugawa Ieyasu Shogun (1542-1616) in 1600, Confucianism had not much contribution in the Japanese society. This unified Japan under the house of Tokugawa Shogun lasted until 1868, i.e., until the "Opening to the West (開 港)".[7]

Japan had already a direct contact with the Western culture before the "Opening to the West (開 港)". In 1543 the first European from Portugal came to Japan. In 1549 the Jesuit priest Franz Xaver came to Japan, but what the Japanese deeply impressed was not the new Western religion but the new Western technology, especially guns. With the great help of guns Japan could

---

[6] Hoobler, Thomas and Dorothy, Confucianism (New York: Facts On File, 1993), p 62

[7] The typical Japanese ethos, which is well known to the world, was already built around this era. Refer to the book: Nosco, Peter (Ed.), Confucianism and Tokugawa Culture (Princeton ,New Jersey: Princeton University Press, 1984). Especially the article of Herman Ooms: "Neo-Confucianism and the Formation of Early Tokugawa Ideology: Contours of a Problem", and that of Paul B. Watt: "Jiun Sonja (1718-1804): A Response to Confucianism within the Context of Buddhist Reform" are helpful to understand why Japanese are strongly Confucian even if their religion is Buddhism.

lead a successful blitzkrieg against Korea in 1592 for the first time in her history but failed against then still powerful China. Thereupon Japan persecuted Christianism since 1637 and purged all European, mostly Portuguese, from its land. Since then Japan stayed isolated from the influence of the West until the forced "Opening to the West (開 港)".

Commodore Matthew Perry of the U.S.A. sailed his battleships into the harbor of Tokyo in 1853 and ended the isolation of Japan, which lasted for 216 years. Japan was the shrewdest country among the peripheral provinces of the traditional Confucian society in the eyes of China. Japan was forced to open her door to the West according to the Kanagawa Treaty in 1854 after a minor naval quarrel with the U.S.A., but she never felt sorry about it and saw rather a chance to be a country as strong as Great Britain, which destroyed then the middle of the world, i.e. China, with ease. Japan began to make every effort to be a modern, i.e., Western like country under the rule of the Emperor Mutsuhito. They called it Meiji Renovation, which lasted for 44 years long until 1912. Here the modernization meant mainly importing and implanting the Western cultures, especially, of economy, industry and technology. Politically Japan became a constitutional monarchy since 1889, and then has begun briskly to be a regional super power. After two successful wars against China and Russia in 1895 and in 1905 respectively, Japan became invincible imperial power in the Far East region. Korea became the first colony of modern Japan in 1910.

As a matter of fact, Japan was never a true Confucian society in the eyes of China. There has never been state examination of Confucian teaching in Japan. There have never been Confucian scholars, who were both teachers and bureaucrats in the Confucian society, in Japan. For the Chinese and the Korean in the traditional Confucian society, the filial duty (孝 道) for one's parents has been the supreme virtue, but for the Japanese the loyalty (忠 誠) for one's master has been the matter of life or death.[8] This kind of warrior culture in Japan was also in China and Korea, but to build a harmonious society on the basis of harmonious family, they preferred the centralized bureaucracy of scholars to the warrior feudalism, which was de facto the sociopolitical system of Japan until the "modernization". This could be one of the most important reasons for the fact that Japan was the first modernized Confucian society in Asia. While the ruling elite of China and Korea in the traditional Confucian society tried to sustain the old centralized bureaucratic society, the warring feudal lords, i.e., Shoguns, tried to win the war with every new means. The Japanese elite in the traditional Confucian society were less ideology-oriented than those in China and Korea, so they could accept the new culture from the West with much ease and adopt it to their purpose.

---

[8] Küng, H., Ching, J., Christentum und Chinesische Religion, (München:R. Piper GmbH, 1988), p110

On the contrary, the rulers of China and Korea in the traditional Confucian society despised war as a means for the solution of political problem, being true to the teaching of Confucius: A virtuous ruler pacifies his opponents with his virtuousness and does not conquer them with force. Face saving of all concerned parties was the most important matter in the traditional Confucian society because there should be no sorry for everybody. On the contrary, in old Japan where many warring parties tried to win over the opponents with every means, surviving was much important than face saving, so they sought first technical help from the West. Especially the German militarism of the Bismarck era had left great impression on newly modernizing Japan. With the Japanese Emperor as incarnated God in the zenith, all components of society must be organized hierarchically with the paradigm of order and obedience. There was also enough favor from the rulers for the blind loyalty of the subjects. This is one of the reasons why there is very small number of Christian in Japan. The Japanese have a living God so there is not much need for the new, and more, very abstract God. In any way, Japan could organize and mobilize her whole society for the modernization, i.e., the Westernization. With the influx of Western technology and economic system, Western culture has found the way to the Japanese society, and it has caused the confusion of value attitude among the people. Economic development for the national wealth without the loss of traditional value system has been the main aim of all Asian countries, but it is very difficult even for the very traditional and peculiar Japanese who still preserve their tradition zealously and relatively well.

3.1.4 The Colonial Model: Incessant Search for Identity

Korea has never successfully escaped from the great influence of China in her whole history, mostly because of her geopolitical situation. It was better for the national interest of Korea not to confront China directly. There was no buffer zone between Korea and China like the strait between Korea and Japan. When war broke out between Korea and China, there was no other way but to fight to the last which meant just the total destruction. That was why Korea under Yi Dynasty (1392-1910) accepted Confucianism as the state ideology. Being friendly to China was much better for Korea than being occupied and exploited by the then sole world superpower. Confucianism was not only the political ideology but also almost the only philosophical theme all through the Yi Dynasty. Following the teaching of Confucius thoroughly, only scholars could become public officers, and when they retreated from public affairs, they studied further the teaching of Confucianism. This ideal society in the eyes of Confucius disintegrated abruptly by the outer force, Japan in 1910.[9]

---

[9] Refer to the book: De Bary, Wm. Theodore, The Rise of Neo-Confucianism in Korea (New

Korea has never been a colony of any Western country, but she was the colony of early-westernized Japan for about 36 years long. Most of the Southeast Asian countries had experiences of colonization by the Western countries as most of the African countries, except Thailand.[10] Korea cannot be regarded quite the same as most of the Southeast Asian countries, but the big sociopolitical vacuum resulted from the colonial era was there both in Korea and in most of the Southeast Asian countries. This vacuum is the main reason for the fact that so many foreign cultures, especially, religions, other than Confucianism and Buddhism could come and flourish in these countries with such ease.

Vietnam was under the great influence of China for a long time. She could resist sometimes against the influence of China because she was far from the heart of China, and China had to fight back mostly invaders from the North. The Great Wall of China was to prevent the invasion from the North. Nevertheless, Vietnam had to accept China as the sole super power in the end. Vietnam gave up its resistance at least officially and developed a friendly relation with China, as the younger brother of China. The Vietnamese Emperor (he called himself Emperor as the Japanese Emperor) paid tribute to the Chinese Son of Heaven, and was, in turn, given a seal to show his right to rule at home. Although the Vietnamese ruler called himself king when he wrote to the Chinese Emperor, at home he gave himself the title of Emperor.[11] He was the Son of Heaven in the Vietnamese universe. Even if Buddhism is the main religion in Vietnam, family oriented Confucianism still prevails in her society. The fully-grown nationalism with the experience with China made Vietnam stubbornly resistant against outer influence. That national sentiment was well shown with the war against the colonial powers. Since 1954 the Vietnamese under the guidance of Ho Chi Minh fought the French, the Japanese, the Americans and even his own countrymen to win an independent and unified nation. Once Ngo Dinh Diem, the ex-president of former South Vietnam, tried to convert his country into a Catholic state in his devout belief in Christianism, but his cruel oppression against Buddhism, the popular religion in Vietnam, led his country into a total chaos. There was at last a military coup against him, and he and his family members were promptly executed. Instinctive disgust against the Western culture made Christianism impossible to be implemented in the soil of Vietnam. In the end the strict policy

---

York: Colombia University Press, 1985). Especially the article of Sa-Soon Youn, "Yi T'oegye's Identification of 'To Be' and 'Ought': Yi T'oegye's Theory of Value", and that of Tu Wei-Ming, "Yi T'oegye's Perception of Human Nature: A preliminary Inquiry into the Four-Seven Debate in Korean Neo-Confucianism" explain well how minute was the metaphysical discussion about the basic theme of Confucianism in Korea. Too much idealism was too good to be realized in this world.

[10] But Thailand was just a buffer zone in the power struggle between Western colonial countries.

[11] Hoobler, Thomas and Dorothy, Confucianism (New York: Facts On File, 1993), p 55

of seclusion against the outer influence made Vietnam one of the poorest countries in the region.

As well known, there are strong influences of Christianism in Korea and Philippine. Hinduism and Islam have some strongholds in Southeast Asian countries even though Buddhism is still the major religion in most of the Asian countries. There are some Christians in China and Japan, but they remain as minorities. China and Japan have never lost their own national identities, so there has been not much room for other cultures, especially religions, than the new technology from the West.[12] On the contrary, Korea and most of the Southeast Asian countries had to rediscover their national identities after the colonial era. These countries tried to rediscover their national identities through the nationalism, and they needed also "national-fathers" for the social integration. To their sorry, most of these national-fathers became easily dictators who exerted unhindered power over their own people. Formally, these countries adapted the democratic political system from the West, but many basic political and civil rights were not allowed to be practiced by the people for the sake of nation building and economic development. As compensation for the limited sociopolitical freedom, many leaders of these countries tried to provide material prosperity for the people, but rash economic development has caused political unrest, and furthermore, a new identity crisis. Before these newly independent countries could find their old identities after the colonial era, they had to first rebuild the economic basis of their countries, which was the basic condition of nation building. However, with the increasing material affluence and the cultural influence from the West, their traditional national identity has been more and more in the danger of extinction.

3.1.5 The New Approach of Mutual Understanding in the Globalized World

The Asian countries, which had experienced the colonial era, have great difficulty with the identity finding, but this identity crisis is common for all modern Confucian societies regardless of their different degrees of development. Adopting the Western technical and commercial culture without the Western political and religious culture has been the principle method in most of the modern Confucian countries. Nevertheless, more and more people realize that they need more than just technology and commerce as the society is getting westernized. Without the democratic political system the capitalistic economic system does not function well. Without the Christian ethos a welfare society cannot have its desirable shape. Even if the traditional Confucian countries

---

[12] China and Japan are the only countries in Asia which have never been a colony of foreign country in their history. In the history of China there were two dynasties which stemmed from other tribes, but they were all assimilated to the Chinese culture, and in the end, lost their own cultures.

cannot be the same as Europe or the U.S.A, they have to find a way to adopt and assimilate the better part of the Western culture in their societies.

In the age of globalization, the traditional family oriented or feudal minded Confucian society has its limit to be a real modern society. In the society of family oriented and feudal minded people, there come easily nepotism and corruption not only in the political arena but also in the whole society, and they result in inefficiency and insecurity. As modern society is based upon the capitalistic economic system, insecurity in economy results in insecurity and disharmony in the whole society. The modern Confucian society needs a new paradigm, which is not in discrepancy with the old Confucian tradition. It should be both democratic and acceptable for the still Confucian minded society.

A new and desirable culture from the West could be the spirit of equality of all people based on the Christian brotherly love. Actually the concept of equality has been the hardest one to be adopted even in the modern Confucian society because it should mean the total restructuring of the still traditionally structured society. The modern Confucian society still retains its traditionally hierarchical structure of society even though it has lost its firm grip especially on the younger generation and women. They do not obey anymore blindly to the authority of the superior. They have acquired the information about the idea of freedom and equality of all men from the West mainly through the mass media. Though this information does not reflect all realities in the Western countries, they believe it to be true because they just like it. The ideal image of women and the young, especially in the U.S.A., is more or less a fabricated picture mostly made in Hollywood. There is still discrimination against women in many ways in the U.S.A., and not all the children in the U.S.A. are rebellious against the older generation. This kind of rebellious and "cool" youngster is also a manmade image in the mass media. This image is virtual, i.e., it is believed to be there even though it never exists in reality. This kind of idealized image made in the mass media can have sometimes a positive function as an ideal role model for the younger generation, but they are not so quite positive in a modern Confucian society where the struggle between older and younger generation reflects exactly the discrepancy between the traditional Confucian moral system and the new Western ideas. This problem could be solved fairly only when it is approached on the basis of the mutual understanding, especially the intercultural understanding.

The clash between modern culture and tradition can have either positive or negative effects on society depending on the mutual understanding of the elements of the society. How should it be achieved is quite a delicate problem when the democratic structure of communication among the social elements is not yet there. This problem must be solved before any new and foreign culture can be adopted. That is why people in the modern Confucian society must look back their tradition to find the common ground of communication. This ground must be both familiar to them and open to the new ethos from the West.

3.2 The Christian Ethos: Phenomenologically Understood

Christianism is one of the two pillars of the modern Western countries. The old Greek democratic political system is quite different from the modern democracy. As the old Greeks discriminated against women and slaves, they cannot be regarded as the true democratic as we understand it now. The modern democracy cannot be established without the spirit of Christianism, which emphasized the equality of all human beings before God and the brotherly love among all human beings.

It is quite difficult for the non-Christian to understand the Christian ethos mostly because of the differences among many Christian denominations: Orthodox, Catholic, Protestant, Anglican, and other small denominations have their own rituals and creeds. Even under the common umbrella of Protestantism, there are further many differences among the sub-denomination of Protestant. Notwithstanding this a little bit complex situation, there is some consensus among them, and the most prominent one is the Bible. Even though there are some differences in translation of the Bible into their own languages, they are all using the same original text of the Bible. That is why we need to go back to the basic of Christianism, i.e., the Bible. Here we can find the unambiguous origin of Christianism: Jesus Christ, regardless the differences among many Christian denominations.

Jesus Christ in the Bible gives rise to another problem for the stranger to Jesus Christ, for example, a Korean manual worker, a woman in Tanzania, and a Marxist in Ceylon, as Walter Jens has described interestingly.[13] Therefore, we need not only the phenomenological motto of "back to the basic (zurück zur Sache)" but also phenomenological ἐποχή to solve the ambiguous problem of the Bible and Jesus Christ. That is why we are here concentrating just on His deeds, not on His many parables, for which both opulent and hermeneutic knowledge about His time are needed.

Jesus Christ was born and died as a Jew in this world. He tried to persuade his contemporary to believe in true God whose nature is love, but most of the Jews at that time did not listen to Jesus Christ but clung to the traditional teaching of the Judaism. So it may be claimed that Christianism must be quite different from Judaism even though the former had been influenced in many ways by the latter. The new law of Jesus Christ (John 13:34)[14] is actually not "new", that is, in the

---

[13] Jens, Walter, "Über die Notwendigkeit einer verfremdenden Betrachtung biblischer Texte", in Die Theologie des 20. Jahrhunderts, Karl-Josef Kuschel (Hrsg.) (München: Piper, 1986), pp. 259-276

[14] A new commandment I give unto you, That ye love one other ; as I have loved you, that yo also love one other.

Old Testaments there are plenty of accounts about the love of God and brotherly love for neighbors, even if its love of God is a limited one: it is just for the "prince of God" (Ge. 32:28)[15], the Israelis, but never for the gentiles. It was for the first time when Jesus Christ talked about the brotherly love for all (Mt. 12:50)[16].

His followers believed firmly in this brotherly love for all as we can witness not only in many letters of St. Paul (Ro. 12:10, 1Th. 4:9, Heb. 13:1)[17] but also in other scripts of the Bible (1Pe. 3:8)[18] This brotherly love ($\phi\iota\lambda\alpha\delta\epsilon\lambda\phi\iota\alpha$) is not peculiar to Christianism, in the Old Testament there is already urge for the brotherly love (De. 15:7,9)[19], but the Christian love is much more cosmopolitan, it means undiscriminating love for all, even for one's enemy (Mt. 5:44)[20].

Such a brotherly love was strongly held by Mozi (墨 子), a Chinese scholar who was born in 479 BC, the same year as Confucius died. He advocated Jian-Ai (兼 愛) which should mean an indiscriminate love for all. He presupposed the Heaven or Heaven's Will which guaranteed this brotherly love for all. This kind of love was unacceptable for the Confucian scholars, especially for Mencius who saw in Mozi (墨 子)'s teaching the destructive chaos of hierarchical order in the harmonious society. Mencius thought that man must love his family first, and then others. So it was unthinkable for Mencius to love all people indiscriminately and simultaneously. The history of China decided that Mencius was right, especially after Dong Zhong Shu (董 仲 舒), who was the first and one of the great scholar politician of the Han Dynasty (206 BC - AD 220), accepted Confucianism as the orthodox teaching of China and established the system of state examination which tested the understanding of

---

[15] And he said, Thy name shall be called no more Jacob, but Israel: for as a prince hast thou power with God and with men, and has prevailed.

[16] For whosoever shall do the will of my Father which is in heaven, the same is my brother, and sister, and mother.

[17] Ro. 12:10 Be kindly affectioned one to another with brotherly love; in honour preferring one another; {with...: or, in the love of the brethren}

1Th. 4:9 But as touching brotherly love ye need not that I write unto you: for ye yourselves are taught of God to love one another.

Heb. 13:1 Let brotherly love continue.

[18] Finally, be ye all of one mind, having compassion one of other, love as brethren, be pitiful, be courteous:

[19] De. 15:7 If there be among you a poor man of one of thy brethren within any of thy gates in thy land which the LORD thy God giveth thee, thou shalt not harden thine heart, nor shut thine hand from thy poor brother:

De. 15:9 Beware that there be not a thought in thy wicked heart, saying, The seventh year, the year of release, is at hand; and thine eye be evil against thy poor brother, and thou givest him nought; and he cry unto the LORD against thee, and it be sin unto thee.

[20] But I say unto you, Love your enemies, bless them that curse you, do good to them that hate you, and pray for them which despitefully use you, and persecute you;

Confucian teaching. After this, Jian-Ai (兼 愛) of Mozi (墨 子) never attracted any serious interest. Only Jen (仁) has become all encompassing concept.

With the Christian love, the Asians rediscovered this brotherly love of Mozi (墨 子) with the new flavor of Christian cosmopolitanism. In the history of Europe, Christianism has played a great role both in political arena and society proper. We may say that the cultural monopoly of Christianism in Europe, at least, until the beginning of our century, was invincible. Therefore, there should be this Christian brotherly love practiced in the European society even if the history of Europe does not always show peaceful coexistence of all men. As a matter of fact, the rulers sometimes forgot this Christian brotherly love. The rulers of the Christian society in Europe had had sometimes more concern on the political power struggle for a long time after the fall of the Roman Empire than the practice of the Christian brotherly love. For them, the Christian virtue was more benevolence of the haves for the have-nots than the brotherly love of equal sharing. It was not until the breakout of the French Revolution in 1789 that people began to understand freedom, equality and fraternity as the most important virtues in the Christian society. And more, against the specter of communism, most of the European countries had to institutionalize the Christian brotherly love with the social welfare system for the less privileged people. Even though the institutionalized Christian brotherly love does not fully guarantee happiness for all men, it can at least show that man needs the Christian ethos of brotherly love to make the society to be worth living in. Some might think that the modern democratic society is the revival of the ancient Greek πολις and her humanism, but in a πολις where women, children and slaves were no citizen, we cannot find freedom, fraternity and equality for all. We see these virtues rather in the teaching and deeds of Jesus Christ. This love of Jesus Christ as the ethos of Christianism should be adopted and reinterpreted by the modern Confucian society where the fraternity is still regarded more as a cause of social disorder than as a basis for social consensus building.

3.3 Sympathy as the Mediating Concept for Intercultural Understanding

When we are doing a comparative study between different cultures, the most common failure we usually make is the mere direct comparison. We can only see the difference of them more clearly with this method. It is not a desirable result especially when we are about to make a mutual understanding. Every culture has its own history, therefore it cannot be correctly interpreted without the preunderstanding of its genetic development. Furthermore, we need a mediating concept, which can be found in both cultures to be compared. This pre-understanding should not be rigorously scientific and reflect exactly the fact. This must be more or less the mass of information. It includes the first impression, and even misunderstanding. Even in the mass of information of the day we may find out a denomination which should not necessary a tangible one. When it can give a clue for the mutual understanding, it can be used as a mediating concept for the tentative beginning.

As a matter of fact, to have sympathy on somebody is not necessarily a religious attitude. This emotive attitude must be rather in the nature of man. As long as we cannot be certain of the nature of man, this could be a disputable argument, but the phenomena of the sympathetic attitude and behavior can be witnessed in everyday life regardless of the difference of religions and cultures. This sympathy has the same character as the concept of life world (Lebenswelt) of Husserl, which cannot be clearly defined, but is a very concrete basis for the phenomenology.

Christian love is based on the pity on the needy as Jesus Christ Himself showed in the Gospels. The Confucian Jen (仁) was originally interpreted by Mencius as the natural sympathy for a baby heedlessly nearing the deep well. With these two concepts, we may begin to make a mutual understanding between two different cultures as long as the concept of sympathy is possibly less tainted with their respective cultural backgrounds.

3.4 The Merit of the Phenomenological Method

When we make a comparative study, we have to pay attention to the fact that a method for this study must be possibly a neutral one. The phenomenology of Husserl is not a new philosophical theory but a method for the scientific study, as Husserl himself explained. Even though it is true that this phenomenology has a strong influence of Kant, it is used for many philosophical theories as a method not as a theory. The main trend of the modern Western philosophy can be arranged in two schools, i.e., the German Idealism and the British Empiricism. As long as man as subject has to experience the world as object, this chasm of idea and experience may be not so easily overcome. Both parties have their own right. They see just other aspects of the same matter respectively. The problem is not their respective points of view but the tendency of the dogmatization for their theory. Without this dogmatization they lose their identity, and without their respective opinion there could be no philosophical discussion, so this tendency of dogma is necessary evil for the development of philosophy.

Nevertheless, for intercultural study man needs no dogmatic theory. Possibly the most neutral point of view is desirable for such a study, but there could be no absolutely neutral point of view as long as everybody has his own opinion. Therefore, we have to adopt a method that could be more neutral than any other theories.

As well known, the phenomenology of Husserl pursues a philosophy as a scientific method without presuppositions even if his original motive for this science was his curiosity about the a priori of correlation between the object of experience and the mode of "the given" (Gegebenheitsweise).[21] For him the concepts without intuition are empty because what is intuitively given is the necessary basis for the truth. By the same token, we can begin an intercultural study with this intuitively given, i.e., the bare phenomena of both cultures without any pre-interpretation. Only the intuitive impression of respective cultures can be the raw basis for the further study. As soon as there comes first an opinion, it becomes a concept not wholly free from the presupposition. Therefore, it may be helpful when the method of the phenomenological reduction is applied especially for the comparative study.

3.5. Mass Media as the Appropriate Medium

The first approach of Christian to Confucianism by Matteo Ricci was confined among the literate of then China. This was not the only reason for the fact that Matteo Ricci's brave and brilliant achievement could not find follow-ups. Without the consensus building among the masses, a true intercultural ethos mediation cannot be accomplished. Especially in our democratic society, the stern and lofty discourse among the scholars does not attract any more the interest of the masses, which is vital for the beginning of mutual understanding. The truth itself does not change but the way of its mediation must always change according to the different sociopolitical environment. When our era is the Information Age and the mass media flourish, we have to have no hesitation in using them. We may ask ourselves what the early Christian would have done if they had the mass media. The answer is clear, they would have willingly used them for the better evangelization of the world.

Nobody can deny that the mass media, with which we have constant contact in our everyday life, are not only the most powerful information messengers but also the strong opinion makers themselves. As long as information plays the most important role in our postmodern society, the mass media, especially an interactive one, can be the most important instrument for the democratic society.

Especially after the fall of communism, democracy stays as the only proper political system in the world. Democracy was originally one of the four forms of government in the Plato's book "The Republic".[22] As a matter of fact, Plato

---

[21] Husserl, Edmund, Die phänomenologische Methode, Ausgeählte Texte I, (Stuttgart:Philipp Reclam Jun., 1985), p. 16

[22] Plato, The Republic, Ch. VIII, (tr. Benjamin Jowett, M.A.) (New York: P.F. Collier & Son, The Colonial Press,1901) , p 349 :

I shall particularly wish to hear what were the four constitutions of which you were speaking.

That question, I said, is easily answered: the four governments of which I spoke, so far as they have distinct names, are

first, those of Crete and Sparta (aristocracy), which are generally applauded;

despised democracy as a lesser form of government. For him democracy was a result of the revolution against the oligarchy.[23] Plato's favorite form of government was aristocracy because there will be chaos when the metals of different races are mingled with each other.[24]

Today democracy is the only alternative for many countries in the world because it is possibly the best egalitarian system of distribution. When there are many people who feel discriminated, it becomes promptly the cause of major social unrest. The communistic distribution system failed mostly because of the apparent oligarchic and tyrannical political system and its vast bureaucracy. One of the most important things in a harmonious society is not the forced consensus but the coexistence of differences. That is why democracy prevails nowadays while communism demised. In a democratic society the minority must follow the majority, not through coercion but through discussion and persuasion.

Democracy is still a very bitter pill to swallow for many countries in the world mostly because of their own non-democratic political culture, which stems from their own history. An example can be found in the modern Confucian society. Traditionally, there was no proper system of communication between the rulers and the plain people. Only between the king and his close attendants the formal discussion about political matters was possible. Even this discussion could not take the form of true open communication either. In the hierarchical Confucian society the rulers were the superior in every respect as long as there is no sign from the Heaven for a new ruler. A man can be an Emperor or a king only according to the Will of Heaven (天 命), so when a

---

what is termed oligarchy comes next; this is not equally approved, and is a
form of government which teems with evils:
thirdly, democracy, which naturally follows oligarchy, although
very different:
and lastly comes tyranny, great and famous, which differs from
them all, and is the fourth and worst disorder of a State.
I do not know, do you? of any other constitution which can be said to have a distinct character. There are lordships and principalities which are bought and sold, and some other intermediate forms of government. But these are nondescripts and may be found equally among Hellenes and among barbarians.

[23] Ibid., p370 :
And then democracy comes into being after the poor have conquered their opponents, slaughtering some and banishing some, while to the remainder they give an equal share of freedom and power; and this is the form of government in which the magistrates are commonly elected by lot.

[24] Ibid., p352 :
In the succeeding generation rulers will be appointed who have lost the guardian power of testing the metal of your different races, which, like Hesiod's, are of gold and silver and brass and iron. And so iron will be mingled with silver, and brass with gold, and hence there will arise dissimilarity and inequality and irregularity, which always and in all places are causes of hatred and war.

man is a king, he must be the embodiment of the Will of Heaven (天 命). This was the strong belief of the people in the Confucian society. This kind of belief still prevails in most of the modern Confucian countries. Such a belief could be also found in the European society as the form of absolute monarchy. But with the rise of the bourgeois and especially through the French Revolution in 1789, the ideas of freedom and equality paved the way to the modern Western democracy. On the contrary, in many modern Confucian countries, there can be no "real" democratic political system not only because of the lack of enough middle class, but because of the strong influence of the Confucian hierarchical political culture.

As the rash development of technology, especially in the realm of communication and the mass media, which are engaged mainly in the information transfer, provides an unprecedented chance in the modern Confucian societies, the situation is necessarily changing. For rapid economic growth the information technology becomes the most important resource in these days, as steel and coal were for Europe in the age of the Industrial Revolution. Most of the modern Confucian countries are eager to use this new technology as they do their best to catch up the industrialized Western countries, but this new technology is not wholly exempt from problem. The new culture from the West through the mass media is not so thoroughly ideologically and religiously colored as the old Western culture in the age of the "Opening to the West (開 港)", in the late 18th and early 19th century, but this new culture cannot free from the democratic spirit mostly because communication through the mass media presupposes freedom of the press, and furthermore, reciprocal and equal dialogue among all people. This new culture is sometimes not only very strange but also very vulgar in the eyes of the Asians who are accustomed to the Confucian culture. Sometimes this new culture could be regarded as danger for the defense of national identity. A rash influx of this kind of culture can be a source of social unrest, which always precedes the sociopolitical change. That is why the Chinese government, for example, tries to control the new way of communication especially through the fax machine and Internet. This is more or less a common dilemma of all modern Confucian countries. To keep the national identity and to catch up the economic standard of the Western countries at the same time are not such an easy matter.

The traditional Confucian culture is not necessarily without flaw. It must not only be reinterpreted but also be changed as the zeitgeist changes. This change could be begun with the interactive mass media with fewer problems because of their double-edgedness: both the driving force of the Information Age and the source of the democratic spirit.

4. The Loci of Sympathy in its Religious Origin

4.1 The Confucian Jen as the Sympathy of Humanism

4.1.1 Whose Jen is it? - Confucius versus Mencius

4.1.1.1 The Etymological Meaning of Jen

There are other great religions than Confucianism in China, for example Taoism and Buddhism. But since the comprehensive compilation of Confucianism by ChuHsi (朱　熹) (1130-1200), who not only interpreted Confucianism with authority but also integrated major contents of Taoism and Buddhism in Confucianism, Confucianism could reign the whole China in every aspect. Furthermore, the books of Confucianism were the only official texts for the state examinations since 1313 until 1905 when China adopted the modern educational system from the West.[25] So when we look into Confucianism, we can find almost all philosophical traditions of China there.

In Confucianism there is no God, therefore no theology. It concentrates itself just on the matter of man, man in this world, not as a metaphysical being, let alone as a spirit in the after life. There is the Book of Change (周　易), which interprets and explains the vicissitude of the universe. It is not for cosmology, which could be found in Christianism where the universe is the result of the creation of God who loves man especially. In Confucianism man and his society are the only matters to be concerned. That is why the matter between two men, which is the etymological meaning of Jen (仁), has become the essence of Confucianism.

The cardinal concept of Confucianism is Jen (仁), as much as love is for Christianism. Jen (仁) appears in "the Book of Odes (詩　經)" for the first time in the history of Chinese literature.[26] Confucius himself referred to the Book of Odes (詩　經) many times with other classics for the explanation of his idea of Jen (仁) in the book "the Analects of Confucius (論　語)". As well known, Chinese is an ideogram, therefore every single letter has its own meaning. Jen (仁) symbolizes two men or persons, Jen (仁) and man (人) sound identically in Chinese.[27] Even Confucius himself once used these two words

---

[25] Feng, You-Lan, A Short History of Chinese Philosophy, I. J. Chung(tr.) (Seoul: Hyung-Sul Pres,1981), p372

[26] The Book of Odes (詩 經), 鄭 風 叔 于 田 巷 無 居 人 豈 無 居 人 洵 美 且 仁....(As Shuzu (叔 于) go on a hunting trip there is nobody (in the town) anymore. How could be there nobody (in the town)? (But) there is not a man as beautiful and **good** as Shuzu (叔　于)....); refer to Waley, Arthur, The Book of Songs (London: 1954), bk 1 ch 7-3

[27] The word Jen (仁) is composed of "Jen (人)" and "Er (二)". "Jen (人)" means a person

indiscriminately.[28] He tried to define Jen (仁) as something that has more profound meaning than a man. As a matter of fact, he spent the rest of his life to teach the true meaning of Jen (仁). Almost all who met Confucius asked him about the meaning of Jen (仁), and Confucius never explained directly but he always used metaphors and allegories as he tried to give an answer. This way of indirect answer has been the traditional practice not only of the Chinese scholars but also of other ordinary people. The ruling class and the learned extremely avoided direct expression of his mind not only in the discussion but also in everyday life. They quoted usually a few verses from the Book of Odes(詩 經), especially when they had to manage diplomatic affairs. This presupposed the thorough understanding of the Book of Odes (詩 經), which was very hard to interpret even for the learned because of its rich metaphors and allegories. But it was an indispensable prerequisite for the rulers and the learned who were mostly bureaucrats because direct and clear expressions were regarded as a way for the uncivilized and the men of ignorance. Loosing face because of the ignorance was one of the most unbearable things for the rulers and the learned. Knowledge about all books of Confucianism was required not only for the state examination but also for the everyday life of the rulers and the learned. But the "civilized" expression of one's mind causes sometimes the arbitrary interpretations of the "true" meaning of the expressed words. This problem has also happened in the case of Jen (仁) in the Confucian tradition. The various schools of Confucius failed to make themselves understandable to each other because of these arbitrary interpretations about the meaning of Jen (仁). Nevertheless, we may draw the common meaning of Jen (仁) from the phenomena of the usage of this word in the Confucian tradition. Jen (仁) should mean first a man, a good man, the good itself, the virtues, loving and helping others. As long as every school of Confucian tradition has its own interpretation of the meaning of Jen (仁), the question about the "true" meaning of it arises first when we are to understand the original Confucian thought. Here we are focusing on two books of Confucianism, "the Analects of Confucius (論 語)" and "Mencius (孟 子)", to carry out the attempt to understand the "true" meaning of Jen (仁) because no other than these two books has been dedicated so intensively to the quest of Jen (仁).

---

and "Er (二)" means two. 仁 and 人 sound the same as Jen (仁)

[28] The Analects of Confucius, chapter 6, 雍 也 宰 我 問 曰 仁 者 雖 告 之 曰 井 有 仁 焉 基 從 之 也... ; refer to Legge, James (tr. & ed.), Confucius : Confucian Analects, The Great Learning & The Doctrine of the Mean (New York: Dover Publications, Inc., 1971), p. 192*

4.1.1.2 Confucian Jen as the Ideal Concept of Perfection

When Confucius (551-479 BC) was born there was still Chou (周) Dynasty (1100-256 BC) but it was actually "the Age of Spring and Autumn Warring" (春 秋 戰 國 時 代). Every single influential provincial ruler tried to expand his power, eventually to be the Emperor of the Land of the Middle (中 國). It was not until the first Emperor of the Chin (秦) Dynasty (221-206 BC) ascended to the throne that there was at last peace. Confucius was at first a small public officer but he was not so fortunate with his carrier that he must after all end his job as such at his age of about 56. He then tried to be a teacher for the doctrine of betterment of sociopolitical environment. He taught not only his own discipleship, but also any political authority. He even tried to persuade the powerful to accept and practice his thought. Even if he never succeeded with it for the rest of his life, he has perennial influence upon the everyday life of almost all Asians. Once, most of his successors were buried alive and all books about his doctrine were burned according to the royal command of the first Emperor of the Chin Dynasty, but the books of Confucius have survived somehow and his fame as "the Master" has had no equal since the 2nd century BC.

The only book about the dialogue of him with his disciples and other people is "the Analects of Confucius (論 語)" which has no known author. There are still six more books about the doctrines of Confucianism, but "the Analects of Confucius (論 語)" has the prime authority over Confucianism because it is the only book which is regarded as containing the firsthand teachings of Confucius. This book has 20 chapters with no logical sequences. It has rather the character of unsorted summary of allegories. The main point of this book is to show how Confucius sincerely tried to explain the meaning of Jen (仁). The true meaning of Jen (仁) has remained rather a vague concept, so there has been many attempts to interpret or find out the "true" meaning of Jen (仁). According to the different interpretations of Jen (仁), there arose many kinds of schools in the tradition of Confucianism. The most influential schools among them were from the followers of Mencius, and later ChuHsi (朱 熹). Mostly, interpretation of a school means showing its own opinion about the idea of their "Master". Mencius and ChuHsi (朱 熹) did no less than this. Mencius had not only his own thought about the meaning of Jen (仁), but also his own theory of society and moral, which not seldom contradicted Confucius. But Mencius himself never insisted that he would dare to talk against the "true" teaching of "the Master". Even though we cannot fail to notice the discrepancy between these two great thinkers of the Confucian tradition when we have the chance to compare them directly, it is still almost a blasphemy for most Confucians to do such a comparison. Apart from this kind of emotional problem there surface another technical problem when we are about to compare them. The books of Confucian thought Mencius had read at his time were different from those of ours. Mencius mentioned sometimes the words of Confucius we do not know. Therefore we could not simply compare the contents "the Analects of Confucius (論 語)" and the "Mencius (孟子)" word by word to find out the difference between them. First of all, we have to understand what the Confucians believe to be the thought of Confucius. As long as "the Analects of Confucius (論 語)" is the only source of the firsthand words of Confucius, we have to begin with this book to understand the thought of Confucius, and of Confucianism.

Confucius was sure of the existence of Jen (仁), but he never told where it should be or how it should work. He just talked about when a man or a situation is related to Jen (仁). But it does not mean that Jen (仁) has an ontological meaning. Confucius gave various answers for the questions about the meaning of Jen (仁), but he never made a logical explanation for Jen (仁) even if it was and is the A and Ω of Confucianism.

Nevertheless, the Confucians think that their Master gave the most appropriate answers to the various questioning people according to their intelligence and situation. Here are some examples: When the most beloved disciple of Confucius, Yen Yuan (顏淵) asked about Jen (仁), the Master answered as *"self-discipline and returning to propriety...."*[29] To the same question of his another disciple Fan Chih (樊遲), the Master answered as *"loving all men..."*[30] The Master gave a different answer to Fan Chih (樊遲) when the latter asked the same question in another chance: *"being respectful in retirement, being attentive in working, and being loyal to others..."*[31]

From the viewpoint of Confucius Jen (仁) has something to do with filial duty and brotherly love (孝悌), politeness (禮), courage (勇), reverence, generosity, faithfulness smartness, kindness (恭 寬 信 敏 惠)[32], and fidelity and benevolence (忠 恕)[33]. As we can easily see, they are all virtues of man and ethical concepts, and more, they are from the good nature of man. It is getting difficult to know what Jen (仁) really means because it has become too comprehensive a concept. As a matter of fact, Jen (仁) is everything what is to be regarded as the good of a man or a given society. Mencius had already seen

---

[29] op. cit., chapter 12, 顏 淵 , 顏 淵 問 仁 子 曰 克 己 復 禮 爲 仁 ...; Legge, James, Confucius, p 250
[30] Ibid., 顏 淵, 樊 遲 問 仁 子 曰 愛 人 ....; Legge, James, Confucius, p 260
[31] op. cit., chapter 13, 子 路 , 樊 遲 問 仁 子 曰 居 處 恭 執 事 敬 與 人 忠 ...; Legge, James, Confucius, p 271
[32] op. cit., chapter17, 陽 貨 , 子 張 問 仁 於 孔 子 孔 子 曰 能 行 五 者 於 天 下 僞 仁 矣 請 問 之 曰 恭 寬 信 敏 惠 ... ; Legge, James, Confucius, p 320
[33] op. cit., chapter 4, 里 仁 , 曾 子 曰 夫 子 之 道 忠 恕 而 已 矣 ... ; Legge, James, Confucius, p 170

such a complexity of Jen (仁) and tried to give a more rational and logical explanation for it.

4.1.1.3 Mencian Jen as the Human Concept of Virtue

Confucius and Mencius were born in 551 BC and 371 BC respectively, according to the History of China (史記列傳). Notwithstanding the fact that there was no chance for Mencius to meet Confucius face to face or to learn from him personally, Mencius was and still is regarded as the true inheritor and the only authoritative interpreter of Confucianism. In the history of Confucianism, understanding the conversation between Confucius and his personal followers played a very important role. It was getting all the more difficult for the followers of Confucianism to understand the true meaning of what Confucius said as time passed. In this regard, the authoritarian interpretation of Confucius' thought was the only way to know his true mind. Confucius was the first man who had given emphasis on Jen (仁), but he never explained why we should practice Jen (仁). Mencius was the first man who had tried to give an answer to this question.

According to Mencius the nature of man is intrinsically good. This thought of Mencius was one of the four representative doctrines about the nature of man in his era: the doctrine of Mencius, the doctrine of neutrality of the nature of man, i.e., man is neither good nor bad in his nature, the doctrine of simultaneously good and bad natures in man, i.e., some are good in their nature and the others are bad, and lastly, the doctrine of bad nature of man, i.e., all men are bad with no exception.

Mencius had had to clarify his theory to drive back the other three opinions about the nature of man. Therefore, he developed an elaborate theory about the nature of man, and eventually built a systematic explanation about the nature of man.

According to the theory of Mencius there are four beginnings of the nature of man:

The sympathy for the people who are in need of help is the beginning of Jen (仁).
The ability to feel shame is the beginning of the justice (義).
The modesty, or refrain, is the beginning of the courtesy (禮).
The ability of discerning right from wrong is the beginning of the wisdom (智).[34]

These four beginning of the nature of man are all in the heart of man. These

---

[34] The Book of Mencius, chapter 3, 公孫丑, ...惻隱之心仁之端也羞惡之心義之端也辭讓之心禮之端也是非之心知之端也 ...; refer to Legge, James (tr. & ed.), The Works of Mencius (New York: Dover Publications, Inc., 1970), pp 202-203

natures are called the four cardinal virtues of Confucianism. It was originally not his own idea, but Confucius'. However, Mencius was the first man who had made the clear explanation of the true nature of man.

Confucius himself had made it clear that Jen (仁) means love for man.[35] He meant with it the love of categorical duty, that is, love with the moral sanction, therefore it had not much to do with the nature of man, but with the duty of man in the society. This moral sanction of Confucius stems from the "Heaven's Will (天命)", which is to be interpreted as destiny, or just the Heavenly Command. It is not easy to know the Heaven's Will (天命). Even Confucius himself said that he knew the Heaven's Will (天命) for the first time only when he became fifty years old.

For Mencius it was also the Heaven (天) which gave us the moral principles. The nature of man is just a concrete expression of this Heaven. The fundamental nature of man is Jen (仁), and this Jen (仁) begins with the sympathy for neighbors. For Mencius sympathy is not only a matter of heart, but also of moral duty. When a man is doing a work according to this nature of man, he is doing his moral duty, but when he does not, he is not only morally blamable, but also not a true man any more. So when an Emperor, the "Son of Heaven", does not fulfill his duty as an Emperor, he is not an Emperor anymore, but just a man of mediocrity. It is therefore justified to dethrone such a "nominal Emperor" by someone who is living according to the true nature of man. Nobody can know from the beginning, who is going to be the next or the true Emperor, only the Heaven knows it, but Mencius added that we can see the heavenly signs for a new Emperor when we concentrate our attention on such signs. It sounds a kind of mysticism. Confucius had never talked about the abdication of the pseudo Emperor, but he had talked about the king who is deserved to be a king. From this Mencius developed the basis for his theory of abdication of the Emperor.

Notwithstanding the fact that Mencius had made just a new interpretation of Confucius, not a new theory, as if the tradition of Confucian thought of pure interpretation was for him too heavy to ignore, his interpretation had and still has no equal in Confucianism. Therefore, we are about to go on in line with the interpretation of Mencius to understand the core of Confucianism. One important point cannot be ignored when we are to talk about Mencius in relation to Confucius. Confucius never believed that the ordinary people (民), who were at his time mostly the peasants, could be in the central stage of the Confucian philosophy. He treated them at most the followers of the good rulers. He said:

"The ordinary people can be made to follow, but they cannot be made to understand (why they should follow)."[36]

---

[35] The Analects of Confucius, chapter12, 顏淵, 樊遲問仁子曰愛人 ...; Legge, James, Confucius, p 260

[36] op. cit, chapter 8, 泰伯, 子曰民可使由之不可使知之 ; Legge, James,

He just tried to be a good teacher more for the rulers than for the ordinary people who had almost no chance to be the rulers in reality. The ordinary people had to just follow the rulers of wisdom and virtue, then their life would be a happy one even if they do not quite understand the politics, not to mention the truth. The teaching of Confucius is mainly aimed for the ruling class. Confucius firmly believed that only the philosopher-king could guarantee the harmonious society, which was cherished by him as the ultimate goal of his teaching.

Mencius had quite different opinion about the ordinary people. For him the ordinary people were much more important than the rulers were. He said:

"The ordinary people is the most important, and then comes the kingdom as next, and the king comes as the least important. One can be the Son of Heaven, i.e., the Emperor, only when he earns the hearts of the ordinary people..."[37]

Such an idea was too radical to be accepted by the rulers with no reserve. Therefore for more than thousand years after his death, his idea about the ordinary people was sanctioned by the political rulers while Confucius was cherished by them. But it is quite wrong to see a representative of the ordinary people in Mencius. He tried to be a teacher of the rulers as eagerly as Confucius did. He interpreted the traditional Confucian teaching more freely, but that should not mean that he built a new school of Confucianism. Confucius was already too big for Mencius and his contemporaries to be criticized. Mencius fought fiercely to defend the teaching of Confucius against other contemporary philosophical schools of his time, like that of Yangzi (楊 子) or of Mozi (墨 子). Confucianism would have never come to be the main philosophical and political theory in China but for this brilliant work of Mencius.

It is clear that the interpretation of Jen (仁) by Mencius was new and filled the vacuum which Confucius had left undone. That new interpretation was too good to be revised by the followers, so it could survive more than two thousand years even if his political idea was not welcomed by most rulers. Jen (仁) of Confucius was too abstract and speculative a concept that only YanYuan (顏 淵), his most beloved but short lived pupil, could fully understand what it should mean. Mencius made this highly metaphysical concept of Jen (仁) more concrete. It is clear that sympathy itself is not Jen (仁) itself. Jen (仁) is too great to be just the sympathy of man, but without sympathy there can be no Jen (仁). Everybody, even the ordinary people, has sympathy as the nature of man, not just the three mythical Emperors of the early Chinese history, or the good rulers. That is the main point what Mencius must have intended. In a society, men are different according to his personality and social role, but men are equal because they have the seed of Jen (仁), sympathy, that can be in the end fully

---

Confucius, p 211
[37] The Book of Mencius, chapter 14, 盡 心 章 下 , 孟 子 曰 民 爲 貴 社 稷 次 之 君 爲 輕 是 故 得 乎 丘 民 以 爲 天 子 ... ; Legge, James, Mencius, p 483

blossomed when everybody becomes the Ideal Man of Virtue (君子), who deserves to be the ruler. Everybody has the same chance to become a philosopher-king when he wants. Here is the great difference from the belief of Confucius. Confucius wanted to make the king the Ideal Man of Virtue (君子), but Mencius wanted the Ideal Man of Virtue (君子) to be a king who has sympathy for his subjects.

4.1.2 Jen and the "Ideal Man of Virtue"

The incarnation of Jen (仁) is the Ideal Man of Virtue (君子). Confucius has used this expression very often to explain the meaning of Jen (仁). The Ideal man of Virtue (君子) is good, wise and courageous.[38] He learns the Tao (道) and he loves every man.[39] Everybody has the possibility to be the Ideal Man of Virtue (君子) but they are too small in number because men are quite different in learning even if their natures are the same.[40] As a matter of fact Confucius had never seen the living Ideal Man of Virtue (君子) before his eyes in his whole life. His most beloved pupil "Yen Yuan (顏淵)" was the only man who could rank with Confucius in almost all respects, but Yen Yuan (顏淵) died too early before he could do any significant contribution for Confucianism. For Confucius there were a few Ideal Men of Virtue (君子) in the early days of Chinese history. They were the legendary three Emperors and five Kings (三皇五帝) and some highly regarded men in ancient China. It seems that Confucius had just too an ideal vision of the Ideal Man of Virtue (君子).

For Mencius it was not quite impossible for an ordinary man to be not only a king or an Emperor, but also an Ideal Man of Virtue (君子): *"The Ideal Man of Virtue (君子) has no intention to be a king but he just keeps in his mind the four cardinal virtues of Confucianism, Jen (仁), justice (義), courtesy (禮) and wisdom (智)."*[41] *"An Ideal Man of Virtue (君子) is a man who is pleased when his parents are alive and his brothers are safe, and when he has nothing to be ashamed before the Heaven and his contemporary, and when he could have the chance to find the brilliant pupils, and to teach them.*[42]

---

[38] The Analects of Confucius, chapter 14, 憲問, 子曰君子道者三我無能焉 仁者不憂知者不惑勇子不懼 ... ; Legge, James, Confucius, p 286
[39] op. cit., chapter 17, 陽貨, 子游對曰...君子學道卽愛人 ... ; Legge, James, Confucius, p 319
[40] Ibid., 陽貨, 子曰性相近也習相遠也 ; Legge, James, Confucius, p 318
[41] The Book of Mencius, chapter 13, 盡心章句上, 君子所性仁義禮智根於心... ; Legge, James, Mencius, p 40
[42] Ibid., 盡心章句上, 孟子曰君子有三樂而王天下不與存焉 父母俱存兄弟無故一樂仰不愧於天俯不怍於人二樂 得天下英才而教育之三樂 ... ; Legge, James, Mencius, pp 458-459

4.1.3 The Anthropological Aspect of Jen

It is clear that Mencius put great emphasis on the dignity of a man as a person. Every man has a chance to be an Emperor, even like the legendary kings "Yao and Shun (堯 舜)".[43] Such a thought was impossible for Confucius who always thought that there should be rigorous hierarchy for the ideal society to be established. Confucius despised the men with a small mind (小 人) and women together as unteachable from the beginning.[44] They had no chance to be the Ideal Man of Virtue (君 子) according to Confucius, they were those subjects who were just to be loved and to be helped. Women and the men with a small mind (小 人) were for Mencius as much unimportant as for Confucius. He mentioned about women just once in his whole books, but never despised women and the men with a small mind (小 人). He just talked about the womanly virtues and the behavior of the men with a small mind (小 人).[45] He believed that even an Ideal Man of Virtue (君 子) like Confucius had no chance to be a King or an Emperor when the Heaven's Will would not cooperate. The legendary Emperors of the Chinese history were also ordinary men at the beginning.[46] Even the saints are the same men as you and me.[47] Therefore, in principle, everybody has the same chance to be anybody whom he wants to be. The foremost reason for this assertion is the assumption of the intrinsic good nature of man.[48] What is then a man? Mencius said Jen (仁) is the man himself.[49]

As we can see, Confucius had never explained why we should practice Jen (仁), but Mencius had tried to give an answer to that arguing that the nature of man is good.[50] When man is not good in his nature, there is no difference between man and animal. Only the Ideal Man of Virtue (君 子) keeps this good

---

[43] op. cit., chapter 12, 告子章句下，曹交問曰人皆可以爲堯舜有儲孟子曰然...; They are the first three legendary Emperors with Wu(禹﹚i n the Chinese history. ; Legge, James, Mencius, p 424

[44] The Analects of Confucius, chapter 17, 陽貨，子曰唯女子與小人爲難養也近之卽不遜遠之卽怨 ; Legge, James, Confucius, p 330

[45] The Book of Mencius, chapter 6, 藤文公章句下,...女子之嫁也...往之女家必敬必械 ... ; Legge, James, Mencius, p 265

[46] op. cit., chapter 9, 萬章章句上,...匹夫而有天下者德必若舜禹而又有天子騰之者故仲尼不有天下 ; Legge, James, Mencius, pp 359-360

[47] op. cit., chapter 11, 告子章句上，...聖人與我同類者 ; Legge, James, Mencius, p 405

[48] Ibid., 告子章句上, 孟子曰...人性之善也... ; Legge, James, Mencius, pp 395-396

[49] op. cit., chapter 14, 盡心章句下,...仁也者人也... ; Legge, James, Mencius, p 485

[50] Feng, You-lan, op. cit., p106

nature.[51] That is why there are so many men who are like animals according to Mencius. Notwithstanding the fact that it is extremely difficult to keep this nature and to be an Ideal Man of Virtue (君子), it is still true for the Confucians that the nature of man is good. So man is man as his nature is good, and he has a chance to be an Ideal Man of Virtue (君子) sometime in the future.

Mencius argued his theory of the good nature of man a little bit too far, but he had to do so because there were many other theories about the nature of man which he did not agree with and wanted them to be refuted. Some said that the nature of man was neither good nor bad. Another said that it was possible that the nature of man was both good and bad. And the other said that the nature of some men was good, and the nature of the other men was bad.[52] In the opinion of Mencius all these theories about the nature of man could not guarantee man the chance of being the Ideal Man of Virtue (君子). Mencius accepted the fact that man could be bad but he did not see the reason of it in the nature of man.[53] The problem was not the nature of man but the situation around man and his will or wisdom to choose the right way to be the Ideal Man of Virtue (君子).

As a matter of fact, ChuHsi (朱熹) supplemented the theory of Mencius about the nature of man. Since AD 1113, 113 years after the death of ChuHsi (朱熹), his interpretation of the "Four Books (四書)" of Confucian thought became the official text for the state examination to choose the officer for the Emperor or king not only in China but also after a while in most of the Asian countries where the Confucianism was the state ideology.[54] Japan was the exception. They accepted Confucianism but they never adopted the system of state examination. Not only because of this fact but also because of his brilliant metaphysical interpretations of Confucianism, ChuHsi (朱熹) became the most influential interpreter of Confucianism in the history of China. ChuHsi (朱熹) integrated Taoism and Buddhism in Confucianism, and made Confucianism as the representative Chinese humanism.[55] His interpretation is regarded as both the supplementation and the culmination of Confucianism. ChuHsi (朱熹) thought that Mencius had explained just about the nature of man, not about the character of man. For the explanation about the character of man he distinguished mind, reason and emotion of man. With these concepts he begun his metaphysical explanation about the nature of man, and with the help of the cosmology of Zhou Liam Xi (周濂溪), who died at his age of 56 in 1073, ChuHsi (朱熹)

---

[51] The Book of Mencius, chapter 8, 離婁章句下 孟子曰人之所以異於禽獸者幾希庶民去之君子存之 ... ; Legge, James, Mencius, p 325
[52] Feng, You-lan, op, cit., p106
[53] The Book of Mencius, chapter 11, 告子章句上, 若夫爲不善非才之罪也; Legge, James, Mencius, p 402
[54] Feng, You-lan, op, cit., p372
[55] Küng, H., Ching, J., op.cit., p106

reestablished the whole theory of Confucianism.

ChuHsi (朱 熹) never doubted the existence of the Four Virtues (四 德) of Mencius in the nature of man. He just explained, how these Four Virtues (四 德) could come about in the concrete action of man. He believed that the mind of man (心) had made the Four Virtues (四 德) of man come forward as visible action. He said that the nature of man was reason or principle (理), so it was intangible. But with the help of mind (心) man could understand what the nature of man should be.[56] For ChuHsi (朱 熹) the nature of man was still good. The problem was the character of man. He called it Chi (氣). According to the theory of ChuHsi (朱熹), we cannot see the nature of man but just the character of man. That is why we can say a man is good and the other is bad according to the exposed character of man even though the nature of man is always good. To have the good character we need discipline through education.[57] That is why the tradition of Confucianism emphasizes education. The Confucians believed and still believe that man can give a man the best chance to be the Ideal Man of Virtue (君 子) or somebody like him through the right education, but this emphasis on education was also the main object of the critics of the theory of ChuHsi (朱 熹). An arch-rival and critic of ChuHsi (朱 熹) was Liu Jiu Yuan (陸 九 淵). He and his follower Wang Yang Ming (王 陽 明) had criticized ChuHsi (朱 熹) that he confused being a scholar with being an Ideal Man of Virtue (君 子). They said that learning became the necessary condition to be an Ideal Man of Virtue (君 子) because of the theory of ChuHsi (朱 熹) and therefore those who had never a chance to learn could never be an Ideal Man of Virtue (君 子). They wanted to emphasize the way to the perfection through the instinctive individual decision.[58] However, this theory never prevailed. The metaphysical beauty of the theory of ChuHsi (朱 熹) and the political situation in China never allowed large room for Liu Jiu Yuan (陸 九 淵) and Wang Yang Ming (王 陽 明) even though they had quite a few followers.

Even though there are many schools other than that of ChuHsi (朱 熹), there has always been the common belief that the nature of man is good, and because of this fact man has a chance to be a perfect being, an Ideal Man of Virtue (君 子). Therefore the existence of evil lost its meaning in the tradition of Confucian thought.[59] Without the help of God, man can stand alone to be a good man. Even though in reality this belief of the Ideal Man of Virtue (君 子) has never been realized, it has still strong support from the multitudes in the Confucian society. This fact can explain why the multitudes always yearn for the philosopher-king as their leader, even today.

---

[56] Feng, You-lan, op, cit., p382
[57] Hans Küng, Julia Ching, op. cit., p108
[58] Ibid., pp108-109
[59] Ibid., p107

4.1.4 The Sociological Aspect of Jen

As a matter of fact, the object of Confucian theory was to build a society in which every member can live together in harmony, but in this society there is almost no room for the equality of man. Everybody has his pre-given role in a society and man has to do his best only to complete his role, from the Emperor to the ordinary man. An Emperor has a role to do as an Emperor, a subject as a subject, a father as a father, and a son as a son.[60] There is strict hierarchy in a Confucian society, but it never should be a relation of the exploiters and the exploited, but of reciprocal help for the symbiotic life in a society.

Between father and son there should be intimacy, between the Emperor and his subjects, justice, between man and wife, discretion, between the elder and the young, order, and between friends, trust.[61] When an Emperor does not do justice for his subjects as much as the subjects do for him, the political system must break down. When a man does not respect his wife as much as his wife does for him, their relation must go to end. Everything is reciprocal in the Confucian relation as Yin and Yang (陰 陽) represent. So the symbiotic life in a society is a must for the Confucians. Even though the life in the traditional Confucian society has never been in such an ideal situation, there always has been the yearning for the society of symbiosis. Mutual dependence between the rulers and multitudes has been always there, and in this situation the social justice has been a latent contract for all elements of society because it was the basis for the harmonious society where everybody helps everybody. Nevertheless, we have to admit that even this Confucian symbiosis is strongly hierarchical. We may call it vertical symbiosis in contrast to the horizontal one, which may be found in the form of Christian symbiosis. Jen (仁) plays here the crucial role. As well known, Jen (仁) has great room for diverse interpretations, but in its essence it must be integrating element for the sound society.

4.1.5 The Moral Aspect of Jen

Mencius' theory about the nature of man has always been the main theme of the Confucian scholars. Though there was an authoritative school of ChuHsi (朱 熹), which was the most dominating among the Confucian schools, the interpretation of human nature was one of the most controversial matter in Confucianism. Basically, it is clear for the Confucian scholars that the nature of man is intrinsically good, but brotherly love cannot be tolerated simply because

---

[60] The Analects of Confucius, chapter 12, 顏 淵 , ...君 君 臣 臣 父 父 子 子 ... ; Legge, James, Confucius, p 256
[61] The Book of Mencius, chapter 5, 藤 文 公 章 句 上 , ...父 子 有 親 君 臣 有 義 夫 婦 有 別 長 幼 有 序 朋 友 有 信 ... ; Legge, James, Mencius , p 252

it is not in accordance with the nature of man. We tend to love more our acquaintance than foreigner just because the former is more familiar than the latter. According to Confucianism man must devote oneself to his parents, but he cannot do the same for the other elders, he can just show his respect to them at most. A man can love his wife, but only with respect. Even if Confucianism, seen as a sociopolitical theory, is very keen on the hierarchical structure of society, in its theory about the nature of man, it is still quite egalitarian. As Mencius stressed many times in his "Book of Mencius", everybody has a chance even to be an Emperor, i.e., the Son of Heaven.

Therefore, the sympathy of Confucianism must be interpreted with caution. The hierarchical sociopolitical structure of Confucian society cannot stand alone without the mutual understanding and helping among people, for Jen (仁) is nothing but being faithful to oneself and tolerant to others.[62] Self-respect and understanding for neighbors require sympathy for both directions, for oneself and for the other. It is not only the nature of man but also a virtue that everybody should strive after, but this sympathetic nature of man is mostly hindered by the egoistic greed, one of the seven sentiments[63] which are to be overcome because they are in the way of being an Ideal Man of Virtue (君子). That is why a man is condemned when he pursuits to realize his own egoistic desire, for example, being rich in the traditional Confucian society. Material condition has almost nothing to do with the Ideal Man of Virtue (君子), the ultimate goal of man in this world, and too many material things even hinder this goal. That is one of the important reasons for the fact that there were almost no well developed commercial and financial system and accumulated capital in most Asian countries when they opened themselves to the West. Capital accumulation and speculation for the surplus profit are not for the ideal Confucian society because

---

[62] The Analects of Confucius, chapter 4, 里 仁 , 夫 子 之 道 忠 恕 已 矣 ; Legge, James, Confucius, p 170

[63] According to ChuHsi (朱熹), there are four cardinal virtues in Confucianism, i.e. Jen (仁), justice, courtesy, wisdom, which are to be metaphysical (形 而 上 學 的) and to be realized in a person; on the contrary, the seven sentiments, i.e. joy, anger, sorrow, pleasure, love, hate, desire, are to be physical(形 而 下 學 的), which means inferior part of man. Since ChuHsi (朱熹)'s this decisive definition about the four cardinal virtues and the seven sentiments of man, it has been a show of immaturity for a man to express openly these seven sentiments, and more, it was a hint of disgrace. The goal of "Ideal Man of Virtue (君子)" was almost a categorical imperative for all noble men in the traditional Confucian society. This "Ideal Man of Virtue (君子)" was a noble man who embodied the four cardinal virtues and abstained himself from expressing the seven sentiments, and furthermore, who could keep his mind under control in any given situation. This tradition of self-control is still cherished by many people in the modern Confucian society. That is why many foreigners have difficulties to know the true mind of Asian people for whom expressing one's emotion easily means a immaturity which is despised still in the modern Confucian society.

it makes people more egoistic and greedy, and these two characters of man are most hazardous for the harmonious society where everybody has to live together in symbiosis. We may think that we have less social problem when we can produce enough for the social needs. But there is no "enough" as long as it has to do with the desire of man. The precondition for the harmonious society, where nobody feels sorry, is having sympathy for the other member of society. It is up to the Heaven's Will (天命) whether a man is rich or not as much as life and death is a matter of destiny according to Mencius. When a man is devout and blameless, and furthermore, courteous with others, he has everybody in this world as his brothers and sisters.[64] According to this conviction of Zi Xia (子夏), one of the prominent 72 disciples of Confucius, the traditional Confucian society is a place where everybody helps others with respect. That is why the hierarchical social order could coexist with the sympathetic attitude. This respect for others manifested in the formal courtesy is a sign of the inner maturity of man. A mature man in the Confucian society is the Ideal Man of Virtue (君子), the embodiment of the four cardinal virtues, and of these virtues Jen (仁) is the most important. Jen (仁) is not sympathy itself, but the latter is the basis and beginning of the former. That means, there could be no Jen (仁) without sympathy. The famous simile of Mencius about rescuing a baby approaching the deep well shows us that Jen (仁) is more a helping hand than an attitude. It is not important whose baby it is because the baby is already a person who deserves to be treated as a person.

In the tradition of Confucianism, everybody is born with the seeds of the four cardinal virtues, which distinguish man from animal. A man can find his true identity only when he sees himself as the moral subject, which has at least the intention to practice the virtues. At the center of these virtues stands Jen (仁), which is in the nature of man, coming from the Heaven. The nature of man is decreed by the Heaven (天). To follow this nature is Tao (道), and to search this Tao (道) is education.[65] Man is in his nature from the Heaven (天), man has to do his best to be treated as a being of heavenly nature. This heavenly nature of man can be manifested in everyday life only when man knows himself as the carrier of the four cardinal virtues and behaves according to them. All these four cardinal virtues can be summed up as Jen (仁). And again, as above mentioned, Jen (仁) is etymologically just a matter of "between two man" even if it came from the Heaven. Neither the cosmology nor the life after death are not needed to be taught in learning about Jen (仁). It is purely a matter of human beings in

---

[64] The Analects of Confucius, chapter 12, 顏淵, 商聞之矣死生有命富貴在天君子敬而無失與人恭而有禮四海之內皆兄弟君子何患乎無兄弟也; Legge, James, Confucius, p 253

[65] The Book of the Mean, chapter 1, 天命之爲性率性之爲道修道之爲敎; Legge, James, Confucius, p 383

this world. It is of course too haste to draw the conclusion that Confucianism is humanism. But as long as there is no heavenly being in Confucianism, the Confucians have had to establish and explain the affair of this world with the nature of human and human behavior, which must be always in accordance to Jen (仁), and Jen (仁) is nothing but the helping hands for fellow human beings who is in need.

Even though it is true that the formal sociopolitical hierarchy has been the most important social substrata in the tradition of Confucianism, the Emperor or a king, who was at the zenith of this hierarchical structure, was asked incessantly to be the Ideal Man of Virtue (君 子), which begins with the unconditional sympathy for other human beings. Nowadays, there stays still the hierarchical social structure in most of the Confucian countries, but without this humanism, i.e., only the form of Confucian society stays still while the ethos of it has disappeared since long. The form and its substance must be in harmony, or the society should be in chaos. The rehabilitation of this traditional Confucian humanism has been tried in vain by many scholars of Confucianism. This is almost an impossible task even when the Western culture has influenced strongly the conscious of people in the modern Confucian society. The traditional way of Confucian "back to the old tradition" cannot find any visible resonance any more without new elements when it is disclosed that there lacks conclusively fraternity and equality in Confucianism. The natural desire of man to be respected as any other on the principle of social justice has been awakened by the influence of the Western culture, which is based on Christianism and Hellenism. The fraternal Christian love and the Hellenic tradition of individualism appeal very much to the people in the Confucian society, even though they do not understand quite well what they are. These concepts of equality and freedom, which had no place in the tradition of Confucianism, are too attractive to resist for many people in the Confucian society.

4.2 Christian Love as the Sympathy of Social Justice

4.2.1 The Pauline Interpretation of Christian Love

Christian love is as hard as the Christian trinity for the Asians to understand. Every concept of Confucianism is unequivocally in the hierarchical system. In Confucianism father is father, and son is son. Every other concept begins from this relation between father and son in Confucianism. Father must be affectionate for his son, and son does filial duty (孝 道) only for his own father. For the elders he may show only his respect, never filial duty (孝 道). Everything and every relation are fixed in Confucianism, but in Christianism God is Father and Father is Son and the Holy Spirit is Son. Man can love his neighbor because God loves man. Jesus Christ, the only Son of God, is in God, as God is in Jesus Christ. Love is everywhere in Christianism. That makes a Confucian extremely difficult to understand the meaning of love. By returning to the origin, the Bible, we may find a glimpse of love even if nowadays the meaning of love becomes too diverse to be interpreted in a few words.

Love is not an exclusive phenomenon of the Judeo-Christian tradition. We can see many words for love in different cultures : אָהַב (ahab), דֹּדִים (dodim), חֶסֶד (hesed), and עֲגָבִים (yagabim) in old Hebrew, 愛 (ai) in old Chinese, φιλια ἀγάπη ἔρως in old Greek, and amor in old Latin, but the love of Christian God has very distinctive character, which can be found seldom in other cultures.

Jesus Christ told about love in many ways. One of the famous definition of love is as follows: "*Do for the other as you want from them*" (Matt. 7:12).[66] St. Paul has tried to define this love a little bit longer in his letter for his fellow followers of Jesus Christ in Corinth.[67] Generally, love means an emotional tendency of man to an object, another man or thing. There is also self-love, but this kind of love has its object too, the self. This subject-object relation has always created a dynamic action and reaction, and love itself has never stood alone. It needs its carrier, man as a person. There is love whenever a person does something good for other person. Most of all, love manifests itself as the helping hands. When a man gives food for the hungry and water for the thirsty, and welcomes a stranger, it is nothing less than love itself (Matt. 25:34-40).[68] So for Jesus Christ it is a simple thing to love a man as a person. Love is just an act of love and nothing more.

For St. Paul love is more than just an act. He tried to define love with other rational concepts. Love has something to do with heart, conscience, and belief (1Tim. 1:5).[69] Furthermore love has something to do with science and sense (Phil. 1:9). That means, love is not only a matter of emotion but also of reason. Love is the integration of the whole Jewish commandments from the God (Rom. 13:8-10).[70] When love should be a law then it sounds to be a kind of duty. Is Christian love then a kind of duty that everybody "must" fulfill? At first glance it seems so. St. Paul was incessantly talking about the necessity of loving each other. He even talked about the labor of love (laboris caritatis, του κόπου της ἀγάπης) (1 Thess. 1:3)[71] We have to love till we are exhausted. Here the love is just self-sacrifice, as Jesus Christ Himself explained with extreme parables (Luke. 6:27-36).[72] It sounds even self-denial. Is there then any meaning of love

---

[66] Nesle-Aland, Novum Testamentum Graece et Latine (Stuttgart: Deutsche Bibelgesellschaft,1991), p16
[67] Ibid., p464
[68] Ibid., pp73-75
[69] Ibid., p542
[70] Ibid., p433
[71] Ibid., p531
[72] Ibid., pp173-174

when a partner perishes in love? Love is principally a relation of person to person, or person to any other thing of affection. When it is so, could there be a lasting love when a partner of this relation goes forever? Should love have a limitation for the survival of all participants of this wonderful relation? Jesus Christ saw no compromise. He loved us unconditionally and demanded us the same kind of perfect love (John 15:12-13).[73] He loved us so much that he could not help being with us as a helping solacer (Paraclitos, παρακλητος) even after his ascending to heaven (John 14:16, 26; 15: 26).[74] How could this kind of extreme self-sacrificing love be possible in the mind of Jesus Christ? It might be possible when there were the thought of near end of the world. Jesus Christ himself talked about the end of the world very minutely (Matt. 24:1-51; Mark 13:1-37; Luke 21:5-36).[75] And his disciples and followers believed very strongly in the end of the world, which must be very near. They even hoped that the end of the world and the coming of Jesus Christ would come much sooner (Rev. 22:20).[76] When the end of the world is near, it is quite understandable to love one's neighbor to the extreme because the Last Judgment is so clear and severe in the eyes of the Christians (Matt. 25:31-46).[77] But the end of the world came not so soon as many Christians had expected. After the emotional expectation gone array, there should be a way to explain the situation in which the Christians had to be situated, and as usual, an explanation needed a logical persuasiveness. What St. Paul tried to do was exactly such a logical explanation so that a man with sane mind cannot help just accepting his reasoning. In this way his very brilliant explanation of love might come into being. He never met Jesus Christ personally but his thought about Christian love is in line with that of Jesus Christ Himself. St. Paul had just explained the love of Jesus Christ in his own words for the people who are interested in Jesus Christ who must come again for his love of all human beings.

4.2.2 The Theological Aspect of Christian Love

God is the creator of all, and most of all, he is omnipotent, omnipresent and omniscient. He created simply everything, including people (האדם). From the beginning, people are both male and female(זכר ונקבה) (Gen. 1:27).[78] God created first the man (האדם) and then the woman (אשה) because man needed a to

---

[73] Ibid., p301
[74] Ibid., p298, p299, p302
[75] Ibid., pp68-71, pp133-136, pp229-231
[76] Ibid., p680
[77] Ibid., pp73-74
[78] K. Elliger, W. Rudolph(ed.), Biblia Hebraica Stuttgartensia (Stuttgart: Deutsche Bibelgesellschaft, 1990), p2

him fitting help (עֵזֶר) (Gen. 2:20, 22).[79] With this man God has a dynamic relation of love.

God is not only righteous but also graceful and loving. The man and the woman died not promptly even if they had eaten the fruit from the tree of knowledge of good and bad. God simply let them go out of the east side of the Garden of Eden and live further together, even though they had been strongly forbidden from eating from the tree of life. God gave them even clouds to help them to survive. After this deporting from the Garden of Eden, the woman became the life (חוה) because she was the mother of all living (Gen. 3:20).[80] God never talked about love or forgiving. God did just his best for the man and the woman who did not obey his order. Here we can see that Christian love means unconditional forgiving and helping. It does not matter whether the loved deserves this love. God may need man as much as man needs Him, for love stands never alone but only between the lover and the beloved. God may be not satisfied when He has to love just Himself. In this regard, man is a good partner of God with the matter of love, even though there seems to be a one-sided love between them. Accepting the love from the lover as true love is as much important as loving truly the beloved. Only in such a relation, there is a true love. That may be why God wanted from man love for Him, even though He already knew that man is just His creature, who is much inferior to Him.

This kind of love manifested itself as help and forgiveness reflected in the whole history of Israelites. At least in the time of the Old Testaments, God loved (אהב) especially the Israelites, and He helped to save them from the hand of the Pharaoh of Egypt, the other men who might need as much love from God as the Israelites (Deut. 4:37).[81] God even became a doctor to heal (רפא) the disease of Israelites (Ex. 15:26).[82]

With the coming of Jesus Christ the love of God became to be the love of all mankind, even of the whole world (mundum, τον κοσμον) (John 3:16).[83] God loved and still loves the world he made so much that He even sent his only son to the world. Jesus Christ as the incarnated God loved all men and healed everyone who asked him to be merciful. Because of the coming of Jesus Christ in this world, the blind saw, the cripples walked, the leprous were healed, the dumb spoke, the dead waked up, and the poor preached the Gospel (evangelizantur, ευαγγελιζονται).[84] With the coming of Jesus Christ, this world became a place worth living in because God had shown with His great deeds that He loved and still loves us in "this world" so much. He just loves us. God's

---

[79] Ibid., p4
[80] Ibid., pp3-4
[81] Ibid., p292
[82] Ibid., p112
[83] Nesle-Aland, op. cit., p253
[84] Ibid., p27

love must be unconditional and lasting. His love must be a kind of self-sacrificing because He has suffered hardship for our sakes (Matt. 8:17).[85] Jesus Christ always saw the misery of the multitudes around him and tried to alleviate them in every possible situation (Matt. 9:36, 14:14, 15:32).[86] He emphasized especially the misery of the poor, the grieved, the hungry, and the weak and tried to give them hope to survive (Matt. 5:3-5; Luke 6:20-21).[87] He simply loved all people, especially the needy.

4.2.3 The Anthropological Aspect of Christian Love

God is the Creator and man is the creature. God is omnipotent, omnipresent and omniscient. Man is helpless before God. God is above there and man is down here. In this regard, there could be just one-sided relation between God and man. But God is jealous (קנא) (Ex. 20:5, 34:14), He is unable to bear when man has another God than Him.[88] God needs to be loved by man. God will show his grace (חֶסֶד) several thousand times to the man who loves God and keeps His Commandments (Ex. 20:5-6).[89] God is a perfect being but He still needs love, especially the love of man. We do not know why, but if God needs our love, that means man has love in his inside which can be given when God wants it. It is absurd to assume that God asks man what he does not have. Man has a freedom to love God. From the beginning man has the free will to do anything he wants even if he did not notice that. Therefore, man could have the freedom even not to keep the first prohibition of God and ate the fruit of wisdom. God still loves man even if man is out of the Garden of Eden. What is this man whom God loves so much? What is this man doing sometimes against the will of God even if God loves him so much?

According to St. Augustine, anything natural is good because God, the only Creator, is intrinsically good.[90] He is the summum bonum, so man must be also good because he is one of the natures of good God. Man is good in nature, and can do anything what he wants because he has the free will, but for man to abuse

---

[85] Ibid., p19
[86] Ibid., p23, p39, p43
[87] Ibid., pp8-10, p172
[88] Ex 20:5 Thou shalt not bow down thyself to them, nor serve them: for I the LORD thy God am a jealous God, visiting the iniquity of the fathers upon the children unto the third and fourth generation of them that hate me;
Ex 34:14 For thou shalt worship no other god: for the LORD, whose name is Jealous, is a jealous God:
[89] K. Elliger, W. Rudolph(ed.), op. cit., pp118-119
[90] Sahakian, William S., Ethics: An Introduction to the Theories and Problems (New York: Barnes & Noble Books, 1974), p77

it by choosing to pervert nature renders it evil.[91] Even if it is evil, the nature of man is still good, for the turning from the superior to the inferior becomes bad, not because the things whereunto it turns are bad, but because the turning is bad and perverse.[92] Is a man as a person then really good? Is he the same as God? No, he is not. When we understand person (as the carrier of dignity) as a social function, a metaphor for the social role which is given not individual but rather conventional (as the diverse functions in the matter of court), then a man as a person has something to do not only with God but also with his fellow.[93] Man as a person has a relation with fellow man as much as with God. Being loved by God and loving God is simple because there is no precondition for this kind of love. Man has to just do what God has ordered before, but love among persons in society is a complicated matter because it presupposes the good and loving nature of man. It is true that the nature of man is inferior to that of God because man is a part of the whole creation of God. Even though we cannot identify the nature of man as person with God who is the summum bonum, the autonomy of the human mind is the best precondition for the idea of truth and possibility of knowing it.[94] Man alone has the supreme kind of autonomy. That is the free will. Free will is surely a trait of the identity of man as person. Normally, we distinguish man from animal with the argument that man has reason, which is independent from the natural evolution of life, since reason is a law standing against any life span of man. Nevertheless, reason alone is not enough for a man to be a man. We need a principle, which is called mind. Mind encompasses not only the act of idea but also the intuition which is the "Urphenomenon" or a content of essence, and furthermore, a kind of volitional and emotional act as kindness, love, repent, reverence, spiritual awe, beatitude and despair, and most of all the free determination.[95] We call the center of the act, where the mind appears within the limited sphere of the being, as person who is absolutely distinguished from all functional centers of life, which could be called mental center.[96] The mind of person is the only being that can objectify itself. The center of mind is the person and it is neither objective nor physical being, but just the always self-realizing (substantially regulated) order units of actions.[97] In this regard a person is a being which has not only any other trait of living creatures but also free will and mind.

---

[91] Ibid., p78
[92] St. Augustine, de civitate dei, Bk. XII, Ch. 6, John Healy (tr.) (from. the Christian Classics Ethereal Library server at Wheaton College in Internet, last modified Sep. 16. 1996)
[93] Wils, Jean-Pierre, Mieth, Dietmar (ed.), Grundbegriffe der christlichen Ethik (Paderborn: Ferdinand Schöningh,1992), p110
[94] Scheler, Max, Die Stellung des Menschen im Kosmos (Bern: Francke Verlag,1975), p64
[95] Ibid., pp38-39
[96] Ibid., p38
[97] Ibid., p48

In relation with God man has a special position in the universe because man alone is created after the form of God, of all His creatures. Man alone has free will and mind, and man alone is person as the center of mind. He can love, and is the carrier of ethical action, therefore the subject of duty.

4.2.4 The Sociological Aspect of Christian Love

Living together and helping each other were not the exclusive character of the early Christian community. There were three philosophical schools among the Jewish before the time of Jesus Christ. They were the Pharisee, the Sadducee and the Essene.[98] The Essene shared their goods among their members equally. They lived not for the individual profit but for the interest of community. They lived not in a single city or town, but they were ubiquitous. They helped each other literally. For example, when brethren came to visit other brethren in another city or town, the former did its best for the latter even though they had never met before. The latter could use anything, which belonged to the former. They helped even nonmembers when these were in need of help. The members of Essene had no individual freedom but two: helping others and having mercy on the other.[99] As the worshiper of God, who was then Jewish God, they lived like the true Christian. What does it mean here the "true Christian"? Literally a true Christian is a follower who listens to Jesus Christ and does exactly what he has asked for. What has Jesus Christ asked for? When somebody forces you to go one mile, you have to go with him two miles, when someone asks you something, you should give him, and when somebody will borrow something from you, you should not refuse (Matt. 5:41-42).[100] Jesus Christ Himself has showed that we can have more than enough, when we share what we have with the other (Matt. 14:15-21).[101] What Jesus Christ really wanted was not the sacrifice for God but mercy for the needy (Matt. 12:7).[102] Jesus Christ was the good shepherd who gave his life for the sheep (John 10:11).[103] As Jesus Christ had asked his followers several times the same thing, his followers lived together like the Essene. They met together and shared everything together. They sold what they possessed and property and distributed them to all according to the need (Acts 2:43-47).[104] Nobody of the believers in Jesus Christ told that it was his own what belonged to him, but it was for all commonly.

---

[98] Flavius Josephus, Geschichte des Judaeischen Krieges, Heinrich Clementz(tr.) (Leipzig: Verlag Philipp Reclam jun. Leipzig,1990), p 158
[99] Ibid., pp159-161
[100] Nesle-Aland, op. cit., p11
[101] Ibid., p39
[102] Ibid., p29
[103] Ibid., p282
[104] Ibid., p326

Nobody among them was poor. Those who had fields and houses sold them and brought the money and deposited the money before the feet of the apostles. And the money was divided to every single member according to his need (Acts 4:32-36).[105]

It is the core of Christian doctrine that man lives in symbiosis. It is very important for Christian that man has mercy on the needy and helps them. Love in Christian spirit means nothing but understanding the situation of the needy and doing best for them even if sometimes it demands one's own life. When someone loves the needy so much, it means that his sin is already forgiven (Luke 7:47).[106] He who helped the needy, will be judged for the eternal life at the day of the Last Judgment (Matt. 25:31-36).[107] How can a true Christian then have no mercy on the needy and not help them? Loving others is not the duty of the Christians but the privilege of them.

4.2.5 The Moral Aspect of Christian Love

Jesus Christ had never used the word of love before he practiced love for the needy around Him. He just had sympathy for the people in need and helped them. But it was not giving alms indiscriminately but having pity on the needy and giving help what they needed. He did not make a promise that He could not keep. He even gave them before the needy had asked Him for anything. This is an active kind of sympathy in contrast to that of Mencius. Active sympathy cannot be always better than the passive one, but the former has advantage in persuading the multitudes who explain their indifference for the needy in the society with their not knowing about the situation.

The true Christian love means not just wishing a well for the poor, but actively knowing and giving what they need. As St. James had once said, a belief without action is dead, and stays just as a belief itself (Jas. 2:17).[108] As the body without the spirit is dead, so faith without works is dead also (Jas. 2:26). This could provoke a very profound theological controversy, because St. James said, "...*You see then how that by works a man is justified, and not by faith only...*" (Jas. 2:24) It has been one of the most controversial theological problems whether we can be saved through our good deeds or through our faith only. We can see many cases of faith that healed the sick and the cripples in the Gospels. Jesus Christ saw their faith and healed them immediately. Christian faith means trusting in God and Jesus Christ, and this trust means not only the belief in His promises but also doing what He taught us. Both for the Augustinian and for the Thomist there is no doubt that God is the summum bonum, but there can be no

---

[105] Ibid., p331-332
[106] Ibid., pp178-179
[107] Ibid., p74
[108] Ibid., p591

sure answer to the question if His grace alone without the virtuous behavior of man guarantees the best way leading to Him. If St. Augustine has right, it is almost of no use that we are doing good for our neighbor because everything in this world is already predestined. All we can do is just waiting and hoping for His amazing grace. St. Thomas saw this problem, and his adherence to the philosophy of Aristotle made him more generous for the good human efforts. His intellectualism showed us that the human will must subject to the human intellect, with the final goal of will and intellect being the contemplation of God, a vision of the divine essence.[109] By virtue of the papal encyclical of Leo XIII in 1879, Thomism has been declared the official philosophy of the Roman Catholic Church, but not all Roman Catholics adhere to Thomism, as is evidenced by members of the Franciscan order, who embrace Scotism, and members of the Augustinian order, who adhere to St. Augustine's teachings. Protestant has been greatly influenced by St. Augustine, particularly through Martin Luther, who was an Augustinian monk.[110]

In his book "de civitate dei" St. Augustine argued many things, which are still regarded, as very Christian, among them: the strong distinction of good and evil, of love for God and love for the world. Accordingly, two cities have been formed by two loves: the earthly by the love of self, even to the contempt of God; the heavenly by the love of God, even to the contempt of self.[111] Even the conjugal affection must not be based on the earthly "passio" of sex because the latter is not from heaven. The carnal life is to be understood not only of living in bodily indulgence, but also of living in the vices of the inner man.[112] When everything earthly is evil and only the heavenly thing is good, there is no room for man to do something for the betterment of this world. This attitude of two cities, the city of God and the city of earth, can be very crucial when we have to think about the Last Judgment, but it is not quite plausible attitude when we have to live in this earthly and "evil" world as long as the Last Day does not come yet. When the goal of the city of God is peace, and war is the goal of the city of man, as St. Augustine argued, we have no chance of peace as long as we live here in his world.[113] It is true that we have to wage war in everyday life, regardless of the scale. Especially in the world of capitalistic economic system, we have to do our best to win the struggle to survive, for a kind of Darwinian survival. It is quite true that a man who survived the competition does not always have to be the morally good one, especially from the Christian point of view. Nevertheless, it is necessary evil that man has to win the competition in this world even man sometimes has to victimize his neighbor for his interest. We

---

[109] Sahakian, William S., op. cit., p84
[110] Ibid., p85
[111] St. Augustine, op. cit., Bk. XIV, Ch. 28
[112] Ibid., Bk. XIV, Ch. 2
[113] Ibid., Bk. XIX, Ch. 27-28

have to have victims who are our neighbors as long as we live in this world of war. We may simply say that the needy in this world are the losers of the struggle for survival regardless of their intention. The losers are also beloved children of God, and they deserve everything from God as much as the winners. That is why we need the sympathy of Jesus Christ for the needy in this world, not in heaven.

The ideal love of Jesus Christ is quite radical for the earthly life. Man cannot practically give his neighbor everything he has, let alone his own life. As long as we are brothers and sisters in the Christian belief, we have to treat our neighbors with respect, not as a means for our conscience alleviation but as a true object of Christian love. As Kant said:

"*Man is indeed unholy enough, but he must regard humanity in his own person as holy. In all creation every thing one chooses and over which one has any power, may be used merely as means; man alone, and with him every rational creature, is an end in himself.*"[114]

When this attitude is appropriate for the Christian fraternity, it can be fittingly described with the concept of sympathy for others.

To tell the truth, the people whom Jesus Christ helped so sincerely were mostly not "normal" members of the society, they were all not fit for the society: the sick, the deformed, prostitutes, the hungry, and so on, but they deserved the mercy and bless of God who created man. This Christian justice comes first from God not from man, but man has the responsibility to do just for his fellow human beings, as God has done for them. Jesus Christ told many times that to love him is to do justice for the socially unfit, especially for the least fit.[115] When we want to have a right and just relation with God, we have to first be right and just for our fellow human beings. To come into the Kingdom of Heaven or the Kingdom of God man has to do the justice of God, which is nothing but loving fellow human beings.

This tradition of Christian social justice based on the fraternity has lost much of its appeal in the Western society since the dawn of the Industrialization and capitalism. To make possibly the greatest output of profit with the least input of investment has become the paradigm not only of industry but also of the whole society. In such a society, in helping others, especially the socially unfit, man needs much more careful reckon, lest man becomes himself one of the socially unfit. To survive the severe competition in the modern society, man has to be more egoistic, or he is going to be a loser, which means literally social trash with no human dignity. With the help of individualism of the modern society, capitalism pushed the Christian love to the edge of a precipice. Especially after

---

[114] Kant, Immanuel, the Critic of Practical Reason, Thomas Kingsmill Abbott (tr.) , 1788, p 81

[115] Mt 25:40   And the King shall answer and say unto them, Verily I say unto you, Inasmuch as ye have done it unto one of the least of these my brethren, ye have done it unto me.

the demise of communism, in the modern society based on the capitalistic motto of productivity, man is weighed by his efficiency, i.e., when a man cannot produce concrete goods for the society more than he consumes, he must be blamed as the unwanted of the society. Human dignity is no more dependent on what he is, but what he produces. Even if everybody knows that this is not a good situation for human beings, there is not much room for the old Christian virtue of love as the capitalism has become the almighty paradigm of the day. Capitalism without social justice is as bad as communism with the dictatorship of communistic party. There has been Jacques Martain, a Neo-Thomist, who saw the root of the evil of the modern society in the anthropocentric humanism. He tried to cure the society with the Christian humanism, true humanism, integral humanism, and theocentric humanism.[116] Theocentric humanism gives history a meaning, a direction, and a supreme ideal, namely, the institution of a brotherly city where standards of justice and friendship will be continuously perfected.[117] The static world of the traditional Christian point of view does not fit anymore for the modern society, so it was not a successful approach to rebuild the old Christian humanism on the new soil of modern society. The traditional Christian humanism must find a way to the modern anthropocentric humanism to make its appeal to the modern society more plausible. As long as the concrete modern social justice can be established without the direct help of the theocentric justice, i.e., man can help other fellow human beings with his own determination based purely on the anthropocentric humanism, the Christian humanism has to find its place as a part of social justice, not the sole one. This approach could be begun when man understands the love of God more as the sympathy of man for his fellow human being than as the celestial mystery of God, as Jesus Christ Himself showed us concretely in this world.

Jesus Christ gave bread and wine, which were his body and blood of the New Testament, even to Judas Iskariot, the man who was going to betray Jesus Christ. Judas Iskariot was the only disciple who was told by Jesus Christ personally that he had better not to be born. Notwithstanding the evil nature of Judas Iskariot, Jesus Christ washed even his feet to purify him. This shows dramatically the essence of Christian love. It is the sympathy of social justice. Christian love does not discriminate people according to their nature and ability. It is quite of no importance what a man is going to do in the future. It was very clear for Jesus Christ that Judas Iskariot was going to commit the severest sin: betraying the only Son of God, but Jesus Christ loved him as much as any other disciple. By the same token, a true Christian society lets not only the socially productive member, i.e., anyone who makes contribution to GDP (gross domestic productivity), but also the socially unfit live side by side. Every single person is

---

[116] Sahakian, William S., op. cit., p 85
[117] Ibid., p 88

God's beloved child, and this is enough for a man to be treated as a person. The motto of "live and let live" is manifested in the true Christian society. This Christian society can be sustained only when every member has sympathy for others. This Christian sympathy was practiced very well by Jesus Christ Himself. Christian love is not just a good relationship between men, but a testament between God and man.

We may discuss about the theological concept of Christian love, as much as the ontological and sociological one, but for the purpose of this paper, we may concentrate our attention to the social ethical aspect of Christian love. The welfare system of the Western countries cannot be established without the social ethical idea derived from Christian love. This Christian love begins with the compassion for the needy, as Jesus Christ showed Himself too many times for us. This compassion is nothing but the sympathy for the needy. More minute analysis of the concept of sympathy should be in the following chapters.

5. Sympathy in its Phenomenological Context

5.1 The Etymological Exposition of Sympathy

5.1.1 συμπάθεια: The Western Understanding of Sympathy

In old Hebrew there is a word "חמל (hml)" which should mean having pity. We can see its usage in many passages in the Old Testaments, for example, in Exodus 2:6, 1 Samuel 23:21, Isaiah 63:9, Jeremiah 15:5, Joshua 2:18, and so on. And furthermore, we can see many usage of the word "המה (hmh)" and its derivatives which originally meant the growling or the screaming of animal, and has acquired the meaning of pity later. In Jeremiah 4:19 or Psalm 42:6,12 this word should mean the beating heart. And in Jeremiah 31:20 we can see again that the word "המה (hmh)," with the reflexive pronoun following "ל (l)," is used to mean the feeling of sympathy of God for Ephraim.[118] And the word "רחם (rhm)" followed, which means the mercy of God.

In the New Testaments there are many usage of such words as "ἐλεέω (having mercy on)" and "σπλαγχνίζομαι (having pity on)" in the presence of Jesus Christ.[119]. Whenever the blind or the cripple requested Jesus Christ to have His ἔλεος on them, He responded with σπλαγχνίζομαι and He healed them all. St. Peter used in his first letter the word of συμπάθεια (sympathy) with other

---

[118] K. Elliger, W. Rudolph(ed.), op. cit., p845

[119] for example in Matt. 9:27, 15:32, 18:33 and in Mark 6:34, 8:2 10:47 and in Luke 7:13, 10:33, 17:13, 18:38 and so on.

associated words like φιλάδελφια (brotherly love) and εὔσπλαγχνος (compassionate) (1 Peter 3:8-9).[120] Here we can see the three kinds of loving and helping minds even if there is still a room for various interpretations for those words. St. Paul also talked about σπλάγχνα with παραμύθειον ἀγάπης (persuasive appeal of love) and οἰκτιρμοί (compassion) in his letter to all the saints in Jesus Christ, who live in Philippi(Phil. 2:1-2).[121]

It is noteworthy that Jesus Christ had never used the word of love like φιλία, ἀγάπη, or ἔρος when He truly loved and healed the sick, the blind, and the cripples. He just felt the same feeling as they did, and had such a great pity on them that He could not help helping them. He knew just how they suffered under their respective situations even though He Himself was a perfect being who never had to have such an experience personally. Without having the same experience, to know and to understand the situation in which others are, is not impossible though it is not so quite easy as Jesus Christ Himself showed us.

Etymologically, we may understand the word of sympathy to mean having the same feeling with someone else in a certain situation, and moreover, having an attitude or a readiness to help the person in need. Even if we still cannot explain exactly how it comes into being, i.e., how the human brain functions when it comes the emotion of sympathy into being, one thing is certain that there has been such an emotion called sympathy and it has a positive function for the collective survival of the human beings in the world since man had come into this world and started to live together. At first glance, it seems to be one of many instincts useful for the collective survival shared with other relatively highly developed animals in the world. When it is true, sympathy must be a psychological phenomenon, which can be described as a kind of automated reaction of man in a certain situation.

If sympathy is an instinct, why Jesus Christ should urge us incessantly to love each other as he loved us. When to love each other and to have mercy on others are just a kind of instinct, it needs not to be taught and learned. When only God or the Supreme Being can do love others unconditionally, Jesus Christ needed not to tell us how to love each other. Love must neither an instinct, nor a heavenly phenomenon. It is still extremely difficult for man to love others as Jesus Christ loves us because love must not be the wholly a posteriori acquirable trait of man. It must be somewhere between instinct and reason of man. As long as we are not certain what the conscious or the conscience of man is, we may be forced to accept such phenomena just as they are there even though we do not know what they exactly must be. That is why we need to understand first what a person is when we are about to scrutinize the concept of sympathy. In chapter 5.2 we will handle this matter.

---

[120] Nestle-Aland, op. cit., p603
[121] Ibid., p 517

5.1.2 Tong Quin: The Asian Understanding of Sympathy

In the history of Chinese philosophy we can see many usage of the word "Tong Quin (同 情)" which means sympathy. Si Ma Qian (司 馬 遷) talked about Tong Quin (同 情) in his history book "Shi Ji"(史 記 , the History of China). He said that when people have the Tong Quin (同 情), they can help each other in achieving something worthwhile. Han Fei Zi (韓 非 子) and Zhun Nam Zi (准 男 子) also talked about the positive effects of the Tong Quin (同 情). Literally, Tong Quin (同 情) means the same sentiment among the concerned people.[122] As time goes by, it has acquired more ethical meaning, and nowadays it means exactly the same feeling as sympathy. Until the "Opening to the West (開 港)" most of the people in the traditional Confucian society suffered mostly from hunger and political oppression. The most important economic basis of Confucian society was agriculture, especially the rice cultivation. To have a good crop of rice man needs a well-organized and very intensive labor force because the cultivation of rice needs a tremendous amount of water and very precise work process according to the seasonal change. That is why the irrigation was developed so early in old China. Controlling the perennially overflowing rivers and building and keeping reservoirs for the coming drought season could be archived only through the well-organized work forces. The royal budget depended not only on the good crop but also on the efficient logistics for the tax collecting, which was in fact rice management. This job could be done only through the strongly centralized bureaucracy. However, the bureaucracy alone could not make people work voluntarily for the Emperor. Only when the Emperor understood the mind of his people and shared with them what he had, people followed his command willingly. This spirit of sharing is Tong Quin (同 情). Mencius once talked with a king who has his private hunting ground and shared it with nobody. He even killed anybody who hunted in his game reserve. The king asked Mencius why his people think that his hunting ground is too big when the people of Wen Wang (文 王), one of the legendary kings in the early Chinese history, had thought that their king had small hunting ground even though he had had much bigger hunting ground than his. The answer of Mencius was simple: Wen Wang (文 王) had shared his hunting ground with his people.[123] He had understood the mind of his people and did what people wanted. This attitude of Tong Quin (同 情) of the rulers for their people was cherished through the history of China. When a king

---

[122] Mordhashi, Tetsuji (諸 橋 轍 次), Great Chinese-Japanese Dictionary, Bk. 4 (大 漢 和 辭 典, 卷 四) (Tokyo, Japan: Taishukan Publishing Co. Ltd. (株 式 會 社 大 修 館 書 店), 1984), p. 1899
[123] The Book of Mencius, chapter 2, 梁 惠 王 章 句 下 ,...與 民 同 之 民 以 爲 小 不 亦 宜 乎; Legge, James, Mencius, p 154

understands the mind of his people and does what they want, and furthermore, enjoys with them, he is the embodiment of Jen (仁) according to Mencius. This Tong Quin (同情) is more than just mercy or alms of the rulers for the poor. Living together with others in harmony stemmed from Heaven is the ideal society for which the Confucians must strive.

This harmony can be achieved through the Tong Quin (同情). It is true that Jen (仁) is the ultimate basis of the harmonious society but it has very wider room for various interpretations, as we can see in "the Analects of Confucius (論 語)". It is not to be denied that sympathy in the tradition of Confucianism cannot be the same as that of Christianism. Even Tong Quin (同情) presupposes the equal human dignity, it cannot be interpreted as a kind of fraternity. In Confucian society, where the hierarchical harmony has the paramount importance, there is no room for the Christian brotherly love. This kind of brotherly love was even loathed by Mencius, so even Tong Quin (同情) has to be a hierarchical love which is rather the favor of rulers for subjects. However the favor with bad intention was called self interest (私利) which was loathed by both Confucius and Mencius. The social status has to be in accordance with the inner maturity of man in the Confucian society, or the harmony of society will be disrupted. Once the duke Ching of Chi (齊景公) asked Confucius about governing. Confucius answered, "When ruler is ruler, subject is subject, father is father, and son is son, then there is a true governing."[124] In Confucian society a social status is not a function but an embodiment of the virtue of man, so Tong Quin (同情) must be a natural expression of the inner virtue, not a disguised hypocrisy. Even Tong Quin (同情) is not the mutual understanding based on social equality, it presupposes the coherent mind of concerned people, so it could be the beginning of sympathy, which was interpreted by Mencius as the beginning of Jen (仁).

5.1.3 συμ and πάθος : The Synthesis of Emotion and Will

Etymologically συμ means together or same and πάθος means experience, destiny, misery, agony, anxiety, desire, mental state, and so on. Sympathy has synonyms like empathy and condolence. "Empathy" stems from the Greek "εμ" and "πάθος", which should mean "(going) into the mind of others". "Condolence" stems from the Latin "con" and "dolor" or "doleo", which should mean togetherness for the agony and anxiety of others. In this regard, we may understand that the mental attitude of the good Samaritan in the New Testaments is nothing but a condolence. As a matter of fact sympathy has nothing to do directly with the agony of other, but without the resonance of the hearts or minds

---

[124] The Analects of Confucius, chapter 12, 顔淵, 君君臣臣父父子子 ; Legge, James, Confucius, p 256

of the concerned people, there could be no ethical action of helping hand for the needy or those in the extreme situation. In this situation a man is not a man anymore, he is a carrier of the dignity of humanity, i.e., a person. It does not matter what he is, or who he is. He is a person, and that is enough to help and to be helped. Sympathy is human, i.e., only man can have the lasting sympathy for others. With free will and determination man helps other people in need. This deed follows always the emotional attitude of sympathy. It is quite difficult to know how much sympathy is a matter of will. It is true that sympathy is not entirely an emotion or an instinct because it requires intuitive understanding for the situation of other. A daughter can sometimes see what her mother thinks, but she cannot always understand why her mother thinks so. To understand something man needs intellect. Originally "πάθος" has something to do with the experiences of man about the matter, which happens around him. As nature cares not much about the condition of man, man has to depend on the luck of his life, which is mostly beyond his ability. From this awareness of helplessness man feels sorrow or wrath. Under such an environment, only man can help others willingly even he knows very well that it must sometimes mean a great self-sacrifice. Therefore, having sympathy and helping others mean more than instinct even though they have something to do with the nature of man. It is true that not all men are sympathetic enough to help others in every possible situation. Only a man as a person who is the carrier of moral good, can truly love others. However, we may presume that every man has the ability of sympathy for others because it is in the nature of man, like a seed, which needs nourishment to come into full bloom. Every man must be treated as a person as long as he has a potential to be manifested later with experience and learning.

5.2 Person as the Subject of Sympathy

5.2.1 The Dynamic Relation of Mind and Body

The word "πρόσωπον" or "persona" meant originally not only the mask but also the role, the figure, and the character in theater. This person is a function as the carrier of human dignity in our society.[125] Therefore it is difficult to deny that a person can exist only in a society, but before a man has become a person in a society, he was and still is a biological body with soul and mind. As the saying goes, man is a social animal, which has every trait of animal, and a soul for the understanding of others. Modern sciences about man, for example psychology, anthropology and biology have unveiled many unknown secrets of man, both physiological and psychological. Most of all, biochemistry has a devastating

---

[125] Wils Jean-Pierre, "Person und Subjektivität" in Grundbegriffe der christlichen Ethik, Jean-Pierre Wils, Dietmar Mieth (ed.) (Paderborn: Ferdinand Schöningh, 1992), p110

impact on the understanding of man, especially after the impressive decoding of the human genes in our century. Nowadays we know that the human body is composed of about 60 thousand billions of cells, most of them being born and dying constantly as long as they live. As knowledge about the biological function of the human brain is getting richer, understanding about human mind, soul and spirit is accordingly getting rather biological. In the earlier way of thinking, the mind was thought of as acting on the "spirit" which in turn acted on "matter", and spirit was not thought of as totally immaterial. "Spirit" was just the in-between sort of stuff that the medieval philosophers' tendency to introduce in-betweens between any two adjacent terms in the series of kinds of being naturally led them to postulate. It was like a gas with just a little bit of push. As soon as "spirit" is dropped out, and the mind is really thought of as totally immaterial, then the push of the mind on even very ethereal matter in the pineal gland appears very strange. One cannot quite visualize that.[126]

Modern biological interpretation about the mind of man is still an on-going process, so there is no conclusive theory about the nature of man yet. Nevertheless, the natural scientific explanation about the nature of man is becoming the most persuasive one because of the strong scientific and verifiable evidences. Even if it has become quite diminutive, there is still room for philosophical and religious explanation about the nature of man not only because of the still unknown secret of man but also because of the fact that man is the only being of can-say-no, the ascetic of the life, the eternal protestant against the naked reality.[127] No other living being in this world can do anything against the will to live. Saying no to the world is substantially absurd. Such an absurdity cannot be explained scientifically. Man is from the beginning not scientific. He has something more in his inside than flesh and bone. In the Old Testaments we can read that God shaped man (אדם) from the dust of the land (אדמה) and then blew in his nose the breath of life (נשמת חיים). Then the man began to breathe.[128] This kind of theological anthropology has lost much of its charm, but as long as there is no scientific explanation for the relation of body and mind, we may presume the existence of God who made man to be man. Moreover, as long as we do not know the origin of man, we still need all kinds of anthropology, i.e., the biological, the philosophical, and the theological theories when we are about to understand the true nature of man.

Nowadays we can diagnose the functions of human body very minutely and explain how they perform, but we still cannot give a satisfying answer to the question: "What is the body?" For many years many theologians and

---

[126] Putnam, Hilary, Reason, Truth and History (Cambridge: Cambridge University Press, 1981), pp 76-77
[127] Scheler, M., op. cit., p 55
[128] K. Elliger, W. Rudolph (ed.), p 3

philosophers have relatively quite ignored the importance of body. For Plato, body was just a shadow of the Idea. For many ascetics of almost all great religions, body was even an obstacle, which was in the way of searching for the true freedom of mind. After Descartes had found the thinking "I", many philosophers on the Continent until recently tended to regard the reason of man as the sole reason for a man to be a man. Man with reason might exist even alone, i.e., without the help of God of the Middle Ages. As the founder of modern philosophy, Descartes was praised because he had seen the new autonomy and the sovereignty of mind, even though he confused mind with reason, and could not distinguish the latter from intelligence.[129] Especially after the two World Wars in our century, we lost much trust on the human reason. Man is no more a reasonable being who is much superior than other creatures in the world but just one of them, even a handicapped being who cannot well adapt himself to his environment as other animals or plants.[130] He is even worse with the matter of harmonious living in nature. Man behaves rather with emotion than with reason, and he is not seldom an absurd being. At any street-corner the feeling of absurdity can strike any man in the face.[131] After the long search for the nature of man, we return to the point of departure. We still do not know what a man really is.

The soul (ἡ ψυχή) of man cannot be confused with the mind (ὁ νοῦς) of man. The former is more religious side of man and the latter has something to do with the reason of man. Both are cherished by many philosophers and theologians more than body, but without the body (τό σομα) they can have no place to dwell in this world. The body is unjustly despised for a long time even though it does all chores in everyday life. For the eschatologically oriented Christian the end of the world will come soon, and in the Heaven body plays not an important role. Body is just a vessel for the soul which is much precious. For Plato in the world of Idea body plays no role. Not only the scholars in the Middle Ages but also the philosophers in the Modern Age did not change this attitude much.

Nowadays we know very well that body is more than a wonderful autonomous machine. It just does its best to survive, as it is coded in the human gene from the beginning. When a bacterium or a virus attacks the human body, it defends itself from that intruder with all possible means. Neither the reason nor the will of man can do the same job. The body follows when the will of man dictates, but that does not prove that body must be subordinated to the will. When we pay enough attention to body, we can see that body tells us what is going on with it, and what we have to do for it. Not body but the excessive desire of mind is the

---

[129] Max Scheler, op. cit., p72
[130] Ibid., p59
[131] Solomon, Robert C. (ed.), Phenomenology and Existentialism (New York: Harper & Row, Publishers, 1972), p489

main source of evil. Body has been unjustly discriminated especially by the learned for a long time. Even though we pay much attention to the body as we are being informed more about the body nowadays, there is still a great tendency for man to ignore body as a mere vessel for much sublime soul or mind. We have to stop to be a hypocrite by intentionally ignoring body because soul or mind without body is implausible. Too much attention to body is a problem of the will of man, or of the desire of man. It is like the indulgence of man. Body is just instinctively reacting to the outer world, and doing its best to survive. Buddha learned after his long journeys for the truth that not only too excessive indulgence in body but also too much contempt of body hinders the way to the Nirvana. Even if Jesus Christ did not care much about body, His body plays a great role as a symbol for the coming salvation.[132] As a matter of fact, not only a dead body, but a disabled body was despised in the Jewish tradition, which cherished cleanness as the divine character.[133]

We still know that man is not just a mass of chemical chain reactions but a being with mind and soul, which demands the human reason and God respectively. One thing is certain that to know the identity of man we need a complete point of view, which takes into account every aspect of man, i.e., soul, mind and body, and treat them equally.

5.2.2 "I" and "Me": The Complexity of Identity with Mead's Theory

It may be absurd that we are to talk about the identity of man when we still do not know who we really are. One fact is clear, nevertheless, that the identity of man comes into being only in the relationship with others. The word of identity

---

[132] Mt 6:25 Therefore I say unto you, Take no thought for your life, what ye shall eat, or what ye shall drink; nor yet for your body, what ye shall put on. Is not the life more than meat, and the body than raiment?
Mt. 10:28 And fear not them which kill the body, but are not able to kill the soul: but rather fear him which is able to destroy both soul and body in hell.
Mr. 14:22 And as they did eat, Jesus took bread, and blessed, and brake it, and gave to them, and said, Take, eat: this is my body.
Mr. 14:23 And he took the cup, and when he had given thanks, he gave it to them: and they all drank of it.
Mr. 14:24 And he said unto them, This is my blood of the new testament, which is shed for many.
Mr. 14:25 Verily I say unto you, I will drink no more of the fruit of the vine, until that day that I drink it new in the kingdom of God.
[133] Le. 21:18 For whatsoever man he be that hath a blemish, he shall not approach: a blind man, or a lame, or he that hath a flat nose, or any thing superfluous,
Le. 21:19 Or a man that is brokenfooted, or brokenhanded,
Le. 21:20 Or crookbackt, or a dwarf, or that hath a blemish in his eye, or be scurvy, or scabbed, or hath his stones broken; {a dwarf: or, too slender}

stems from the Old Latin "idem" which means "the same". Later, there came "identitas". When we are talking about the identity of man, it means literally "agreeing with oneself". So long as we do not know who we really are, we are in the identity crisis in some measure, that is, we cannot agree with ourselves quite well.

As Aristotle argued, all men by nature desire to know.[134] We all tend to know our identity. We are living in this world in the dynamic relation of subject and object. The personal identity is built up from the subjectively and intersubjectively structured sediments of socially delivered impressions, basic models and behaviors.[135] So we may say that the identity of man is some mixture of subjective and objective, i.e., social traits. This is not all we can be sure of the meaning of identity because there is still the identity crisis somehow. As our sense organs tend to receive only those sense data, which they can and want to receive, our subject may tend to accept just what it wants to accept. Through the process of socialization we are forced to accept some social norms, even if we are to feel sometimes the sense of disapproval. We have no choice but to accept them without grunts.

Standing against outer influences, the subject of man reacts with its will. There could be various explanations for the existence of the will. Theologically, we may say that being a person signalizes that to him comes a quality which is entrusted before the "being subjective" and the individualizing, and which he must not first put into practice.[136]

It is true that we have to adapt ourselves to the norms of society when we want to live in it. To adapt oneself to those norms is quite different from to accept those norms and internalizing them. It is not only the matter of intelligence but also of will. We know well that every single pupil learns quite differently under a teacher. One pupil achieves a brilliant result, but the other not. First of all, it is because of the difference of intelligence of the pupils, but different attitude and will play a great role too. Man does not learn like a robot, he always "actively" reacts to the stimuli of the outer world.

We may presume that there are two things to be concerned when we are to talk about the identity of man. As Descartes has concluded, there must be "I" who thinks that I am somebody whom even the devil needs when he wants to deceive "me".[137] Though many scholars have tried to know what this "I" must be, since Descartes found this "I" in 1641, we still do not have a clear picture about this

---

[134] Aristotle, Metaphysica, W.D. Ross (tr.) (New York: Random House,1982), p689

[135] Hunold, Gerfried W., "Identität" in Grundbegriffe der christlichen Ethik, Jean-Pierre Wils, Dietmar Mieth (ed.) (Paderborn: Ferdinand Schöningh, 1992), p32

[136] Wils, Jean-Pierre, "Person und Subjektivität" in Grundbegriffe der christlichen Ethik, Jean-Pierre Wils, Dietmar Mieth (ed.) (Paderborn: Ferdinand Schöningh, 1992), p127

[137] Descartes, Rene, Discourse on Method and meditations, Laurence J. Laufleur (tr.) (New York: The Bobbs-Merrill Company, Inc.,1960), p82

"I". There are many kinds of explanations about the "I" of man.

Theologically, man is a subject who is totally dependent on the mercy of God because man is a sinner before God for good since the fall of Adam. But who God must be and what He is in His divinity show and reveal God not in an empty space of the divine for-self-being (für-sich-sein) but authentically just in the fact that God exists, talks and behaves as the partner (clearly as a better half) of man.[138] In this dynamic relation with God, we can see the identity of man not as a fixed but a variable one. Here the identity of man is not only given but also to be made in the interaction with God. According to Aristotle, man comes to the position of his own being only in a πολις, i.e., the comprehensive and ethical contact of all human behavior and usefulness can be established only in the community of experience of the freemen.[139] Here man builds in the interaction with other men not only a πολις but also his own identity, as man can be a man only in relation to God for the Christians. There are also psychological, anthropological and biological definitions about the identity of man. On the whole, we may say that the identity of man never stands alone, it always needs a relation with other men.

Here we may borrow a few concepts of George Herbert Mead for the better understanding of the identity. He used "self", "I", and "me" to explain what the identity of man should be. The "self" means the reflective ability of a subject to act for oneself the same way as for the other subject. However this is not a lone self-reflection. The social behavior comes into being as the behaving subject preoccupies the attitude of every other partner of the interaction, while thinking in them, and perceiving from their perspectives (empathy). The "me" is used for the part of the experience of individual, which comes into being from the sum of external expectations ("the generalized others"). The "I", the unequivocally identical "I", means the court of spontaneity and creativity, and its formation cannot be explained from the experiences of the interaction alone. Genetically the by others determined "me" comes before the "I", the court where I pass judgment on everything. The "person" forms himself from the internalization of the external expectations, which every subject faces in the interaction. The expression of the "I" needs the method of manifestation given by the socially formed "me". This fact means the same as the "institution" which is defined by Mead as the collection of the empirical attitudes that all individuals carry for themselves. The identity, the "self", is the result of the arrangements of the individual specialty ("I") with the social generality on the way of the clear understanding of every single "me" as the "generalized others". Here the identity is understood as a dynamic mass growing from the process of behavior

---

[138] Karl Barth, "Von der Göttlichkeit und Menschlichkeit Gottes", in Die Theologie des 20. Jahrhunderts, karl-Josef Kuschel (ed.) (München:R. Piper GmbH & Co. KG, 1986), p155
[139] Hunold, Gerfried W., op. cit., p34

among men which concludes the understanding of the past social relation among men, and according to that understanding individual adapts oneself to the social reality of norm without phase.[140]

We still have a problem in understanding the "self" because we still do not know exactly how and why the "I" can adapt itself to the given social norms and make them "me". There are many attempts to answer such questions. Here we will employ the phenomenological method for the better understanding of "self", i.e., the identity of man. However the definition of man could differ according to various theories, the essence of man stays always there invariably. Not only as a beloved image of God but also as the unique existence of the universe, man is important, as Hermann Hesse once said:

"*Jeder Mensch aber ist nicht nur er selber, er ist auch der einmalige, ganz besondere, in jedem Fall wichtige und merkwürdige Punkt, wo die Erscheinungen der Welt sich kreuzen, nur einmal so und nie wieder. Darum ist jedes Menschen Geschichte wichtig, ewig, göttlich, darum ist jeder Mensch solange er irgend lebt und den Willen der Natur erfüllt, wunderbar und jeder Aufmerksamkeit würdig. In jedem ist der Geist Gestalt geworden, in jedem leidet die Kreatur, in jedem wird ein Erlöser gekreuzigt.*"[141]

The unique importance of every person can be manifested more clearer when we may intuitive apprehand his essence. A way of this intuition can be found in the Phenomenology of Husserl.

5.2.3 The Transcendental Ego as the Center of Identity

The science of phenomenology was founded by Edmund Husserl (1859-1938), who regarded Descartes and Kant as his most important philosophical predecessors. His phenomenology takes the Cartesian attention to the primacy of first-person experience and the Kantian search for basic "a priori" principles as its modus operandi.[142] Like Kant Husserl tried to identify and defend the basic a priori principles of all human experiences and understanding.[143] First of all, Husserl wanted to gain a radical, preconception free understanding, i.e., ἐπιστήμη, a true understanding through the phenomenological method, not δόξα, an opinion.[144]

As a matter of fact it has been a job for almost all philosophers in the history to find out the true understanding of man. Without the help of such a true

---

[140] Ibid., p37
[141] Hesse, Hermann, Demian Die Geschichte von Emil Sinclairs Jugend (Frankfurt a. M.: Suhrkamp Verlag, 1997), pp 7-8
[142] Robert C. Solomon (ed.), op. cit., p1
[143] Ibid., op. cit., p1
[144] Husserl, Edmund, Die Phänomenologische Methode, Ausgewählte Text I, Klaus Held (ed.) (Stuttgart: Philipp Reclam Jun, 1985), p13

understanding there could be hardly a true moral theory. So we have to understand what and where the ἐπιστήμη must be, and how it functions before we could begin to talk about the ethics.

It is clear that the thinking subject of Descartes exists though it is not certain where it should be in time and space. Husserl called this the transcendental ego. For Husserl its being is prior to all "objective beings" in the order of knowledge: In a certain sense it is the underlying basis on which all objective cognition take place.[145] To show or to prove the existence of this transcendental ego is as difficult as Kant's the thing itself (Ding an sich). Husserl had to use the transcendental ἐποχή and the transcendental reduction to find out the transcendental ego in the end. According to Husserl it is a sine qua none for us to begin with a kind of radical and skeptical ἐποχή when we are about to be a serious philosopher who has to have a philosophical cognition, which must be direct and apodictic.[146] The transcendental ἐποχή means "to doubt about everything which is accepted as a matter of course". Not only the validity of all existing sciences, including mathematics, which claims the apodictic evidence, but also the validity of the fore- and unscientific life world (Lebenswelt) which is a always with indisputable self-evidence given world of the sensual experience, and every unscientific and scientific life of thought which lives on it. Husserl named this kind of doubt as "Cartesian ἐποχή", and he distinguished it from the antic skepticism of Protagoras and Gorgias, which did not go beyond the denial of the rational substructure of a "philosophy", which presumed the rational it-self with its presumptive truth it-self, and believed that it could be achieved.[147] What can this transcendental ἐποχή give us? Husserl's answer is minute. The phenomenological ἐποχή lays open (to me as a mediating philosopher) an infinite realm of being of a new kind as the sphere of a new kind of experience, a "transcendental experience". When we take it into consideration that for each kind of actual experience and for each of its universal variant modes (perception, retention, recollection, etc.), there is a corresponding pure fantasy, an "as-if experience" with parallel modes (as-if perception, as-if retention, as-if recollection, etc.), we surmise that there is also an a priori science which confines itself to the realm of pure possibility (pure imaginableness) and, instead of judging about actualities of transcendental being, judges about its a priori possibilities, and thus at the same time prescribes rules a priori for actualities.[148] This kind of transcendental thought is similar to that of Kant but Husserl saw in the transcendental realm the relation of cogitatio and

---

[145] Robert C. Solomon, op. cit., p119

[146] Edmund Husserl, Die Krisis der europäischen Wissenschaft und die transzendentale Phänomenologie (Hamburg: Felix Meiner Verlag, 1977), p83

[147] Ibid., pp83-84

[148] Solomon, Robert C., op. cit., p120

cogitatum, which his predecessors overlooked.

When we see something, we know that there are observed objects and observing consciousness of our own. As a matter of fact the two main philosophical thoughts of the modern Western philosophy distinguish from each other in stressing one of these two components of consciousness, i.e., cogitatio and cogitatum, and they built the British Empiricism and the Continental Idealism respectively. Many philosophers saw that the chasm between subject and object is unbridgeable. We build relations with the objects in the world through our sensory organs, which react chemically and physically to the outer sensory data stemming from the objects. Visible rays of light for eyes, audible waves for ears, water-soluble chemical compounds for nose and tongue, and for skin there are pressure and temperature. Here the sensory organs of man react only to the sense data, but these kinds of sensory data and sensations alone do not make any sense unless the human brain processes such data, i.e., learns and memorizes. The brain gathers, analyses, stores, and remembers the information primarily stemming from the sensory data. Nowadays, to explain the function of the human brain we use mostly biological knowledge because of the brilliant progress of the neurobiology in recent decades. We have found out that there are tremendous amounts of biochemical and electrical chain reactions in the human brain when it functions, i.e., when it processes the information. As Professor Steven Rose, head of the department of biology at the Open University in Milton Keynes, outside London, has said, it is impossible to ask where in the brain a particular memory is located because memory is a dynamic property of the brain as a whole rather than of any one specific region. Memory resides simultaneously everywhere and nowhere in the brain.[149] We can no more find out where the memory is than locate where reason and emotion of man are. It is like the quantum physics.

It is true that the dignity of a man is totally ruined when he loses memory because of the disease like Alzheimer's neurodegenerative disorder. That does not mean his reason or will is wholly dependent on the biological function of the brain. Reason and will command how a man processes the information, i.e., how he learns and memorizes. Reason and will might be influenced by the experiences acquired a posteriori, but they cannot be made from those experiences. Apart from the biological explanation, there is psychological one for the human reason and for the scientific theory like mathematics and logic. Husserl refutes exactly this kind of "psychologism" vehemently. It is true that psychology is a positive science in its every empirical and eidetic discipline, a science in the natural attitude, in which the simply given world is the thematic ground.[150] It is also true that all our experiences in the world are individual or

---

[149] TIME, May 5 1997, p42
[150] Husserl, Edmund, Die Phänomenologische Methode, Ausgewählte Text I, Klaus Held (ed.)

subjective and can be explained somewhat psychologically, but describing phenomena is quite different from providing the basis of sciences, especially when it comes to the science of logic and mathematics. As long as psychology depends upon the empirical data it cannot be a sole foundation of logic, especially the "pure" logic that does not stem from experiences. The law of syllogism does not need empirical data to be established as a "pure" logical law. It is just applied to the empirical facts to ascertain the truth or falsehood of them, not vice versa.

Another problem with the psychologism is the fact that it is in all of its form a skeptical relativism.[151] What we need to understand the facts of the world is not just the sense data and our memories about them. We have to have the ability of analysis and generalization, which belongs to our innate and a priori domain. Psychologism cannot be an appropriate method for the explanation of the whole phenomena of the human mind, as long as it tries to draw the necessity of law from the contingency of facts of the world as any other relativism.[152] In fact the most radical skeptics in the past did not attack the world in its ordinary meaning, but made its relativity to be valid with the intention of negation of the ἐπιστήμη and philosophically in it based (substruiert) world itself. Here its agnosticism comes into being. So here comes the world enigma of unprecedented style on the plan and it conditions a wholly new kind of philosophizing, i.e., the "epistemological", "rationalistic" and soon also systematic philosophies of a wholly new kind of goal setting and method. This biggest revolution is named as the conversion of the scientific modern objectivism, and also of all the philosophies of the past thousand years into a "transcendental subjectivism".[153]

The transcendental ego comes as the center of the transcendental subjectivism. Even though there are many different theories concerning the "ego" because of the vagueness of this subjective being, in regard of the question of what this being in me must be, it is simply true that there must be a being in me who has relation to the objects in the world. It is the ego, and for Husserl it must be a kind of transcendental. Husserl described the ego as two-folded being: On the one hand, the ego must be an existence for itself in continuous evidence; thus, in itself, it is continuously constituting itself as existing. On the other hand, Husserl understood the ego as the 'I' who lives this and that subjective process, and who lives through this and that cogito as the same 'I'.[154] As long as this transcendental ego has relation with the concrete objects in the world, it must be also concrete, not abstract. It means that the transcendental ego can describe

---

(Stuttgart: Philipp Reclam Jun, 1985), p211
[151] Robert C. Solomon, op. cit., p94
[152] Ibid., p95
[153] Husserl, Edmund, Die Crisis der europäischen Wissenschaft und die transzendentale Phänomenologie (Hamburg: Felix Meiner Verlag, 1977), pp74-75
[154] Solomon, Robert C., p393

concretely the objects in the world even though it accepts the existing objects in relation of noema and noesis, i.e., intentional conscious and intentional objects. How concrete the world can be in the phenomenological point of view is a matter of discussion, but the perennial chasm between subject and object in the traditional philosophy can be overcome with the phenomenological intuition, though this may be a very hypothetical one. Aside from this philosophical problem, we are about to concentrate ourselves more on the matter of mutual understanding between men because the identity of man comes into being only in the relation itself.

5.2.4 The Intersubjectivity as the Prerequisite of Mutual Understanding

The main limit of Husserl's phenomenology was the subjective validity of the a priori phenomenological intuition. The truthfulness of the subjective cognition can be acquired with the notion of the transcendental ego. As long as the ego stays just as a subjective one, there could be hardly a reasonable argument about the nature of the phenomenological ego. So it was necessary for Husserl to assume the intersubjectivity of the transcendental ego. In fact this is a transgression of his own doctrine of presupposition-free science because this notion of intersubjectivity presupposes the ideal existence of others. Therefore, for example, the existentialists reject the idea of knowing others and replace it with the analysis of experiencing others. As Maurice Merleau-Ponty said, the existence of other people is a difficulty and an outrage for the objective thought. For Jean-Paul Sartre other people were even the hell.[155] Husserl risked the criticism of the existentialist to avoid the danger of solipsism of the phenomenology. My phenomenological perspective about the objective world is clear for me through the phenomenological ἐποχή. In this phenomenological conscious the being of other people as object is also clear, but the problem is the clarity of the conscious of those other people. The clarity of my presupposition free transcendental ego is indisputable for me because of the phenomenological ἐποχή. On the contrary, the clarity of the transcendental ego of other people is not clear for me as long as other people stay out there just as objects of my conscious. But other people must be beings with the same conscious as mine because I see them as such in my conscious. Therefore, Husserl had to say:

"*My own essence can be at all contrasted for me with something else, or that 'I', who 'I' am, can become aware of someone else, who is no 'I' but other than 'I', presupposes that not all my own modes of consciousness are modes of my self-consciousness. Since actual being is constituted originally by harmoniousness of experience, my own self must contain, in contrast to self-experience and the system of its harmoniousness, the system, therefore, of self-*

---

[155] Ibid., pp418-419

explication into components of my ownness, yet other experiences united in harmonious systems."[156]

Here we can see the resemblance of Hussel's logic to that of Descartes. The only difference is that Husserl did not presuppose the existence of God as Descartes. But the harmoniousness of experience must presuppose the absolute being like God, therefore we can find not much difference between Husserl and Descartes with this matter of "pre-given."

Logical consistency was less important here than the necessity of explaining the world as it is, therefore Husserl presupposed the intersubjectivity of the phenomenological ego even though he must have beforehand anticipated the criticism of his theory. The other must be the same being as "I". This fact must have been so clear for Husserl that he willingly risked the critics.

But where are all these phenomenological egos? They should not be in someone's primordial sphere because the fundamental task of the intersubjectivity theory of Husserl consists in the fact that we have to delimit the copresence (Appräsentation, Mitgegenwärtige) of the experience of others from that of normal perception of things which does not go beyond the sphere of one's own, and put it out in its peculiarity.[157] This was the basic task of Husserl in answering the question : "How could the objects of various persons appear in the same way in spite of their different situations of experiences?"[158] He used the theory of association, which he called "Paarung" to transcend the primordial sphere of subject, and he needed the body which existed "here" to have the conscious of my existence "here".[159] As it is well known, Husserl's theory of intersubjectivity is very disputable one, therefore he needed more concrete basis for his theory. That is why he postulated the life-world (Lebenswelt) in the end. This world is a normal world where we experience ordinary things. This is a necessary world for sympathy because sympathy presupposes a common field where all participants come together and do something interactively. Should then this mean Husserl's return to the ordinary world from that of his famous transcendental, or phenomenological ego? Not entirely. Husserl was the son of the German Idealism from the beginning to the end. He could not be a kind of empiricist as those of England.

5.2.5 The Life World as the "Common Sense" for Sympathy

Why we should "go back" to the life world from the rigorous scientific world of the phenomenology? To this question, we can give as an answer what Hilary

---

[156] Ibid., p423
[157] Husserl, Edmund, Phänomenologie der Lebenswelt, Ausgewählte Texte II, Klaus Held (ed.) (Stuttgart: Philipp Reclam Jun, 1985), p35
[158] Ibid., p31
[159] Ibid., pp31-32

Putnam has told: "the common sense." Even Bishop Berkley, who never wanted to accept the physical reality of our world, and regarded it just as our fantasy, had to eat when he felt hunger, and had to suffer under the stomachache when he had eaten too much. The understanding of the world on the basis of the common sense tells us always that the world is much bigger than we understand, categorize and conceptualize. Even the most advanced field of science, i.e., the quantum physics cannot fully explain the phenomena of the world. To understand the world correctly is very important, but to accept as it is much more important. When we accept just what we want to accept and make a theory from it, it becomes a dogma, not a science. Philosophical arguments need always supportive arguments, which are based on the ultimately indisputable theory. This theory should be always valid through time and space. But as Albert Einstein had proposed in his theory of relativity, and his followers and opposite parties together showed, time and space are not anymore the unchangeable basis of existence. There are more than what we have known in this world, not just in the physical term, but also in the matter of idea. Our idea comes with experiences. Experiences are acquired always through our sensual interaction with the real world where we live. We can have just a small amount of experience of the world, not only because of our very limited sensory organs but also because of the character of the vast world itself. When Isaac Newton wrote his Principia, explaining the laws of gravity and motion, the world was still a static place for man. After the advance of the new perspective of Albert Einstein, the picture of the world has become very relative. Even the relativism cannot explain the whole phenomena of the world as much as the traditional theories. When our intelligence is not enough for the truth, we have to let the world be there as it is, as inconceivable. We should not make a truth from what we know, even from what we want to accept. That is why the phenomenology of Husserl is much cherished as open science with the concept of the life world. Tomorrow, we may be a little bit brighter than today with new experiences.

It is quite natural for Husserl to emphasize the importance of the life world (Lebenswelt) because his science was from the beginning a kind of concrete one. Only on the basis of the concrete life world, which we experience everyday, we can construct our subjective idea about the world, and further more, we can build the objective concepts of the world. In the life world we do live a "normal life". We share this world with others, not only with other people but also with other living beings. This Lebenswelt does present itself, actually or virtually, in such experience, perceptual experience as well as its derivative forms like memory, representation, imagination, etc.[160]

Nowadays, we have to be familiar with the purely mathematically constructed viewpoint of the world. Many people thought they could even explain the whole

---

[160] Solomon, Robert C., op. cit., p350

universe only with the mathematical method, especially since Newton had found the law of gravity. In the course of such a mode of thought we have forgotten the importance of the world itself, which has been main object of our thought. Instead, the human understanding itself and its function have been main concern for most of the philosophers since Descartes. Even though we can understand the world proper clearer with the help of the mathematical method, it does not guarantee that we can explain the whole world. The world is so big for the human understanding that it remains still incomprehensible.

A part of this world is the life world where we not only encounter our fellow-men and take for granted that they exist in the world, but also aware that they are confronted with the same things and objects as we are, though to each of us, depending upon his point of view, the objects and the world at large may and do appear under varying aspects and perspectives. It is one of the unquestioned and even unformulated certainties of common experience that the world is one and the same for all of us, a common intersubjective world.[161]

This common world for all egos is very important for the ethical behavior of the persons in a given society. In this common world man can be a person with the sense of duty not only for others but also for himself. Especially in the modern society we are living in our own world with not much ethical concern about others. There is not so much sense of responsibility for others mainly because of the objectivism and the belief of the technological progress. Much of our sense of duty, which we have learned mostly from the teaching of the great religious leaders, should lose its persuasiveness more and more as the advancement of technology becomes uncontrollable. Literally, the word "technic" stems from the Greek "τεχνη", which means art, skill, craft, efficiency. It has something to do more with the mundane and physical things than with the transcendental and celestial things. With the progress of technology, we as human beings are bound to have the humanistic (ἀθρώπειος) point of view instead of the divine (θεόθεν) one. Our relation with God is getting feebler and more fragile as the technological progress is getting fiercer. As this change is getting more apparent, the sense of divine duty is also becoming fainter. The technological complexity of our modern society makes it more difficult for man to have the sense of duty. Everybody takes part in the gigantic system of modern society in this or that way, but nobody could see the whole system or take control of it. It is extremely difficult to find out the accountable when something goes wrong in our society. Everybody is accountable in a way but it means nobody takes responsible for matters that go wrong totally.

The main culprit for this phenomenon of unaccountability is the objectivism, or rather the mathematicalizing of the world. According to Husserl this kind of mathematicalizing of the world had begun with Galilee, so he named it as

---

[161] Ibid., p352

Gallilean mathematicalizing (Galileis Mathematisierung).[162] One of the most prominent discoveries in the era of Renaissance was this mathematical view of nature. Through the whole Middle Ages the world itself was just the harmonious creatures of God who loves especially man in his image.(Gen. 1:26)[163] Without the help of God we could explain the nature not in a single case until the beginning of the Modern Age. Suddenly man could explain almost all phenomena of the nature mathematically without the help of God's providence. Modern scientists found even the fact that the medieval theocentric explanation of the world did not fit to the objective world. Only the mathematical explanation was self-evident, i.e., it agreed with the matters of the nature which were the objectives of the observing and investigating new scientists. After the Copernican system of the universe had been found, we could not say anymore like Leibniz, who said, "...the soul follows its own laws, and the body likewise follows its own laws; and they agree with each other in virtue of the pre-established harmony between all substances since they are all representations of one and the same universe."[164]

People in the modern age have lost the direct contact with nature along with the contact with God. Nature, which God made, does not exist anymore as the common field of life with other creatures but just as the object of mathematical analysis and technical manipulation. Indirect relation with nature through the mathematical formula of natural science has made us to be indifferent to the sense of responsibility, a responsibility not only for the nature but also for our fellow human beings.

Husserl was aware of this danger and concluded that this trend of the society was a crisis. He talked about the crisis of science as loss of its meaning for life.[165] In ancient Greece the natural science was for man to understand the phenomena of the nature and to use the natural force for the human benefit. Nowadays, especially, the natural science and the technology exist mainly for the efficiency of the production process. Efficiency means nothing but cost saving and maximum output. Natural scientists and technicians cannot and will not see that this efficiency must be principally for all persons in the society. Mostly, they issue the maxim of utilitarianism, the greatest happiness of the greatest number, as their excuse.[166] But the greatest number is just a speculative concept that has nothing to do with the living concrete persons. Natural

---

[162] Husserl, Edmund, Die Krisis der europäischen Wissenschaften und die transzendentale Phänomenologie (Hamburg: Felix Meiner Verlag, 1969), p22
[163] Ellinger, K., Rudolph, W. (ed.), op.cit., p2
[164] Leibniz, Gottfried Wilhelm, Monadologie(Frankfurt a.M.: Insel Verlag, 1996), p61
[165] Edmund Husserl, Die Krisis de europäischen Wissenschaften und die transzendentale Phänomenologie (Hamburg: Felix Meiner Verlag, 1969), p3
[166] Bentham, Jeremy, "Constitutional Code", vol. I, in The Collected Works of Jeremy Bentham, J.R. Dinwiddy (ed.) (Oxford: Clarendon Press, 1984), p 18

scientists and technicians today do their job for the smallest number of people who want the maximum profit with any means. The sense of responsibility disappears in the blind pursuit of profit and the anonymity of the masses. In this way, not only the merchants but also almost all other people in a given society see the world mathematically. When a politician says that we have a good economy, almost all people promptly demand the precise statistics, without these data nobody is willing to believe what he says. It does not matter whether he lies with these statistics or not. The masses have no means for the verification of those data. This phenomenon is not peculiar in the arena of politics. In almost every corner of our society the mathematical data dominate. Even the value of a person is mathematicalized, or rather quantified. This quantified person is not anymore a peculiar being with dignity but just one of the anonymous masses. What it cannot be quantifiable is not considered much. Whether a person is good or bad is counted not much, but whether such a character can be useful and profitable for someone plays very important role in our society. In almost all deals of the people of our age, there is this medium of mathematicalization, and it hinders the essential human contact.

For all its faults we cannot live without this mathematicalized environment, especially, in our "Information Age", where the mathematicalized information plays main role for almost all affairs. Every single interaction between people today happens through the medium of information consisted of numbers and numerical formula. This is an irreversible trend of our age. It is rather a paradigm of our age. It is of no use when we are about to strictly object objectivism and mathematicalization, which were the main culprits for the crisis of the science in Europe, according to Husserl.[167] We have to accommodate ourselves to this new environment of numeric information, but only with the humanistic touch. The humanistic touch means the rediscovery of the irrational human nature. There may be many approaches leading to the rehumanization of our society. One of them is to rediscovering our sense of responsibility for our neighbor. This sense of responsibility for our neighbor begins with the sense of sympathy with and for the neighbor. This is a small step but it will not stay small as it says in the Bible: "Though your beginning has been small, but your end grows very great." (Job 8:7)[168]

Before we begin to find out the way of rehumanizing our society, especially with the diffusion of sympathy with the mass media, we need to scrutinize the concept of sympathy proper.

---

[167] Husserl, Edmund, Die Krisis de europäischen Wissenschaften und die transzendentale Phänomenologie (Hamburg: Felix Meiner Verlag, 1969), pp3-5
[168] Ellinger, K., Rudolph, W. (ed.), op. cit., p1235

6. Sympathy in its Mode and Phenomena

6.1 The Mode of Sympathy

6.1.1 Positive and Negative - Scheler versus Schopenhauer

Of many proponents for the ethics of sympathy, Arthur Schopenhauer (1788-1860) and Max Scheler (1874-1928) might be regarded as prominent because of their respective influences on this matter. Interestingly, they stood extremely against each other even though both of them cherished the human sympathy so much. Schopenhauer defined the sympathy as :

"*The natural compassion which is innate and indestructible in every man, and which has been shown to be the sole source of non-egoistic conduct, this kind alone being of real worth*".[169]

For Scheler, sympathy means the chain of human feelings, which begins with "feeling the same (Einsfühlung)" and ends with the "acosmic person's and God's love (akosmistische Person- und Gottesliebe)."[170] Scheler's sympathy has rather genetic and dynamic phases and functions. Every phase of sympathy has direct relation with each other, which is inevitable for the whole system of sympathy.

Scheler criticized Schopenhauer's theory of sympathy mostly because of his negative (and wrong) interpretation of sympathy. According to Scheler Schopenhauer must have confused the true sympathy with the "follow-up feeling (Nachfühlen)."[171] The true sympathy must be a positive one, which could at least alleviate the pain of others. For Schopenhauer, the world is from the beginning full of pain (Leid), therefore it is quite of no use to try to alleviate the pain of others. The pain itself is inevitable for man as long as man lives because the individual's suffering is for the benefit of the human race.[172] Even if the life in this world is painful, it contributes for the continuation of human generation. It is not a matter of concern for the blind will to live (blinder Wille zum Leben) whether an individual wants to live because the most important matter for mankind is the self-preservation as any other living beings in this world. Just to survive, and to keep reproduction are all those human beings must and can do in this world. In such a dismal situation the sympathy for the "fellow human being (Mitmensch)" is not an unnatural attitude because it is the self-pity itself, which a man in a bad situation must feel for himself. This is a distinctive truth for Schopenhauer who thought :

---

[169] Schopenhauer, A., The basis of Morality (London: Swan Sonnenschein, 1903), p. 264

[170] Scheler, Max, Wesen und Formen der Sympathie (Bern: A. Franke AG Verlag, 1973), pp105-111

[171] Ibid., op. cit. P 63

[172] Sahakian, William S., op. cit., p 159

"*Ultimately there is but one will, not many, which permeates everywhere and penetrates everything; accordingly, the desire and sense of pain in another person are in us as well.*"[173]

Many people talk about the Buddhist influence on this kind of thought of Schopenhauer. It is true that the world is full of pain according to Buddhism, but as a matter of fact, Buddhism is not a pessimism in its core, on the contrary, it is very positive religion, and full of hope that every single person in this world can achieve Nirvana by his own efforts. Every individual can achieve what Buddha had already achieved in the end, it just takes time. Sometimes in the future there will be no pain in this world. There is no one great will of Schopenhauer in Buddhism, everybody has his own destiny according to his deeds. In Buddhism *dharma* plays a very important role. Actually there have been many misuses of this concept by the Western scholars. And it obscured sometimes our understanding of the whole course of Indian religions and philosophies.[174] The endless incarnation is not evidence to show the inevitable misery and the merciless destiny of man, but a chance for all men to achieve the Nirvana, which is the extinguishment of the pain of the world. An individual in Buddhism is no Nietzschean "superman (Übermensch)" either. For Nietzsche, love and practical sympathy, i.e., the Christianity, for the botched and the weak are more harmful than any vice.[175] The helping hand for the needy is very bad thing for the survival of whole mankind. That very sympathy even killed Jesus Christ according to Nietzsche :

"*- 'Thou servedst him to the last?' asked Zarathustra thoughtfully, after a deep silence, 'thou knowest how he died? Is it true what they say, that sympathy choked him;*
-That he saw how man hung on the cross, and could not endure it;
-that his love to man became his hell, and at last his death?' - -"[176]

In Buddhism man is neither a cursed, nor a God-like being. To strike the middle way (中 道) is the right way for the Buddhists.

If Schopenhauer ever had aquatinted himself with Buddhism, he misinterpreted the teaching of Buddha. The existence of pain in this world is a positive phenomenon for the ultimate healing. When we love each other and have sympathy for others to share their pain, the pain disappears, not increases.[177] The most prominent evidence for this phenomenon can be found in

---

[173] Ibid., p 160
[174] Kunst, Arnold, "Use and Misuse of Dharma" in The Concept of Duty in South Asia, Wendy Doniger O'flaherty, J.Duncan M. Derrett (ed.) (India: Vikas Publishing House Pvt Ltd.,1978), p.15
[175] Ibid., p 148
[176] Nietzsche, Friedrich, Also Sprach Zarathustra, Thomas Common (tr.), p 89 in Internet
[177] Scheler, Max, Wesen und Formen der Sympathie (Bern: A. Franke AG Verlag, 1973), pp. 62-63

the Gospels. There were many pains in the people around Jesus Christ. Whenever Jesus Christ saw the pain of them and had sympathy for them He healed them immediately. The pain of the people disappeared when Jesus Christ felt pity in His heart for the pain of the people around Him. He provided them with pleasure. Having pleasure is not just the temporary absence of the blind will as Schopenhauer believed, but the shared pleasure is even a positive value. Not only the sympathy for the needy but also the happy-together with others is morally valuable thing, even though sympathy for the needy is a much ubiquitous phenomenon.[178]

Schopenhauer did not want to discern the peculiar identity of each individual. For Schopenhauer all human beings are just a part of a great will, the will to live. This will to live of all living creature should not have just a negative meaning. The will to live is even the main cause of the reverence for life. Albert Schweitzer confessed that he was full of reverence for the mysterious will of life(Wille zum Leben) in all living beings.[179] His belief in God made him this positive attitude for the will to live possible. As Johan Wolfgang von Goethe explained, man can be free and positive only when he accepts the existence of superior being, God:

"Man is free when he reveres a being, which is superior to himself, not when he does not want to accept it, because man can be the same as the object of reverence when he reveres it."[180]

When there is no difference or distance between persons, there could be no phenomenological and intentional relation between them. The distance between persons itself is not quite substantial for the true love because there should be no distance between the lover and the beloved. As Scheler insisted, love is not sympathy but a value. Love means the creative change of the lover, not of the beloved as the object of love.[181] Love cannot be a feeling but a movement. All feelings are passive functions but love is an action of mind. This action has nothing to do with the "I", but has something to do with the "person". Love is the foundation of all sympathy, and without love there is no sympathy.[182] It may not clear for many whether sympathy must be just a reaction to the outer stimuli as any other feelings of our body, but it is right that love must be the foundation for the sympathy as an ethical act. Just feeling sorry for the needy is not the true sympathy which is the beginning of love. This is why the passive sympathy of

---

[178] Ibid., pp. 142-143
[179] Schweitzer, Albert, Kultur und Ethik (München: C.H. Beck'sche Verlads Buchhandlung, 1955), p 228
[180] Hessen, J., Lehrbuch der Philosophie, 2 bd., Wertlehre (München: Ernst Reinhardt Verlag, 1969), p 26
[181] Spiegelberg, H., The Phenomenological Movement, vol.1 (Hague: Martinus Nijhoff, 1969), p 261
[182] Ibid., p 147

Schopenhauer is not enough to be ethical. Just feeling sorry and staying there is not the true way of sympathy. There must be an act of helping hands. It cannot be denied that there is a spontaneous impulse of feeling of sorry or sorrow when we encounter the poor. This seems to be the pure reaction to the outer stimuli of the poor. Helping hands come after this change of inner emotion. In this way, there can be a genetic development of sympathy.

6.1.2 The Genetic Development of Sympathy

The phenomena of sympathy are ubiquitous, so it is not a special experience, but a common thing for everyone in the world. The most common experience of sympathy is apparently passive. When we see a poor man on the street corner begging a dime or a piece of bread on a cold winter night, we feel immediately some kind of pity on him even though we have no apparent and special relationship with him. At any beneficial events there are always people who are ready to donate some money for the needy. These phenomena can be some evidences of the fact that there are people who are the carriers of sympathy. This kind of sympathy is just the beginning of the true sympathy, or rather the integral sympathy, which should mean the reciprocal interaction of the $\pi\alpha\theta o\varsigma$, heart, between concerned persons.

Sympathy should not always imply just the passive reaction to the poor situation of others. Just having a pity on someone who is inferior to me is not to be considered as the integral sympathy because an integral sympathy should mean having a feeling of pity on others with the sense of "voluntary" duty, which should mean an instinctive feeling of obligation for fellow human beings. Only the integral sympathy, which functions in a reciprocal way, can build a true bridge of mutual understanding and help between concerned persons. Only when two hearts understand each other reciprocally, we can go on to help one another. One-sided help for others, which manifested mainly through the practice of charity, does its function well in alleviating the conscience of the donators. In this way it quite often happens the discrepancy between the giver and the receiver. In the practice of charity, there is no room for the mutual sympathy building, which is a necessary process for the integral sympathy as the result. The problem is not the compensation for the pangs of conscience mainly with the material alms. It is the lack of the communication of hearts.

It takes time to understand each other, especially when the concerned people are in quite different situation. Mutual understanding comes never by itself. The greater the difference is, the harder for them to understand each other. As the learning process of children, the sympathy building needs practice and time. It is clear that all men are born with the ability of sympathy but it needs to be nurtured, as a seed needs water, sunshine, carbon dioxide, and other minerals to sprout out, and to come into bloom. By the same token, the seed of sympathy needs nurture of learning and practice.

We may here discern three phases, or rather modes of sympathy: primary, middle, and integral. In the end sympathy is just one and only, so it is not quite correct when we are talking about the three different kinds of sympathy. The primary sympathy is almost a spontaneous reaction to others under poor situation. Logically, it always precedes the other two modes of sympathy. In the end it is comprised in the integral sympathy as a part of the whole sympathy. Without learning and practice, the primary sympathy stays as unilateral understanding, not reciprocal, so there is no room here for the active helping hand. There is no sense of duty in this stage of sympathy. The sense of duty must be acquired, i.e., it must be learned from someone who already knows and does the duty for others. Here a role model plays very important role.

The ability for the sense of duty resides from the beginning in nature of every human being, it does not come from outside. It just needs learning and practice, as a small child needs nourishment and practice to be a good man later. In fact Jesus Christ had seen in human nature more that this ability, so he could tell us with assurance that we love each other as he loves us(John 13:34)[183]. Loving each other, seeing Jesus Christ in each other, and serving each other as Jesus Christ is the ultimate goal of long journey of love. To have sympathy is the very beginning of this itinerary.

By the same token, there is a long way to be an Ideal Man of Virtue (君 子) who is eventually a man of Jen (仁), which was authoritatively interpreted as sympathy for others by Mencius. We cannot identify the Christian love with the Confucian Jen (仁), but in the basis there is common ground of sympathy as they are related with the feeling of sympathy as the moment of beginning of ethical action. As long as the true sympathy should always come with the act of helping hand, a developing sympathy plays an important role, it is not important whether it is through the rigorous and long lasting study as seen in Confucianism, or through the belief in the good will of God who comforts us through His own deeds in His incarnated son of Jesus Christ.

6.1.3 The Extension of Sympathy in the Society from Individual

There is quantitative and qualitative difference of sympathy in relation to society and person. Normally, in almost all societies, regardless of the differences of region and culture, there exists very strong family tie, which is formed natural without a specially organized institution. Every member of a family is united very closely, not only biologically but also psychologically. This smallest unit of society cannot stand without its building brick, i.e., the individual. The family bond is reinforced by the noema and noesis relation of

---

[183] Nestle-Aland, op. cit., p296

sympathy among family members. Sympathy is a phenomenon between at least two concerned people. But there is no physical transaction between them. There happens only a subjective change, which amounts to be a creative one. This subjectivity does not hinder that there happens a mutual resonance between concerned people. Even if it is delicate matter what happens in this individual sympathy because it is very natural, we can describe it phenomenologically because it happens in the relation of noema and noesis.

As soon as sympathy extends itself in a society, it disappears behind the institutionalization. Especially in the modern welfare society, we can easily find the institutionalized sympathy in the form of charity organizations. When the conscience of man can be lighter with the sympathetic act, i.e., charity, there is no better way of doing it than building and operating the organization of institutionalized sympathy. Here are still many problems, for example, the anonymity of individual as person, and intolerable suffering of personal dignity in the masses. The helped must be treated as a man with dignity, but in reality there are many incidents of the contrary cases. This leads not seldom to the humiliation of the helped who must suffer twice. And to tell the truth, it is by no means so true, as is said, that it is self-evident that a sufferer will ask for help as long as someone can help him. It is far from the truth, though the counter-examples are not always cases of despair as great as this. The fact of the matter is this:

"someone suffering has usually one or more ways in which he could wish to be helped. If then someone helps him, well yes, he is glad to be helped. But as soon as the question of being helped begins, in a more profound sense, to be serious, especially when the help is to come from a superior, or the most exalted of all - then comes this humiliation of having to receive unconditional help, in whatever form, of becoming like a nothing in the hands of the 'helper' for whom everything is possible, or even just of having to give in to some other person, to give up being oneself as long as one is asking for help. Ah! indeed, there is much, even prolonged and agonizing suffering in this way of which the self does not complain, and which it therefore fundamentally prefers so as to retain the right to be itself."[184]

However, there is no other alternative than the social sympathy in the form of charity organization, as long as there are many people in need, and the individual sympathy for them has its limits. As the saying goes, we have to give fishing gear and teach how to use them when a man wants a fish from you even if we have to give him first the fish lest he starves to death.

As long as there is personal relation, the individual sympathy functions well as the helping hands, but it cannot cure the whole social problem. Only the merit of scale can help the needy in mass. Here we can see the difference of the

---

[184] Kierkegaard, S., The Sickness unto Death (London: Penguin Books, 1989), pp 102-103

individual sympathy and the social one. Individual sympathy can provide the fish, which is mostly accompanied with personal warmth and intimacy. In the social sympathy, there is always a distance between people, but it can provide fishing gear so that the needy can survive without the help from others, and furthermore, he may help others who are in need in the future. With the social sympathy, we can reproduce the sympathy ostensibly in the public. With the individual sympathy, we can give a personal impression or teaching how to help others, and later it can be useful for people to have an understanding for the social sympathy. With the distance between people, the personal intimacy grows fainter, but sympathy itself stays there, i.e., even though the modes of sympathy are different, the essence of sympathy as the helping hands is always there because the true sympathy does not depend on the spatiotemporal distance between people.

Even though we can easily see that the individual sympathy is the basis of the social sympathy, we cannot claim that the social sympathy is the extension of the individual sympathy. The individual sympathy and the social sympathy are the same in their essence. The social sympathy is more extended, but without the individual sympathy which we can easily identify among family members and peer groups, it cannot stand alone. These two sympathies are rather complementary for each other.

6.2 The Phenomena of Sympathy

6.2.1 Sympathy with Other as the Receptive Concern for Fellow Human Beings

6.2.1.1 Empathy as the Primary Phase of Passive Sympathy

We may see some people who really "love" their dogs very much but "hate" some of their neighbor because the latter does not like their dogs. We may see some people who really care so much about the whales, which are said to be endangered species, but not pay much attention to the people in Africa, who are starving to death. We may see some people who really feel very sad and even cry when they see poor people, but find it very hard to give them what they have because they have sons and daughters, who have to eventually inherit the whole property of their parents intact. We may have to guess what happens in the mind of such people, who truly love and care what they want to love and care. In their mind it happens just the feeling of empathy.

A human feeling does not always arise simply, but there is a lump of interwoven complex of feelings. We may first say that empathy is a kind of contagion, as far as man identifies the other "I" with one's own "I." To be lost in someone or something is not the true sympathy but just a kind of emotional ecstasy, like the effect of the addictive drugs. However, we cannot begin to feel the way others feel when we are not emotionally contagious. Without the emotional contagion, it is very difficult for us to have a Mitgefühl, and furthermore the helping hands for others.

One important ethical matter in our world is not if a deed is right or wrong, but if it can be helpful for the peaceful coexistence of people. It is true that we can see the danger of the blind empathy with their pop "stars" among the younger generation, especially when it goes mad with the vulgar cultural idols, like pop singers and movie stars. Much serious problem is not the fact that the younger generation is mad about somebody whom it does not know well, but that somebody is not seldom morally blamable in many ways. Many of the "stars" of the pop culture do not care much about their social responsibility. They just want to have wealth and fame as much as possible, with all means. They are using the empathy of the younger generation, which is mostly not immune to the bad contagion, as much as to the "good contagion". The messy sexual life and the irresponsible behavior of the "stars" have tremendous negative effect not only upon the younger generation but also upon society proper. This bad influence is extremely magnified through the commercially oriented mass media, which do anything to have the maximum profit. Like the leaders of religious fanaticism, they are using the immature souls of the younger generation for their own profit.

The pure passivity of empathy is not enough for the truly sympathetic society. Just to have the same feeling without action means a bad case of sympathy. A true sympathy must be in a situation where two "I"s face each other with their respective own identities and feel and do something together. There must be no immersion of one identity into the other. In most cases of empathy, there happens a kind of ecstasy regardless of the duration. Ecstasy has just an effect of escape. There may be many different reasons why there are so many young people who find empathy with the pop stars, but one of the most important reasons may be their despair.

Not only the fundamental and existential despair but also the concrete fear arising in everyday life makes people in the world helpless. In the postmodern society where the blind drive for the achievement and aggressive competition are cherished, too many people must recoil from the world, lest they become sick to death. Regardless whether the despair is feminine or masculine, according to Kierkegaard's distinction, a man is in danger of death.[185] Whether a man does not want to be himself or he wants in despair to be himself, there must be a conflict, which leads to the need of ultimate help. There is still less hope in our age than ever before when people are much far from God as the ultimate help. There are always more losers than winners even though nobody wants to

---

[185]Ibid., p 80, p 98

be a loser. Especially the environmental disaster and the economic uncertainty, which are all caused by the uncontrolled desire of man, drive them into constant stress, not seldom into despair. The problems are mostly beyond one's ability, therefore there is pervasive resignation among people about the future. That is why there are so many people who want to escape from the real life. As opium was the only way for many Chinese in the 18th and 19th century to escape from then China with no future, there is tendency of escaping from this world of today. One of the easiest ways to escape from the reality is just forgetting it, forgetting that the "I" is in this uncertain world of pain. However, to become addicted to narcotics is not the ultimate escape from the reality, on the contrary, it makes one more dependent on the real world as long as he or she has to find the narcotics in this world. By the same token, the sick empathy for the pop stars results in frustration in the end.

Empathy does not last long when it should mean losing oneself in someone else, or, even seldom, something else, which ends with self-frustration and search for the next ecstasy. This bad case of empathy must be sublated (aufgehoben) and carried into the realm of the true Mitgefühl, where the identities of everybody are preserved. Without the individual identity, there is no true emotion (Gefühl), which can be shared together. For all those limits of empathy, we cannot simply discard it because it is the very beginning of the Mitgefühl. It is much similar to the Einsfühlung of Max Scheler, which has very great scope of its limit. The problem is, in fact, that we cannot lose ourselves totally to someone else or something else for a long time in our normal life. The phenomena of empathy are evidently there in our daily life, so we can go on from these phenomena to search the true sympathy.

6.2.1.2 Mitgefühl as the Social Prerequisite for Sympathy

We may easily find a girl who is crying just because her friend is crying. At first sight, it seems to be rather empathy than Mitgefühl because of its contagiousness, but it stays as Mitgefühl as long as there is an intact relation between the lamenting and the solacing. There is interesting theory about Mitgefühl by Max Scheler. He distinguished four facts about Mitgefühl :
"*1. To feel the direct sympathy (mitfühlen), for example, the one and same sorrow with someone else;
2. The Mitgefühl for something : to be happy together with someone's happiness and to feel sorry together for his sorrow;
3. The simple contagion of feeling;
4. the true Einsfühlung.*"[186]
These four facts of Mitgefühl are quite different from each other. The first

---

[186] Scheler, Max, Wesen und Formen der Sympathie (Bern: A. Franke AG Verlag, 1973), p 24

case of direct sympathy can be found in the sorrow of father and mother who have just lost their loving little child. They seem to feel the same sorrow but it does not mean that they feel the same sorrow, which is there. They feel just the sorrow with each other (miteinander). For the third party, their sorrow can be just an object of sorry. The second fact is phenomenological one, i.e., it is intentional. The sorrow of others can be here present only through the act of understanding or Nachfühlen. My sorrow and his sorrow are phenomenologically two different facts, not the same fact as in the first case. We can have Nachfühlen without Mitfühlen. The third case has something to do with the developmental theory of the positivist, like Herbert Spencer. Scheler named it as contagion of feeling (Gefühlsansteckung). Here, there is no need for the intention of feeling or the participation in the feeling of others. The contagion of feeling happens just between the states of feelings, and therefore there is no need for the knowledge about the happiness of others. Without the experience of the feeling of others, the contagion can be happened. Having pity on someone cannot be confused with this contagion of feeling, but not only H. Spencer but also Friedrich Nietzsche made the same mistake. When sorrow is an infection, as F. Nietzsche has claimed, there will be no need for the sharing of the sorrow. The fourth and last case about Mitgefühl is the Einsfühlung (respectively, Einssetzung). An acrobat can take my whole heart for a moment when he is doing very difficult stunt. There are two kinds of empathy according to Scheler: idiopathic and heteropathic types respectively. These two types are different in their duration, but they are the same in the end because they are just kinds of emotional contagion. And Scheler dismissed them as not the true Mitgefühl.[187]

Scheler enumerated, further, many cases of Einsfühlung. They are the totem cult, the religious antic mystics, the hypnotizing, the Freudian mass-psychology, the childish imaginary role playing, the split of the consciousness, the truly loving sexual act, the Führer and the blind followers, the Soseins-Einsfühlung of mother and child, and the instinctive reaction of the primitive animals to the outer stimuli in relation to the biological survival.[188]. Scheler was right when he said that all these cases could not guarantee the individual identity to be sustained along the way of Mitfühlen. We can here see the anti-evidences of the true sympathy. A true sympathy should never mean losing identity of every individual who is taking part in the act of sympathy.

As long as we are feeling something like sorry or pity with someone who is in need, but doing nothing, there is no true sympathy in the moral sense, even though the feeling of pity is the beginning of the true sympathy. It is clear, nevertheless, as Scheler claimed, that those phenomena of sympathy in

---

[187] Ibid., pp. 23-29
[188] Ibid., pp. 30-48

everyday-life do have a function of "chain of grounding" for sympathy in general, i.e., Einsfühlung founds Nachfühlung, and the latter founds Mitgefühl, and Mitgefühl founds human love. This human love founds the acosmic person- and God-love, which is Christian, i.e., not from the Resentment, but from an autonomous and healing love of God for the individual "center" of person.[189] As long as the Mitgefühl encompasses the whole phenomena of sympathy, it cannot be denied that the act of feeling is the most important factor with the matter of sympathy. As the neo-platonistic mystics of the early Middle Ages in Europe, who searched the true love of Jesus Christ only in the intellectual insight, there was the tendency of intellectual interpretation about the matter of feeling in the traditional Confucianism, especially with the concept of Ce Yin (惻隱).

6.2.1.3 Ce Yin: The Confucian Understanding of Sympathy

There are two other words which have similar meaning to Tong Quin (同情): Ci Bai (慈悲) and Ce Yin (惻隱). Ci Bai (慈悲) is a Buddhist concept which means universal love. Literally, it means to love and to have pity for every living being so that there could be no sorrow for them regardless whether they are men or animals. In many Buddhist scripts we can see explanations about the Ci Bai (慈悲). It said that the mind of Buddha is nothing but Ci Bai (慈悲) itself.[190] And Ci (慈) means to be able to be happy with the happiness of others, while Bai (悲) means to be able to understand the misery of others.[191] Moreover, there is Lian Min (憐愍) or Lian Min (憐憫). These words have almost the same meaning as pity or compassion for the misery of others, or simply sympathy. In the Chinese history it meant mostly the merciful mental attitude of the Emperor or the king for his subjects who are in need of help.[192]

Mencius had used the word "Ce Yin (惻隱)" many times, which should mean pity proper. As we have already seen in chapter 4.1.1, Ce Yin (惻隱) is the mental attitude, which is the beginning of Jen (仁). In Confucianism there is rather a beneficiary act of the rulers for the poor, which must be interpreted rather alms than a humanitarian (and egalitarian) act of sympathy. In the rigidly hierarchical Confucian society, man (人) means mainly a man of higher status

---

[189] Ibid., pp. 105-108
[190] The Book of Great Sun (大日經), 佛心者大慈大悲., refer to Mordhashi, Tetsuji (諸橋轍次), Great Chinese-Japanese Dictionary, Bk. 4 (大漢和辭典卷四) (Tokyo, Japan: Taishukan Publishing Co. Ltd.) (株式會社大修館書店), 1984), p 4550
[191] The Secound World of Buddhism (法界次第), 能與他之樂心名之為慈 能拔他之苦心名之為悲 ..., refer to Ibid.
[192] Yi, Xin (庾信), 謝藤王集序啓, 聖慈憐愍遂垂存錄 ..., refer to Ibid.

with the appropriate influence on the society. Between a king and his subjects, there was not seldom the relationship of mutual benefits, in the disguise of blind royalty and care. In the traditional Confucian society, when someone brings about the emotion of sympathy of others because of his bad situation, the latter cannot be a subject with the human dignity, but just an object of pity which was interpreted as more alms than a humanitarian understanding and caring. According to the teaching of Confucius, there must be the Ideal Man of Virtue (君子) in our world, not in the Heaven (天), but this man is so scarce that even Confucius himself never met him in his whole life. All other people who cannot be the Ideal Man of Virtue (君子) were called the "men with a small mind (小人)", or man with the narrow mind. They were despised together with women by Confucius himself. Confucius once said :

"I cannot put up with woman and the men with a small mind (小人). They become too arrogant when I treat them very well. They make a grievance against me when I do not care about them much."[193]

Even if Confucius never gave up his life work of searching for the conditions of ideal society where everyone must live a decent life, there were many cases of laments about the decadence of his era. He understood exactly what the problems of the society were, and he knew the right answer for those problems, but he could never put it into practice because of the indifference of the rulers against him.

Confucius had the feeling of Ce Yin (惻隱), as the beginning of Jen (仁), about his contemporary, and understood them, but he could not make them to live a better life. He strongly believed that man had to voluntarily learn to be a truly virtuous man, while just to have the intention to be such a man did not much matter for him :

"When man loves Jen (仁) but does not learn, he becomes foolish. When man loves knowledge but does not learn, he becomes unreliable. When man loves belief but does not learn, he becomes dangerous. When man loves honesty but does not learn, he becomes narrow-minded. When man loves courage but does not learn, he becomes rebellious. When man loves rectitude but does not learn, he becomes maniac."[194]

Only through thorough learning and understanding with many experiences, man can be an ideally virtuous man. This is a theory, which is very similar to that of Socrates. For Socrates, virtue is knowledge (knowledge of the good); the

---

[193] The Analects of Confucius, chapter 17, 陽貨, 子曰唯女子與小人爲難養也近之卽不遜遠之卽怨 ; Legge, James, Confucius, p 330
[194] Ibid., chapter 17, 陽貨, 好仁不好學其蔽也愚好知不好學其蔽也蕩好信不好學其蔽也賊好直不好學其蔽也絞好勇不好學其蔽也亂好剛不好學其蔽也狂 ; Legge, James, Confucius, p 322

two are equated. A person who knows what is right will by virtue of such knowledge do what is right; conversely, to do wrong stems from ignorance, evildoing being an involuntary act. While virtue and knowledge are identified as one, in a sense, actually virtue is the result of knowledge and dependent upon it. Genuine knowledge as Socrates understood it was moral insight, which he assessed as the best thing in the world. Virtue (*arete*) is excellence, ability, or efficiently functioning at one's task. Since all knowledge is virtue, then it follows that knowledge is the most excellent of all possessions. Knowledge not only results in right conduct, but knowledge per se is good conduct. "No man errs of his own free will" implies that while men seek what is good, moral disagreement among individuals results from the different degrees of knowledge that each possesses. Inasmuch as virtue is knowledge, then it is teachable and can be conveyed to other persons merely through instruction; and since knowledge is a single body of learning, the seemingly multiple virtues are ultimately not many, but one entity.[195] This was exactly the conviction of Confucius who tried to teach the people the right way, but in the end he failed not because his theory was false, but because he did not give enough attention to the feeling of man, even if his intellectualism has become the core of Confucianism.

With this regard, there has been incessant controversy about the nature of man in the history of Confucianism. The "Seven Emotions (七 情)"[196] of man cannot have any meaning for being a virtuous man, but just the "Four Cardinal Virtues (四 端)"[197] have to be learned and practiced. Man tends to act according to feeling even if it not seldom results in failure. That is why the traditional Confucians favored intellectualism. We do sometimes help spontaneously others in need, but mostly, in this case the scale of help is relative small. When the scale of help, both in quantity and in quality, must be very big, there comes a fundamental reasoning : "Should I help others in need even it means great self-sacrifice of mine?" We do not know the answer until we learn more about the "morally right and valuable".

The feeling of Ce Yin (惻 隱) comes up as spontaneous reaction as soon as man sees the pitiful situation of the needy. The action of helping them comes later after some reasoning. As a matter of fact, the modern education for the socialization of children is based on the belief that man can be morally mature by learning, which is exactly the essence of the moral intellectualism, but as a matter of fact, the intellectual awareness alone cannot guarantee the moral behavior. There must be also consideration for the emotional aspect of human being. The human reason alone cannot make man reasonable, as we have

---

[195] Sahakian, William S., op. cit., pp. 9-10

[196] i.e., happiness, wrath, sorrow, joy, love, hate, desire (喜 努 哀 樂 愛 惡 慾)

[197] i.e., Jen, righteousness, courtesy, wisdom (仁 義 禮 智)

already seen in the history, especially, in the two World Wars in our century. The much-cherished reason of man, which has its deep root in the intellectualism, could not stop the greatest catastrophe of human history. On the contrary, the mathematical human reason helped to destroy the human dignity systematically. We still need to find out the better trace of man not only in the realm of reason but in the realm of emotion when we want to find the way to the society where people feel no resentment. A good society must be a place where nobody feels sorry not only in the matter of material needs but also in the matter of human dignity. As long as one must feel shame when he receives help from someone else, there is no good society, even if the act of help is happened after the moral reflection. Help begins with the feeling of Ce Yin (惻 隱), but it must not hinder the egalitarian relationship between people when they do the act of the true sympathy. The giver and the receiver must be treated as the same people who have the same human dignity. In the strictly hierarchical Confucian society, there was not much room for the egalitarian relation between people. That is why the modern Confucian society still needs to learn from the Christian moral of sympathy, which leads to the love of God in the end. Before God, everybody is equal. This thought has been hardly acceptable in the traditional Confucian society.

6.2.2 Sympathy for Other with the Sense of Responsibility

6.2.2.1 Condolence as the Primary Phase of Active Sympathy

St. Thomas Aquinas once made a systematic argument about the pragmatic usefulness of sympathy in his work of Summa Theologica.[198]

---

[198] St. Thomas Aquinas, Summa Theologica, (tr. Fathers of the English Dominican Province), First Part of the Second Part (QQ. 1-114), 38. Of the Remedies of Sorrow or Pain, A(3) Whether Pain or Sorrow Are Assuaged by the Sympathy of Friends? :
FS Q[38] A[3] Thes. Whether pain or sorrow are assuaged by the sympathy of friends?
FS Q[38] A[3] Obj. 1
OBJ 1: It would seem that the sorrow of sympathizing friends does not assuage our own sorrow. For contraries have contrary effects. Now as Augustine says (Confess. viii, 4), "when many rejoice together, each one has more exuberant joy, for they are kindled and inflamed one by the other." Therefore, in like manner, when many are sorrowful, it seems that their sorrow is greater.
FS Q[38] A[3] Obj. 2
OBJ 2: Further, friendship demands mutual love, as Augustine declares (Confess. iv, 9). But a sympathizing friend is pained at the sorrow of his friend with whom he sympathizes. Consequently the pain of a sympathizing friend becomes, to the friend in sorrow, a further cause of sorrow: so that, his pain being doubled his sorrow seems to increase.
FS Q[38] A[3] Obj. 3
OBJ 3: Further, sorrow arises from every evil affecting a friend, as though it affected oneself:

Here, St. Thomas Aquinas wanted to show the positive effect of sympathy lessening the pain of others. Needless to say about Buddha who saw the world as the sea of pain, there are many theories talking about the painful life of man in this world. Not only pessimists like Schopenhauer or Nietzsche, but also optimists, who are mostly religious, accord in the opinion about the hardship in this world. As long as there is great sorrow or pain in this world, it is welcomed fact that friends are there to alleviate this pain. Only a true friend can do this job, but the problem is that the true friendship must be always limited in its number. Man can be a philanthropist who loves his neighbor and helps them. However, without the feeling of sympathy for others, and just with the reason, or the enlightened self-interest, we can hardly have condolence. We may be nice to our neighbor. It can be motivated by the enlightened self-interest because mutual benefit may be the cause of the trade.[199] However, we cannot have a happy society just with the concept of mutual benefit. Condolence is what happens only between two true friends. And a true friendship does not presuppose the mutual benefit, the latter is rather the results of the former.

We may enumerate many causes of the pain and misery of man in this world. The real remedy for the sorrow of man is to eliminate its causes. There are two main causes of the misery, which cannot be easily removed. They are the outer

---

since *"a friend is one's other self"* (Ethic. ix, 4,9). But sorrow is an evil. Therefore the sorrow of the sympathizing friend increases the sorrow of the friend with whom he sympathizes.
FS Q[38] A[3] OTC
On the contrary, The Philosopher says (Ethic. ix, 11) that those who are in pain are consoled when their friends sympathize with them.
FS Q[38] A[3] Body
I answer that, When one is in pain, it is natural that the sympathy of a friend should afford consolation: whereof the Philosopher indicates a twofold reason (Ethic. ix, 11). The first is because, since sorrow has a depressing effect, it is like a weight whereof we strive to unburden ourselves: so that when a man sees others saddened by his own sorrow, it seems as though others were bearing the burden with him, striving, as it were, to lessen its weight; wherefore the load of sorrow becomes lighter for him: something like what occurs in the carrying of bodily burdens. The second and better reason is because when a man's friends condole with him, he sees that he is loved by them, and this affords him pleasure, as stated above (Q[32], A[5]). Consequently, since every pleasure assuages sorrow, as stated above (A[1]), it follows that sorrow is mitigated by a sympathizing friend.
FS Q[38] A[3] R.O. 1
Reply OBJ 1: In either case there is a proof of friendship, viz. when a man rejoices with the joyful, and when he sorrows with the sorrowful. Consequently each becomes an object of pleasure by reason of its cause.
FS Q[38] A[3] R.O. 2
Reply OBJ 2: The friend's sorrow itself would be a cause of sorrow: but consideration of its cause, viz. his love, gives rise rather to pleasure.
FS Q[38] A[3] R.O. 2 And this suffices for the reply to the Third Objection.
[199] TIME, Special Issue, The New Age of Discovery, Winter 1997/98, p99

nature and the inner nature of man. The outer nature is not friendly for man. It nurtures man only when man does hard labor. This nature does not care what man wants to do. Nature punishes man mercilessly with floods, draught, and storms. Many say that man is the enemy of nature, and furthermore, nature does not need man. It is true that man is part of nature, and therefore man has to live in harmony with nature. Nevertheless, nature is not generous even to most of the animals that live according to the law of nature. Man is relatively prosper in this world, not because man obeys nature but man does his best to survive the harsh conditions that nature provides all living creatures indiscriminately.

As long as man tries to survive, man has to endure such conditions. Enduring means mostly pain and misery. Man cannot change the whole nature at his will, therefore there is always pain, as long as man has to survive. It is not only the outer nature that hurts man, the nature of man does hurt fellow human beings, sometimes harsher that the outer nature. For a man to survive in a society means to win the competition with other men. A winner is always an offender who hurts his loser, direct or indirect. It is true that nobody wants to be a loser. That is the nature of man. As long as this nature of man cannot be changed, there is always pain in this world.

As long as there is pain, man needs condolence of friends. Condolence is not just a psychological trust for the "loser" but it is a great help for the survival. As Kierkegaard said, the disease that leads to the death is despair, which is caused mostly from the pain of loosing. In a competitive society nobody cares much about loser, mostly because the latter does not give any help for the former in the matter of surviving the society. This kind of nature of man is called egoism. As a matter of fact, egoism is necessary for man to survive in this world. Too much egoism does hurt too many fellow human beings, but total self-sacrifice for the neighbor means in reality being a total loser in society, therefore everybody needs some amount of self-interest, which is called the enlightened self-interest. Nevertheless, it is extremely difficult to find the appropriate amount of self-interest, mostly because this is not seldom confused with the greed of man. And greed hurts not only the weaker in society but also the society itself. To know what greed is as much important as to control it. And to control greed is as important as to condole the grieving for the continuing existence of society.

Condolence is an ethical act not only because it mitigates the sorrow of man but because it helps the whole society to survive. Without society there is no need of ethics. In an ideal society all men have to live a happy life. As Ernst Bloch once formulated:

"*The social utopia has to do with the happiness of man, the natural right of human dignity.*"[200] And... "*there is no human dignity without the end of need, as*

---

[200] Bloch, Ernst, Naturrecht und menschliche Würde (Frankfurt a. M.: Suhrkamp, 1985), p 13

the happiness fitting for man without the end of the old and new lower social stratum."[201]

The problem is neither the absence of the idea of freedom in the history of mankind, as manifested in the Article I. of the Amendment of the Constitution of the U.S.A.,[202] nor the idea of equally happy life of all men, as we can see in the Declaration of Independence of the U.S.A. in July 4. 1776:

"We hold these Truths to be self-evident, that all Men are created equal, that they are endowed by their Creator with certain unalienable Rights, that among these are Life, Liberty and the Pursuit of Happiness---"[203]

That means there should be no pain, sorrow, and resentments in a society, which are the opposites of the endowment of God.

Before we can accept a man as our friend, we have to accept him as a man. Not only in the era of Aristotle but also for a long time after him, there has been a strongly lasting concept of class in society. Only the people who happened to be in the upper class were generally accepted as "true man". There was only the social justice from above, whether it is from God or the political authority. Only after the Declaration of Independence of the U.S.A. in 1776 and the French Revolution in 1789 respectively, people have really begun to think about the true concept of man and his right. Before these two historical events, there were already many philosophers who advocated the freedom and equality of man, but the theory of Thomas Hobbes has been seen as the true explanation of the history of man for a long time: *"homo homini lupus, bellum omnium contra omnes."*[204] Even if it is true that there is more than a wolf in the nature of man, it is quite hard to believe in the good nature of man as long as there is social injustice. This has been also the main cause of pain and sorrow of man in society.

We may propose many remedies for social injustice, but, most of all, we cannot have a social justice before we can accept all other men as a carrier of human dignity. Religiously, the equality of all human beings was already proclaimed by Jesus Christ Himself when He told to His followers:

"For whosoever shall do the will of my Father which is in heaven, the same is my brother, and sister, and mother. (Mt. 12:50)"

Here the only precondition of the equality of all mankind was just the belief in God. After two thousand years since this proclamation, there is still many cases of injustice in the world, and therefore, there are still pain, sorrow, and

---

[201] Ibid., p 16

[202] In Internet, www.emory.law.edu :
"Congress shall make no law respecting an establishment of religion, or prohibiting the free exercise thereof; or abridging the freedom of speech, or of the press; or the right of the people peaceably to assemble, and to petition the Government for a redress of grievances."

[203] The Declaration of Independence of the U.S.A. in July 4. 1776 in Internet, www.emory.law.edu

[204] Bloch, Ernst, op. cit., p 61

existential despair. That is why we still need condolence even if it could be practiced only between true friends, and such friends are very seldom. When we cannot find a true friend, we have to find a medium, which is much pervasive and easy to access. Compassion may be an answer for that search even if it still needs more religious resolution with a passion for fellow human beings. Only Jesus Christ could show us well how it should practiced. So we are here to find out what He exactly has done for us.

6.2.2.2 Compassion: The Action with the Sense of Responsibility

As the Gospels have well shown, Jesus Christ was always full of pity on the people who seek help from Him. An example shows it in Mt. 9:36:

"*But when he saw the multitudes, he was **moved with compassion** on them, because they fainted, and were scattered abroad, as sheep having no shepherd.*"[205]

Literally, compassion means "to be moved as to one's bowels", for the bowels were thought to be the seat of love and pity.[206] In 1Jo 3:17, we can see exactly this usage of the word of compassion.[207] There are some examples of Hebraic words of compassion in the Old Testaments :

"*And when she had opened it, she saw the child: and, behold, the babe wept. And she had **compassion on** him, and said, This is one of the Hebrews' children*"(Ex. 2:6)[208] "*That then the LORD thy God will turn thy captivity, and have **compassion upon** thee, and will return and gather thee from all the nations, whither the LORD thy God hath scattered thee.*"(De. 30:3)[209]

In the New Testaments, we can see other kinds of usage of compassion. Except "σπλαγχνίζομαι", there are "ἐλεέω and "οἰκτείρω". While the former, which comes in Matt., Mark, Luke and some letters of St. Peter, has much to do with the mercy of God, the latter, which comes only in the letters of St. Paul, is a reaction for the sorrow or pain of others. The interesting word of "συμπάθεια" comes only once in the letter of St. Paul :

"*Finally, be ye all of one mind, **having compassion one of another**, love as brethren, be pitiful, be courteous:*" (1Pe. 3:8)[210]

---

[205] ἰδὼν δε τους οχλους *εσπλαγχνισθη* περι αυτων οτι ησαν εσκυλμενοι και ερριμμενοι ωσει προβατα μη εχοντα ποιμενα

[206] Timnathserah Inc., Online Bible (Ver. 7.05/ Win32) (Winterbourne, Canada: Timnathserah Inc., 1998)

[207] But whoso hath this world's good, and seeth his brother have need, and shutteth up **his bowels of compassion** from him, how dwelleth the love of God in him?

[208] Ex. 2:6 ותפתח ותראהו את-הילד והנה-נער בכה ותחמל עליו ותאמר מילדי העברים זה

[209] De. 30:3 ושב יהוה אלהיך את-שבותך ורחמך ושב וקבצך מכל-העמים אשר הפיצך יהוה אלהיך שמה

[210] το δε τελος παντες ομοφρονες *συμπαθεις* φιλαδελφοι ευσπλαγχνοι ταπεινοφρονες

Regardless of all these variances, the most important thing in the Christian compassion is a passion for others who are in need, not only with mind but with action. Whenever Jesus Christ feels compassion for the people around Him, He helps them in a secret way but with concrete results : healing the sick, giving the bread and fish for the hungry, and condoling the grieving in sorrow. Compassion is much similar to condolence than sympathy in its etymological meaning because there is the dynamic action of emotional Leidenschaft (passio) between people. Even Jesus Christ Himself once wept for Lazarus.[211] Passion has something to do with suffering, which means having pain both in body and soul. This kind of compassion is not the peculiar Christian virtue. We can witness many usage of compassion and mercy of Allah in the Quran. The most frequent passage containing these words is :

"*He is Oft-Returning with compassion and is merciful.*"

Here Compassion never stops just as a feeling, it induces always the act of help. A compassionate act means always the manifestation of the spontaneous, therefore, natural good of human being. It is still controversial whether the nature of man is good or bad. But it is very clear that the dignity of man must be considered as one of the highest priorities. The dignity of the poor, who are mostly the receiver of help from the helper, must be also as much revered as that of the rich and famous. There can be raised another question about this matter of the dignity of man. In ancient Greece, women and slaves could not be citizen in Athens, they were not "men". Even Aristotle, the great philosopher of our history, thought the slaves had no soul. Therefore, moral virtue, intellectual virtue, and even friendship, which he praised in his great book "The Nicomachean Ethics", did not have anything to do with the slaves.[212]

Nevertheless, slaves did not eat liver of their friends, contrary to the guess of Aristotle, they even raised a loud voice against the tyrannical politics and asked for social justice, not only in the Roman Empire but also in old China. Nowadays, there are no official slaves in the world, but there still exists an invisible wall in the mind of people, which is much harder to eliminate than the

---

[211] Hoh. 11:34 ff

[212] Aristotle, Nichomachean Ethics, (Tr. David Ross) (Oxford: Oxford University Press,1980), P 212 :

"*But in the deviation-forms, as justice hardly exists, so too does friendship. It exists least in the worst form; in tyranny there is little or no friendship. For where there is nothing common to ruler and ruled, there is not friendship either, since there is not justice; e.g. between craftsman and tool, soul and body, master and slave; the latter in each case is benefited by that which uses it, but there is no friendship nor justice towards lifeless things. But neither is there friendship towards a horse or an ox, nor to a slave qua slave. For there is nothing common to the two parties; the slave is a living tool and the tool a lifeless slave. Qua slave then, one cannot be friends with him. But qua man one can; for there seems to be some justice between any man and any other who can share in a system of law or be a party to an agreement; therefore there can also be friendship with him in so far as he is a man.*"

tangible one.

Even after the Civil Rights Bill was passed, the Afro-American were not "normal" citizen in the U.S.A. Bull Conner, a white public-safety commissioner of Birmingham, Alabama, thought in May 1963 that he was doing right thing when he was ready to use water cannons and attack dogs on a group of civil right demonstrators led by Rev. Dr. Martin Luther King Jr.[213] After long struggle for social justice, there is no more official racial segregation against Afro-American in the U.S.A. Nowadays, the Afro-Americans in the U.S.A. have the equal right as their fellow white citizens, but there are still many white people who does not want Afro-American as their neighbor, let alone as their friend. Without the sense of duty to accept and love others as one's neighbor, it is not easy to practice the love of Jesus Christ. Law alone cannot make a just society where all men are equal. Kierkegaard briefly defined the content of Christianity's joyous good news as man's kinship with God:

*"Therefore, Christianity sets as a task man's likeness to God. But God is love; therefore, we can only resemble God in loving, just as, according to the Apostle's word, we can only be 'God's co-workers in love.' With God there is no partiality; therefore, a person first resembles God when he loves his neighbor. Through God's law, summarized and articulated with divine authority in the double love-command, one learns to recognize love. The law describes that position in which the human person must be placed for love's radical humanity to emerge as every individual's original possibility. However, the law cannot actualize love. For this reason, Christianity's talk about love must contain 'this apparent contradiction: that **to love is duty**.'"*[214]

Nevertheless, two cases shown above tell us very well how difficult it is for a man to understand the other man, let alone to have sympathy for him. Compassion does not come by itself because it means, most of all, self-sacrifice. What Jesus Christ said and did was not just a reaction for the emotional and physical poverty of the people, it was a creative action from the core of Himself: the love. But his preach of love is for many people too ideal. We cannot easily give up ourselves for the good of others, even when the others are our enemy.[215] Nevertheless, a true Christian never gives up this love. They keep them at least

---

[213] TIME, March 9. 1998, p 40

[214] Müller, P., Kierkegaard's Works of Love, Christian Ethics and the Maieutic Ideal, Stephan & Jan Evans (tr.) (Denmark: C.A. Reitzel, 1993), p 23

[215] Mt 5:38 ff.

38 Ye have heard that it hath been said, An eye for an eye, and a tooth for a tooth:

39 But I say unto you, That ye resist not evil: but whosoever shall smite thee on thy right cheek, turn to him the other also.

40 And if any man will sue thee at the law, and take away thy coat, let him have thy cloke also.

41 And whosoever shall compel thee to go a mile, go with him twain.

42 Give to him that asketh thee, and from him that would borrow of thee turn not thou away.

as the ideal model, which they must follow, sometime, somewhere. Idealism belongs not exclusively to Christianism. After Plato, philosophy has never given up the idealism that it could be possible to make people and nations feel at ease with good human reason. Philosophy has given up just the wrong idealism, according to which it was enough just to raise high the picture of perfection without the consideration of how to achieve that.[216] As M. Horkheimer indirectly expressed, philosophy still has not found out the "how" :

"Our present task (as philosopher) is rather to ensure that the ability for theory and action, which comes from the theory, never get lost in the future, also not in the late epoch of peace, when the daily routine may promote the tendency to forget the whole problem again."[217]

Truth itself is very important, but when it cannot make all people live in a happy society, it is hardly truth anymore. Compassion is one of the core idea and attitude of the happy society. Not alms but compassion, which presupposes the true fraternity of all people, is the true sympathy for others. This still remains just as a project for the future, like Christian love, or the other great ideas of philosophy, but as long as we keep searching for the "how" of Horkheimer, there must be a way through the wall in everybody's mind.

Compassion is more than just a theory, but not just a praxis as Christian love. It is an amalgam of theory and praxis, which is as contagious as empathy but never means to lose one's identity or to sacrifice oneself totally. For compassion there must be always, at least, two partners that react to and for each other. Compassion does not mean giving up everything what one possesses. It means rather an optimal sharing and participation with each other. In Christian love, I have to first empty myself to be filled with the true love of God, and without the love of God, man is nothing.[218] Like philosophy where there is no praxis without theory and vice versa, compassion needs also practice even if it is rather feeling than reason. A feeling that is not controlled with reason cannot guarantee the positive attitude for neighbor. Compassion is more latent but pervasive phenomenon of sympathy than condolence. The true condolence is, of course, a very difficult act of love, even self-sacrificing one, but existential pain and passion we share do a role of common ground for the awareness that we are all having same problem of survival as long as we have to live in this world. This compassion, therefore, should be based on fraternity, as Jesus Christ proclaimed his followers as his brothers and sisters as long as they believe in God who loves them and tells them that they have to love each other as He loves them.

---

[216] Horkheimer, Max, Die Gesellschafliche Funktion der Philosophie (Frankfurt: Suhrkamp Verlag, 1979), P 288
[217] Ibid., p 290
[218] 1Co. 13:2 And though I have [the gift of] prophecy, and understand all mysteries, and all knowledge; and though I have all faith, so that I could remove mountains, and have not charity, I am nothing.

Compassion is more than the attitude of moral sense, it comes always with the sense of responsibility for the person next to oneself. This sense of responsibility does not come from outside, but from inside, i.e., from conscience. Etymological origin of conscience is "conscienta", which means knowing together, and this Latin word comes from the Greek "συνείδησις", which has the same meaning. There is another word of Socrates for conscience: "δαιμόνιον", which means the divine voice. In Chinese it is called Liang-Xin (良 心), which means literally good heart or good nature. They all presuppose the knowing of good deed. Education plays here an important role, but moral education alone cannot draw the attention of man to the sense of responsibility because the nature of man cannot accept and understand what is not adaptable to his nature. We can make this point clearer when we watch closely the sensibility of man. When the frequency of a sound goes beyond the audible limits, man just says that there is no sound even if there really exists the vibration of the medium like the air. With the help of sensible machine man can ascertain the existence of non-audible "sound", but it is not a sound any more for man as long as man cannot "hear it as it is". It is just beyond the nature of man. We can see objects as long as there is light, which stems from energy, reflects on the surface of thing, and stimulates our visual nerves. When the frequency of light exceeds the limits of the visible ray, man can see nothing even if there are still enough protons in the air. Man has to use a visual machine to reduce the frequency of the light until it falls within the limits of the visible ray. Man sees only what he can see, and man hears only what he can hear. By the same token, man is as moral as he can be. Man cannot be so good as angel, or even as God.

As a matter of fact, we cannot tangibly demonstrate the existence of God, therefore we cannot define God, but we attribute every possible good, the summum bonum, to God. There must be good which goes beyond our ability of understanding because it is beyond our "antenna". We may understand it partly within our limit. We may attribute this narrowly understood good to God. There is nothing wrong with this venture, as much as there is no wrong when we call only the visible ray light even if there are much wider scopes of ray in the world. Conscience must be our "antenna" to understand what good is. That is why compassion must always come with the sense of responsibility based on conscience, which tells us what good is within the scope of our ability. Jesus Christ must have told us to do what He did to us, i.e., to love each other as He loved and still loves us, because He already new that it is within the scope of our ability even if it is very limited one. His love must be much greater than ours, but our love is as good as His because it is part of it. To have compassion upon the needy and to help them are the essence of Christian love, which we understand within our limit. There is still another aspect of love, which can be understood by the concept of sympathy even if it is much divine than any other phenomenon of sympathy: benevolence.

6.2.2.3 Benevolence: The Ideal State of Sympathy

The grace of God comes from His Good Will because God is only good, the summum bonum. He can just do good, nothing else. What is good? Why there is evil, which is, at least, the perversion or privation of good according to St. Augustine.[219] The definition of good, especially the absolute good, the summum bonum, has been always one of the main theological and philosophical themes of dispute. For most of the traditional Christian theologians good is simply the nature of God. God created this world and He was happy because it was "good" what He just had made. But suddenly, the world was not good anymore after man had eaten from the tree of the knowledge of **good and evil**.[220] Since then, the sorrow of woman has been multiplied by God, and man has to eat from the by God cursed ground, with sweat in his face until he goes back to that ground (Genesis 3:16-19).[221] There is pain for man and woman who want to live and prosper in this world, as God told them. When the situation for man in this world is so desolate, there is just one chance of regaining the happiness in the Garden of eastward in Eden : the grace of God. It is eventually God who ordered the sorrows of man and woman, therefore only He has the right to undo that negative condition. In this regard, benevolence is much beyond the ability of man. It needs the unconditional affection of the lover for the beloved : His good will (benevolentia).

What is good? As Aristotle said, it can be the fulfilled potential.[222] According to Aristotle, when God is good, it should mean that He is perfect. Or as G. E. Moore has defined, we cannot define what good itself is, or we are just making a naturalistic fallacy.[223] We are just making a natural fallacy when we are talking about good. Hence we cannot talk about good God. He is just God who must be good of which we cannot talk about it.

What is good will? Is it just wishing a well being, and doing nothing? Maybe not. Especially in the tradition of Christian fraternal love, it should mean

---

[219] Sahakian, William S., op. cit., P 77

[220] Ge. 2:17 ומעץ הדעת **טוב** ורע לא תאכל ממנו כי ביום אכלך ממנו מות תמות

[221] Ge. 3:16 Unto the woman he said, I will greatly multiply thy sorrow and thy conception; in sorrow thou shalt bring forth children; and thy desire shall be to thy husband, and he shall rule over thee.

17 And unto Adam he said, Because thou hast hearkened unto the voice of thy wife, and hast eaten of the tree, of which I commanded thee, saying, Thou shalt not eat of it: cursed is the ground for thy sake; in sorrow shalt thou eat of it all the days of thy life;

18 Thorns also and thistles shall it bring forth to thee; and thou shalt eat the herb of the field;

19 In the sweat of thy face shalt thou eat bread, till thou return unto the ground; for out of it wast thou taken: for dust thou art, and unto dust shalt thou return.

[222] Aristotle, Metaphysic, (tr. W.D. Ross) (New York: Random House,), p 692

[223] Moore, George Edward, Principia Ethica (Cambridge: Cambridge University Press, 1980), P10

forgiving and serving as the word itself (εὔνοια) connotes. Just saying go in peace for the needy is not enough for Christian love, as shown in James 6:3. It is clear that just wishing שלום for the needy when they should suffer under hunger and cold out there, even though שלום could be the best for the peace of society as shown in the Old Testaments.[224] God's benevolence for man is rather a mercy (חסד) than grace (חן), because it is a kind of compassion for the miserable who have no chance to survive without His help. Of course it is thanks for His grace that man lives a decent life in this world, and that man will be saved at the Day of Judgment. Benevolence presupposes the "good" in the lover, which flows later to the needy who are in a miserable situation. This kind of compassion can be found in Buddhism. Gautama Siddhartha, who became later Buddha[225], left his wife and son in search of the ultimate truth. It symbolizes his distaste of this world, which is full of desire and pain as the result of it. After he had become a Buddha, he came back to this world. He tried to convey something good what he had found in his heart to the people in this world who were still suffering under their destiny. This compassion was from his good will for the people, who were in a miserable situation, mostly because of their ignorance. But he could not "give" them what he had found. He could just help them to get by themselves what he had already found. Buddha could do this because he was already good by himself. His good will for the people was natural for him.

We can see this attitude in Christian God. God is good in His essence. Man in this world is in miserable situation because of his sin against God. God helped him to make good (שלום) again with God, but He cannot give man the "good" in Him which is divine. He can just help man to be as good as Himself. This good will of God can be possible because He is already good, good enough to help man to be good as God Himself.

There is very delicate difference between the good will of Buddha and that of Christian God. Man committed sin against God as he did what God had forbidden. As the result, man could not have anymore the good old relation with God. Man was in urgent need of rebuilding that relation with God, or he must be condemned. In this desolate situation God took the initiative to make it good again with man even though man was very wrong. Here, the good will of God is unconditional love, which is just forgiving. And through the passion of His only

---

[224] Ge. 44:4 And when they were gone out of the city, and not yet far off, Joseph said unto his steward, Up, follow after the men; and when thou dost overtake them, say unto them, Wherefore have ye **rewarded evil for good**?
Ex. 21:34 The owner of the pit shall **make it good**, and give money unto the owner of them; and the dead beast shall be his.
[225] "Buddha" stems from the Sanskrit word of Budh, which should mean waking from the sleep. It connotes the spiritual awakening from the mundane life which flows just like a meaningless dream. This awakening is called Nirvana in Buddhism, which should mean extinction of the fire, the fire of human desire in this world.

Son, Jesus Christ, man became as good as he once was in relation with God. Man is no more a sinner because he has made good again with God, with the help of Jesus Christ. God could just do good, and nothing else. On the other hand, the good will of Buddha is rather human. He could not help coming back to the people who had no idea to escape from the misery in this world. Buddha became quite different being, much better than any other people. So he could see the problem of people exactly. He knew the right answer for that problem. It was not from the feeling of duty that he helped people. He had seen the potentiality of man, which was good. He saw the other people were as good as himself to be a Buddha. He could help them because they had the ability to be a Buddha. There has been no other Buddha in this world after the departing of the first Buddha from this world, but Buddha did good for man. He saw and encouraged the good of people in this world. He had parted with this world and came bake to make good again with the people in this world. He could not make people good once and for all as Christian God, he needed time, about 5.67 billion years as some say. That is why benevolence must be always very optimistic.

7. Sympathy in the Modern Confucian Society

7.1 New Challenges in Understanding the Confucian Society

7.1.1 The Disruption of the Traditional Concept of Time and Space

With a little bit knowledge of the new quantum physics, we have to accept that time and space are not any more the absolute scale to which everything in this world must be measured. Time and space change according to the gravity of matter, which is in turn just the condensation of energy in a given time and space. When there is enough gravity, time stops forever and space shrinks.

Day and night are just our subjective interpretation of the phenomenon of the rotating earth. A year is just one completed cycle of the earth around the sun. The sun is not in the middle of the world. Our sun will die in 4.5 billion years as any other stars of the same size in the universe. This world called the earth on which we live should perish before our sun dies because the sun becomes such a giant red star that it could touch the earth and swallow it with its tremendous gravity and heat. Even our galaxy is positioned on the edge of our visible universe. The universe is just expanding world of matter after the Big Bang, in contrast to the anti-matter. According to the Big Bang theory, the universe exploded from a tiny point of matter about 12 billion years ago and is still expanding. At the time of the Big Bang, there were both matter and anti-matter. All anti-matters were fused with almost all matters and become nothing. There remained very small amounts of matters, and they began to build the visible universe, which we can see now.[226] This material world is not directly opposite to the spiritual world because matter is just a condensation of energy, which is not tangible and quite difficult to distinguish from the invisible thing like spirit. The new astrophysical and quantum physical knowledge show, the universe becomes increasingly open field of speculation. The whole traditional human knowledge about the world has become chaotic or relative since the dawn of our century. It was a great confusion for the Confucian society where the fixed picture of lasting harmonious society was cherished mostly.

In old China only the Emperor had the right to have a calendar and his subjects had to wait until their Emperor bestow the calendar on them even if it became more ritual ceremony. Nobody but the Emperor had to know the movement of the Heaven and the secret of nature because he was the only Son of Heaven. Most of the Asian countries used the lunar calendar when the Western solar calendar was introduced for the first time after the Opening to the West. Even though this lunar calendar was not accurate and needed one or two intercalary months in every year, there could be no objection against this lunar calendar. It must be absolutely in accordance with the Will of Heaven (天 命) because it was from the Emperor who was the Son of Heaven. But as soon as people had found out that a month is neither exactly 30 days, nor a year is 365 days, the hierarchical system of the imperial authority could not exist anymore.[227] And more, there is 24 time zone which means the sun rises in different time in different region. For the old Chinese the world was a fixed flat place, and in the middle of it was China as the center of the world. The world is in truth round and there is no place to be a center in this world. The hidden mystery of four seasons and the system of day and night are not the Will of Heaven (天 命), but just the result of the revolution and rotation of the earth around the sun. Even the sun is not the center of the universe but just one of the millions and billions of stars in the galaxy. Time and space are relative for everyone in this world. This means again the break up of the absolutely centralized picture of the world.

This vacuum of authority is still very clearly visible in the everyday life of people in the modern Confucian society. The younger generation does not respect any more the older generation as before. This is a ubiquitous phenomenon in almost all society in the world but it is distinctive when it happens in the Confucian society, where the elders deserve to be respected just because of their age, and where the respect for the elders was the basis of social order. Aside from this Confucian sociopolitical order, there came the modern Western democracy, which was foreign for the people who never played a major

---

[226] In Internet, www.nasa.org
[227] Ibid., The moon revolves around the Earth once in 27 days 7 hours, and 43 minutes. The rotation period of the Earth is 23 hours 55 minutes, and 48 seconds. And the revolution period of the Earth is 365 days 6 hours 14 minutes and 24 seconds.

role with the sociopolitical matter. The ideology of democracy must have had the authority, which the rulers had in the traditional Confucian society, but democracy needs time to find its root in the soil of Confucian society. In many Asian countries, there is still the political system of one man dictatorship, which finds its root in the rule of the Ideal Man of Virtue (君子). The ruler must be always perfect in every respect. As long as he keeps the social order and fulfills the needs of the multitude, it is quite all right for the people in the Confucian society, even if he may be a dictator in the eyes of the Westerner. In the modern Confucian society, this belief in the traditional Ideal Man of Virtue (君子) has vanished largely because of freedom of the press, but it still lingers very strongly in the mind of the older generation. With the new idea of time and space, the younger generation does not care much about the "old" and "too ideal" picture of their leaders in the society. They see in their leaders the normal persons who must take charge of state affairs with the sense of responsibility. The leaders are just the representatives of people. This generation gap is extremely manifested in a country where social change happens too rapidly as the result of economic development.

7.1.2 The Wreckage of the Traditional Intellectualism through the Technological Development

What the people of the traditional Confucian society mostly excited about was the technological progress of the West, not Christianity. Many sociopolitical factors for that technological progress had been ignored by most of the Asians. They just saw the fruit of the technology and wanted them as soon as possible with all means.

Quite different from the West, where the theocratic cosmology had to clash with the modern natural science, the people of the traditional Confucian society had almost no problem with the modern scientific knowledge because there was no God who alone created the whole world for them. In the tradition of Taoism, we may find many divine beings, even the Supreme God(上帝), but he is more like the mundane Emperor who was called the Son of Heaven. There was no elaborate theology in the tradition of Confucianism, There was no need for the divine Providence of God who governs every single affair of the world. After the Opening to the West, the people in the traditional Confucian society saw just the fall of the imperial dignity of the Emperor, which had happened many times before. Confucianism is, as well known, very practical and pragmatic teaching. Confucius himself never wanted to discuss about spirit and death before he could clearly understand man and the mundane life.[228] This teaching has had

---

[228] The Analects of Confucius (論語), chapter 11, 先 進 , 季 路 問 事 鬼 神 子 曰 未 能 事 人 焉 能 事 鬼 敢 問 死 曰 未 知 生 焉 知 死 ; Legge, James,

great influence on the traditional Confucian society. When something facilitates the practical life of people, it is accepted with no reserve.

These are basic reasons for the fact that there are many brilliant progresses in the newest technology, especially in the field of semiconductor. Japan is the biggest producer of the consumer electronics, and Korea produces 35% of the DRAM in 1988, which the world consumes yearly. The other Asian countries produce also many electric gadgets with the merit of low production cost and relative high quality of labor. This could be achieved in a relatively shot span of time mostly because of the new technology. For the new technology there is not much need of consideration for the tradition, mostly religious and cultural. So there is very small conflict when the traditional Confucian society imports new technology from the West.

Problem is that many aspects of Confucian tradition are deserted alongside the technological progress. The mathematicalization does happen not only in the realm of technology, but also in society proper. Traditionally, technology and commerce have played minor role in the Confucian society even if they have been never prohibited. The eternal rule was already there, so all what people had to do was not renovation or improvement of the society but keeping the status quo. The economic basis of the traditional Confucian society was rice cultivation, which was very highly labor intensive. There was much room for the technological renovation with which the productivity could enormously increase. As manual activity was traditionally despised, there were very few incentives and impetus for the technological improvement. Autocracy was favored by most of the ruling classes in the traditional Confucian societies because the rulers were always afraid of the revolt from the enlightened under-class with the affluence stemming from the surplus production.

According to the teaching of Mencius, when an Emperor or a king does not behave as the Ideal Man of Virtue (君子), anybody who is morally correct can enthrone him because he is not a right ruler anymore but just a criminal who misused his power. In reality, being an Ideal Man of Virtue (君子) is extremely difficult. The rulers, who were mostly highly learned with the teaching of Confucianism, knew this very well, therefore they tried to keep silence about this teaching and favored the obscurantistic policy.

With the forced Opening to the West, nationalism came to the mind of the rulers, which was then the mainstream politics for most European countries. Keeping the inner social equilibrium played no role any more, as the outer force as a nation tried to exploit the traditional Confucian society. A total mobilization was needed to make the Confucian oriented country strong enough to become a sovereign one. For this purpose the people of the traditional Confucian society must produce enough national wealth because being a strong modern country

---

Confucius, pp 240-241

meant a productive nation as a whole. Industrialization and colonialism of the European countries were the only model for the rapid growth of national wealth. The technological progress was the sine qua non for that model. In this new situation, obscurantism was of no use. That is why the public school system was rapidly introduced not only in Japan but also in most of the Asian countries.

As much as technology does not mind the difference of cultural traditions, it does not take into account much the preservation of traditional cultures. As new technology is almost always better than the old one, it goes the same to the cultural matters. New culture is better than the old one. There are great cultural vacuums in most of the Asian countries, quite different from the more or less homogeneous Christian culture in the West, or the strongly traditional Islamic lands in the Middle East. Most of the people in Confucian society think that "modern" means just "not traditional", i.e., not Confucian. They are modern as far as they know nothing about Confucianism, and have nothing to do with Confucianism. In reality, they are still very strongly Confucian in their thought and behavior. They have still great difficulty in accepting many parts of the Western culture. Most of the people in the Confucian society are strongly family oriented regardless of their social status. This is the main reason for the fact that cronyism is so pervasive here. Even though the highly developed technology keeps on its progress, the hidden negative influence of the Confucian tradition hinders still the full efficiency of the modern Confucian society.

7.1.3 The Limits of the Adopted Myth of Perpetual Progress

The Asian economic model was already a very hotly debated theme among the Western scholars before the financial crisis that has begun in late 1997. Many believed that there was special remedy in the Asian model for the chronic cycle of inflation and deflation of the traditional capitalistic economic system. As the recent financial crisis in most of the Asian countries has shown, there is no panacea for the socioeconomic problem in the capitalistic society, mostly widening gap between the rich and the poor, not to mention the chronic financial problem. To prevent the social unrest stemming from the economic inequality and the discrepancy between idea and reality, man has to first produce more wealth with all means. At first sight, capitalism seemed to be the right answer, with its efficiency and productivity, as most of the modern capitalistic societies produce enough wealth to provide material comfort for almost all members of the society. Nevertheless there are still much social unrest not only in the developing countries but also in the well-developed countries. The four pillars of capitalistic system, i.e., capital, labor, natural resources, and technology, must always be there and corporate with each other harmoniously to make the most of it. In reality there are always conflicts between capital and labor and between man and nature. As long as capitalism is not a static but dynamic system, a certain amount of conflict is working positively for the progress. But it is not right when the property of 358 richest people in the world is bigger than the whole yearly income of the 45% of the poorest population.[229] The future is not optimistic when nature strikes back whenever man tries to exploit it. The problem is not production but distribution. As the collapse of the communism has shown, artificial distribution does not solve the problem but aggravates it. While the unequal distribution of wealth could be the main reason for social unrest for both the developed countries and the developing countries, the low productivity is still a great problem in the underdeveloped countries. That is why it still seems to be convincing that we have to produce more. Even for the developed countries, there is no other way at the moment than producing more to prevent the social problem, for example, high unemployment. There is really worldly economic growth, at the moment annually around 2%, but that cannot solve the problem. Germany has produced and exported enormous amounts of goods unprecedentedly, but the rate of unemployment grows. China has to keep the 11%-a-year real GDP growth for the next few years to attain its goals of keeping down unemployment and maintaining social stability while pushing state-enterprise reform. If China grows just 4.6% over the next two years, 78 million people would be unemployed.[230] This is the man-made problem. We have begun to build a tower that must perpetually grow up to the sky, but we know from the beginning that it is impossible.

Why do we need a society, what can a society do for us, and what can we do for the society? These basic questions must be asked and answered again before we begin to solve the problem postulated by our society. There is no perpetual progress as long as the natural resources are limited, and furthermore, as long as the mind of person cannot find its true nature.

As long as there are many people who are willing to give away money rather to buy a CD, which contains songs sung by an already too rich singer who wants to have more, than to donate some for the needy, a good society is a far cry. It is true that we have the right to buy freely what we want as much as we earned the money freely. But nowadays, most of the big money in the world is made not by the labor but by the large scale of speculation. Stock speculation, spot trading, and currency speculation are now the most profitable ways of money making. This is not the traditional way of production, which combines labor, capital and natural resources, nevertheless there is always a loser when someone wins profit. With the technological development, the transaction in these markets has become virtual, i.e., there is no human being as the counterpart of the trade, but just mathematical data behind it, which decide everything. It is like gambling, there is someone who is winning in the party, but on the whole the sum is

---

[229]. Meadows, Dennis L, in Die Zeit, Feb. 19., p. 25
[230] Roche, David, in TIME, February 23, 1998, p 31

always zero. There happens just the concentration of wealth for the few, but there never is real growth of productivity in this field. The potential productivity needed for the growth stems from the cost-down, which eventually means exploitation of the poor. Globalization makes it much easier for the people who are searching for the maximum profit to find a place where the production cost is lower and the interest rate is optimal.

The richest people do not want to give up their luxurious life easily to help the needy. Poor people try as usual with all means to be the rich who in the end enjoy the luxury. Hedonism has long history. Everybody knows more or less that this way of life is not the best, but they do not know quite well how to do else in this world. Various religious teachings have still its saying, but they have not much influence on society as before. We cannot wait until all people understand the truth and do only the right thing in the eyes of God. "Rehumanizing" the society must begin with the renewing of conscious, i.e., we have to abandon the false belief in the perpetual progress and it's effect of panacea.

Especially in the modern Confucian society, it is very difficult to dissuade people from the material affluence, which has long been one of the most important goal for most of them. Just the material achievement has become the only thing, which deserves the whole attention of the people. The naïve belief in morally better tomorrow, which meant returning to the ideal primordial society, is replaced with the affluent tomorrow, which will come with the perpetual progress. This tendency seems to be keeping on as long as there is no alternative to the material affluence, which the capitalistic society provides.

7.2 Sympathy Lost as the Result of Misfitted Modernity in the Confucian Society

7.2.1 The Collapse of the Traditional Confucian Humanism

Craving for the material affluence is not peculiar to the Asians. But it has become rapidly a main tendency for most of the Asians, not only because it provides a concrete reward for the physical labor, but also it is the only clear substitute for the lost traditional spirituality of Confucian humanism.

Humanity is the core of Confucianism partly because there is not much room for the divine being in its tradition. The universe is more or less the results of the action and reaction of the Yin and Yang (陰 陽) and five basic elements of the world.[231] Even the creation of the world must be rationally, i.e., human, explained. In such a world the relation between people must be the most important matter. The "fellow-feeling" between people in the Confucian society

---

[231] Chung, Julia, Konfuzianismus und Christentum, Detlef Köhn (tr.) (Mainz: Matthias-Grünewald-Verlag, 1989), pp 128-129

must be strong enough to compensate the lack of Christian God's unlimited love for man.

However, in the modern Confucian society, where the social welfare system is not yet well constructed, the traditional fellow-feeling among people disappears faster than any other traditional virtue. As a matter of fact, the government must care about the socially ignored. It cannot afford it mostly because there still lacks money for the well organized welfare system. Investment for the growth of national wealth is still the priority. So there comes a vacuum of humanitarian concern for the needy. The traditional virtue of mutual care in a family circle cannot stand anymore firm as the traditional family bondage has loosened.[232] The filial duty (孝 道) has, theoretically, very humanistic and pragmatic function. Parents have done their best for their children to raise them, therefore children have to do their best for them in turn when they can, not from the sense of forced duty but from the voluntary humanistic concern and respect for them. It is a respect for them not only because they deserve it but also they need it when they are too old to live alone. In this way the traditional Confucian society solved the problem of social welfare for the elders who could not survive alone.

The filial duty (孝 道) is still cherished as an important moral virtue, but modern society itself does not allow traditional big family which is the ideal hotbed for it. The big family hinders flexibility and mobility, which mostly needed for the social production in the modern society. The old generation becomes the main object of social rationalization, i.e., they are not needed by anybody, and are set aside as useless elements of the modern society. As there is yet no well-organized social welfare system, the old generation has to depend on their children mostly even though the traditional family care system for them has collapsed before a substitute emerges. This discrepancy cannot be solved until both a new social welfare system and a new humanism come to pass.

The capitalistic society, where the struggle for the material affluence is mostly cherished, most of the people have no time to care about the elder people who need total care. The needy hinder even the productivity of society, they are regarded even the "unwanted" of society. Here happened the "Umwertung" of

---

[232] To the traditional Confucian family circle belongs a tremendous degree of consanguinity. Horizontally at least 9 generations belong to a normal family. Vertically there are again 9 degrees of relations in each lineage, i.e., of agnate and cognate respectively. Each family member has his or her own name according to his or her position in a family. A uncle is not just a uncle, according to his position in a family, he has a already fixed own-name except his proper name. In an extreme case, a small town could be composed of just a family. When there is a family member, mostly a man, who rise in the world, he has to take care of all members of the family, or it is a great disgrace not only for himself but also for the family itself. This is the deep root of cronyism in Confucian society. Besides this cronyism there were not much alternatives in the traditional Confucian society for the family care. This cronyism played as a social welfare system in a small scale for the family members. That is why the filial duty was so highly cherished in the Confucian society.

the traditional virtue. Traditionally, an ideal society for Confucian was a society where the "most deprived four (無告)" are cared foremost.[233] They were orphans, old men with no family, widowers, and last but not least, widow. They must be cared firstly by everyone, especially by society. A disease means for a Confucian the lost of bodily harmony. A lethal disease of a family member means a great disaster for the family because it could not only disrupt the harmony of family but also annihilate whole generations, which not seldom before. But when the sick happened to be the elders of family, all members of the family have to do their best to take care of them even if it could mean a disaster for the whole family. This was purely a humanistic attitude.

The modern individualism has made many of the younger generation to have a new thought about the filial duty (孝道): Parents have not right but duty to raise their children. They have done what they should do, therefore it is not an inborn duty but an option whether the children support their parents. However, this cannot eradicate the old tradition of the filial duty (孝道). There is therefore conflict between these old and new concepts about the parents-children relation. As Confucius himself emphasized, the filial duty (孝道) is the basis of Jen (仁), i.e., of the whole Confucian thought.[234] For the Confucians the filial duty (孝道) is the humanism itself. It is not just a forced duty of children for their parents, but their manifested respect for the human dignity of parents as person. Its social function is practically supporting the older generation by the younger generation, but if it had not been based on the humanistic respect for the older generation, it could not have sustained for so long. The filial duty (孝道) has to do more with the moral attitude taught by the Confucian teachers, than with the substitute for the not well-established social welfare system in the traditional Confucian society.

In the modern Confucian society, there is another discrepancy between the expectation of people and the reality. Even though there still lacks public finance for the social welfare system, many people expect conveniently that the government do its "duty" to care for the older generation, which was traditionally a family affair. Not the individual but the society as a whole has to care about the constituent of society in the modern democratic society. This latent evasion of personal moral duty in the name of social justice has its charm

---

[233] The Canon of History, bk. 1, chapter 3, 虞書, 大禹謨, ...舍己從人不虐無告不廢困窮惟帝時克 ; refer to Ryu, Jung-Gi (tr. & ed.), 四書三經 (The Four Books and the Three Classics): 大學 (The Great Leaning), 中庸 (The Doctrine of the Mean), 論語 (The Analects of Confucius), 孟子 (The Book of Mencius), 詩經 (The Book of Odes), 書經 (The Canon of History), 易經 (I-Ching: The Book of Change) (Seoul, Korea: Myung Moon Dang, 1994), p 507

[234] The Analects of Confucius, chapter1, 學而, ...孝第也者其爲仁之本與 ; Legge, James, Confucius, pp 138-139

because it frees people from the personal sense of guilty. But the Confucian tradition of the filial duty (孝道) was not based on the sense of guilty but on the humanism. Therefore it is still a matter of personal duty whether one do the filial duty (孝 道) or not. The outer condition does not have much to do with the filial duty (孝 道) because it is a moral behavior stemming from the nature of man, not like that of beast. In the modern Confucian society people are still taught in the tradition of old Confucian thought, i.e., the filial duty (孝 道) is still cherished at least in the formal education. But as any other developed countries, most of the modern Confucian countries pursuit first the national wealth which can guarantee the social stability. As capitalism still shows itself as the most effective system for that purpose, it is inevitable that the pursuit of material affluence prevails in the modern Confucian society. The old meaning of family as the basis of Confucian society has vanished before new one comes up and substitutes it. This vacuum could not be filled even the social welfare system is completed because there still lacks the moral basis, i.e., humanism, which has been the core of the traditional Confucianism.

7.2.2 The Broken Bondage of Family Relation

The phenomenon of human estrangement is not new in the industrial age. Since the publication of "Das Kapital" by Karl Marx it has become not only a terminus technicus for sociology but also a cliché for the typical phenomena of the deprived individual in the industrialized modern society. In our post-modern age there is an unprecedented phenomenon of double estrangement of human being from the production process. In the age of Karl Marx, human being was alienated from the produced goods, and unemployment was the result of over-production, which was the result of the greed of the capitalist. In such a situation human estrangement meant the estranged condition of production from the producer (die Entfremdung der Produktionsbedingung vom Produzenten).[235]

Today, the unemployment is rather the result of rationalization as the result of the modern technological progress, and human beings are alienated not only from the produced goods but also from the production process. Productivity means less employment and human beings are considered to be put into the process of production only when the technology cannot yet do the job better than man does. In a post-industrial society, unemployment means not only a financial ruin but also social disaster. There goes down the dignity of man with unemployment. Unemployment is a social phenomenon but its effect is rather personal.

Unemployment is a new experience for the people in the Confucian society.

---

[235] Marx, K., Das Kapital, Kritik der Politischen Ökonomie, Band III: Der Gesamtprozeß der Kapitalistischen Production (Frankfurt a.M.: Verlag Ullstein GmBH, 1971), p 562

Traditionally an individual is just a part of the whole organism in the Confucian society. It means that not only an individual has a duty for the whole, but also the whole has a duty for the individual. Even the Emperor is not any more the Emperor when he cannot guarantee his people a satisfied life in the harmonious society. In the traditional Confucian society, the rulers were responsible for the personal misery, but in the modern Confucian society, man has to take care of himself by himself as an independently responsible individual. This is still very difficult task for most of the people of the Confucian society. Not the social welfare system but the Confucian moral has supported well-being of the individual in society. Being an independent individual in a society is even strange thing for most of the Asians who are get used to be a part of the organic society. This is an estrangement not only from the tradition but also from the cozy Confucian life itself. Even if there was a tyrant, it was better to be a part of society than to be alone in the wild. That is why many Asians have still difficulty to be a truly liberated individual. Being an individual means being estranged from the organic society where an individual finds his identity as a part.

With the vast social change after the Industrial Revolution, there happened the drastic shrinking of the traditional big family, which meant more than three generations under a roof, in the Western countries. Nowadays a family means at most two generations in a house, i.e., parents and children. The severe competition in the post-industrial society does not allow to sustain the old big family. Competition itself is not all bad because it promotes the social productivity, which is vital to sustain the modern society. And competition has contributed to the entire progress that man has made until now. This post-modern society has made man more a replaceable part than a not reducible individual with dignity. It is clear that human dignity is not a natural right from the heaven but rather spoils of war, for which man has fought. In the Confucian society everybody has his dignity as a part of the harmonious whole. The human dignity does not stem from the individual uniqueness but from his contribution for the harmony of society in the tradition of Confucianism. When a society should be a field of struggle, not a place where everybody has his function as a part of the society, and family means not anymore the basis of humanism, people in the modern Confucian society must be doubly estranged from the society and from his own identity.

7.2.3 The Partial Understanding of Christianism as Meta-Physical Idea

A famous contact between Confucianism and Christianism was made by Matteo Ricci. He tried to explain Christianism with the concepts of Confucianism, especially in his Book "The True Meaning of the Lord of Heaven

(天主實義)". He even quoted many Confucian classics.[236] He did his best to link Western and Eastern cultures. Nevertheless his method was disputed immediately after his death in the West.[237] It was too much for the Christians to accept the Confucian ritual not as idolatry. The Chinese were also too proud to accept a new religion. They preferred rather the scientific knowledge, which Matteo Ricci had brought. The spirit of Ti-Yong (體用), Chinese body and Western use, was born around this time and it intensified with the bad experience with the Englander in the 19th century.[238] There was not much room for foreign religion and philosophy in China where national identity survived continuously.

God has never been in the center of Confucian tradition. To tell the truth, there is no God in the tradition of Confucianism. There was at most the Heaven (天), which was more philosophical concept than a theological one. That does not mean that man is to be as arrogant as a divine being in the Confucian tradition. On the contrary, man has to do his best to follow the law of nature, which comes from the Heaven (天). When a foreign thing comes into the environment of Confucianism, it can be assimilated as long as it complies to the law of nature. That is why, in most cases, there were very little problems with Christianism in the traditional Confucian society. There was no eradication of the local cultures or mass massacre or martyrdom in the name of God in China.

On the whole, Christianism is minority in the modern Confucian society. Only in Philippines and South Korea there are relative big Christian denominations which can be counted.[239] There were many martyrs in Korea, the Vatican canonized 103 of them for saint. They were killed not because they believed in wrong God, but because they did not care about the Confucian tradition, especially the filial duty (孝道). There was no conflict of religious war. Christianism was accepted as one of many religions. There have been many religious conflicts in the history of China, but they were more or less the interest conflicts among warring factions than a real ideological struggle. Peaceful coexistence of many religions, as many ethnic groups in China, had found out the middle way, with which all concerned parties could make a compromise even if it was not an ideal one.

This a little bit naïve attitude for Christianism was the main cause for the misunderstanding of it. Christianism is monotheism, which allows neither room for other Gods, nor other interpretation about the world and life than those of the Christian church. When Christianism came with the modern natural scientific knowledge about the world, there was a great confusion about Christianism in

---

[236] Tang, Yi-Jie, Confucianism, Buddhism, Daoism, Christianity and Chinese Culture (Peking: The University of Peking, 1991), p 149

[237] Ibid., pp. 152-155

[238] Ibid., pp155-157

[239] more that 90% of Philippines are Catholic and more than 20% of Koreans are Christian.

the modern Confucian society from the beginning. God created the whole world, including man, in seven days about 6,000 years ago according to Christianism, but the age of the earth is much older than that, and human beings seem to be biologically much nearer to the apes than to God, whom man never saw, except Adam, Eve, Abraham and Moses, according to the modern natural scientific knowledge. This knowledge is very persuasive as it has visible evidences for its argument even if it is not wholly sufficient. While the Christian cosmology could not be a persuasive argument for the modern Confucian society, the Christian moral teaching is new and attractive because of its concept of fraternity. Equality and fraternity have been almost tabooed concepts because they did not fit the ideal Confucian society where hierarchy was cherished for social harmony. Fraternity meant for the traditional Confucians a chaotic relationship among people, which must result in a chaotic society in the end. The basic relation between father and son cannot be substituted by any other virtue than that of the filial duty (孝道). If this virtue cannot be accepted, then there must be banishment from society. The filial duty (孝道) is much important than any other virtues in Confucian society. When a man have to choose between the filial duty (孝道) and the law, he never hesitate to choose the former. A man should never serve both his father and his friend's father with the same devotion. A man should never love any other woman more than his wife. A man should never save the other man's son at the sacrifice of his own son. When a man does more for others than his family, it is against the nature of man.

The fraternal love of Christianism does not allow discrimination. Before God, everybody is equal, everybody is brother and sister of Jesus Christ as long as he or she believes in God. This is partly the renewal of the long deserted theory of Mozi (墨子) in the eyes of the devoted Confucian. There should be no hierarchical order in a family, a community, and furthermore in a country in Christianism. Not the omnipotent and omniscient Christian God, but this fraternal love of Jesus Christ was the prickly matter for the Confucian society in the eyes of the rulers. Actually, the difference between the Christian and the Confucian understanding of God is mainly in the Person of Jesus Christ, and His meaning for the mankind. In the center of Confucianism is the teaching of the unity of Heaven and man. In the center of Christianism is Jesus Christ as the Savior, in whom God revealed Himself in a unique way.[240]

A man have to keep the two-year mourning after his parents' death as the sign of his filial duty (孝道). But this was regarded by quite a few Christian missionaries as the ugly idolatry. A true Christian must worship no any other idol than God. This is one of the most evident intercultural misunderstandings.

---

[240] Chung, Julia, Konfuzianismus und Christentum, Detlef Köhn (tr.) (Mainz: Matthias-Grünewald-Verlag, 1989), p 154

Moreover, the Opium War between China and England made the image of the Christians much worse. The Christian missionary came always with soldiers and merchants who altogether tried more to get from than to give and help the people in the Confucian society. They were not much better than the old bad rulers in Confucian society. When Christianism is not better for the society, it is not needed by the people of the Confucian society.

The thought of hierarchical social order which lasted more than two thousand years, and the bad image of the Christian Westerners in the 19th century made it extremely difficult for the Asians to make a sincere approach to Christianism, which is needed for the right mutual understanding. Christianism found its place mostly among the social underclass and outsider who suffered under the rigid structure of Confucian society. In Korea the situation was a little bit different. As Korea was the colony of Japan, even some of the Korean intellectuals tried to find a way to the independence from Japan in Christianism. Christianism as a way of resistance against the unjust secular rulers has become a tradition in Korea, and it was once a form of resistance against the military dictatorship, which was named as Min-Jung theology. Even if Christian love must mean more than a means for civic struggle for freedom, there has been not much room for other interpretation.

The other extreme case of misunderstanding of Christianism is begging personal fortune from God, as most Asians have done in their traditional way before. The undiscriminating Christian fraternity among whole people could not be found in this situation. The essence of Christian society is the social justice based upon fraternity, i.e., brotherhood and sisterhood of all mankind before God. Every single person is very important because he or she is the beloved creature of God. Exactly this idea has been very difficult to be adopted by the people in the traditional Confucian society mostly because of the lack of the concept of fraternity in Confucianism.

7.2.4 The Bad Case of Capitalism Lacking the Spirit of Christian Morality

Capitalism itself cannot be stigmatized as the root of all evil of our era, on the contrary, it has become the basis of all social productivity without which no society can survive anymore. Nevertheless it is also true that the unbiased search for profit from the side of capitalist hurts the whole society in the long run. We may need check and balance between capitalist and other elements of society.

Capitalism was introduced in most of the modern Confucian countries with the political system of democracy, but the latter has had great difficulty to be implemented in the soil of Confucian society because it just does not fit to the traditional Confucian society, not only because of the small clan of politically power-thirsty dictators but also because of the character of the hierarchical system of the society itself. The sharp increase of social productivity through the capitalistic economic system might promise the welfare society like that of the West. But the chronic cycle of inflation and deflation must hurt the belief of the bright future. Even the world economy survived the October Crash in 1987 without the disaster like the Great Depression of 1928 and the World War, and the world economy booms with the longest expansion in recent history, it does not mean the sound basis of capitalistic system is at last found. The world economic boom of the day keeps on expanding mostly thanks to the newly found market in the former Eastern Bloc countries, and the tentatively vast market of China. High productivity depending on the rapid technological progress is another pillar of the economic boom at the moment. The bad case of capitalism still lingers on every corner of the world. The widening gap between the rich and the poor grows steadily regardless of the different stages of the economic development, i.e., it is the same phenomenon both in the U.S.A. and Germany, and in India and Bangladesh. Especially in the post-industrial society where the economic status determines the grade of human dignity, the widening gap between the rich and the poor signifies the deepening fundamental inequality among people, which is opposite to the idea of democracy.

Especially in the modern Confucian society, where the hierarchical inequality is still accepted as a natural phenomenon, capitalism shows its bad side more vividly. As the recent financial crisis in the Asian region has shown, the Asian capitalism is characterized by its cronyism and government-driven economic plan, which have boosted mainly the wealth of the small number of economic tycoons and political rulers. A democratic society needs a harmony in society too, but it should not be confused with the coerced one. A democratic society must be based on the pluralistic system, which works harmoniously, not on the uniform system, which does not allow different minds. Social consensus is important in a democratic society, but the symbiosis of differences is much more important. This fact seems still not to be applied to most Confucian societies, even to the most developed Asian country like Japan. The whole society must follow what the small number of political elite say, almost blindly, to achieve the pre-fixed goal. Until the late 1970s, this system worked well in Japan, until the early 1980s in Korea, and until the early 1990s in most of the South Eastern countries, and even in China. As the recent financial crisis has shown, even the finest elite make failure too, as any other "ordinary" people, especially in a totally globalized world. Most elite in the modern Confucian society did not want to yield to that plain truth. Since middle of the 1980s the economy of Japan wobbled, but not a single political leader in Japan conceded that fact. They did not want to lose their face, which is regarded as the most disgraceful thing in Confucian society even if it is modern. The democratic consensus building is very strange thing in a Confucian society because the elite should know everything, therefore they have no need to ask for advice, especially from the "plain" people. The idea of Ideal Man of Virtue (君子) still survives in the modern Confucian society. In the traditional Confucian society only the Ideal Man of Virtue (君 子) must rule, that means the rulers are the Ideal Men of Virtue (君 子) who make no failure because they are perfect. This naïve and wrong belief has been shared with all people in the traditional Confucian society, by both the elite and the ordinary people. But as the saying goes, nobody is perfect, especially in the post-modern society, where rather the diversity and chaotic way of thought promotes the technological progress, which is the main engine of social progress. At the moment, the most important goal of the Asian governments is just to produce enough wealth to be divided among the people. Even there still is not enough wealth to be distributed, uneven distribution of wealth has become already a routine in the Confucian society, and it gets worse with the bad capitalism which aims just the maximum profit of the small army of the privileged with all means.

At the moment, it is technically impossible to sustain the economic structure of the modern Confucian society without capitalism. Even the People's Republic of China tries capitalism in their own way, mainly to keep pace with the change of the world. It is quite a big experiment what the Chinese government does now for its country. The Chinese government tries to adopt capitalism without the Western democratic political system. She will not give up the paradigm of the government controlled economic system. As recent Asian economic crisis has shown, too excessive control of the government results in very bad confusion. Not only cronyism but also too big bureaucracy hinders the efficiency of the economic system. But the established political stability cannot be sacrificed too much for the profitability of the economic sector of the Chinese society. Totally liberal economic system cannot guarantee the desirable result because of the still influential political culture of old Confucian tradition. Capitalism and democracy must find a middle way to be well adopted in the modern Confucian society, but the tradition does not give way easily to the new paradigm. Capitalism without democracy is bad, but without social justice based on the Christian fraternity, it is the worst.

Most of the Asian countries have tried their best to catch up the material affluence of the Western countries, without much attention to the matter of democracy, let alone social justice. In the old Confucian society, social welfare system was not needed much because of the family supporting tradition. Every member of family had his or her portion of right to be rightly treated according to his or her role and position. In the awkward situation of transition from traditional to modern society, only the visible fruits of material well-being based on the bad capitalism, which is in its essence the wrong justification of the uncontrolled egoistic greed, is cherished. It is true that just distribution can be followed only when there is enough to be shared. But as most of the Western society show, there can be no social justice without the conscious and conscience of every individual who has the sense of responsibility for other members of society. Democracy without social justice is just a form of the dictatorship of majority. That is why capitalism needs not only democracy but also social justice. Here we need not only a political science for the just society but also the moral alliance of the people as citizen of the society. The task of political philosophy is to develop a kernel of political morality that can be at the center of an "overlapping consensus" and hence can permanently resolve the fundamental assurance problem. Such a kernel of political morality must first and foremost settle what it is politically urgent to settle: how to choose now among feasible institutional alternatives. But stability requires that citizens should also agree in broad outline upon the ground of such settlements, that is, upon a criterion of justice. Such a criterion identifies and evaluates the morally salient properties and features of institutional schemes and thereby anticipates how such a scheme may and (especially) how it may not be adapted to changing circumstances. If such a shared political morality assures the various social groups that there will continue to be room for their particular values and way of life, then each such group can develop a moral allegiance to the basic institutions (as they are and will be), including a willingness to uphold these institutions.[241] We can witness no rapider change in our society than in the field of communication, especially in the mass media. To guarantee the overlapping consensus of the citizen in the changing environment, we need the sympathetic mass media, which we cannot find yet. That is why we have to first look into the mass media before we go on to draft the ideal modern Confucian society.

Under the capitalistic economic system inequality means mostly unjust distribution of social goods. The problem is how a man can set a just criterion of the distribution. As long as there is interest conflict, there must be hardly a from all acceptable criterion of distribution. We may refer to the reflective equilibrium of Rawls. In "A Theory of Justice" Rawls advanced two principles of justice and claimed that they are in reflective equilibrium. He defended this claim by appeal to a hypothetical contract; he argued that parties in a position satisfying certain informational and motivational criteria, which he called 'the original position', would choose the following two principles of justice to govern the basic structure of their society.

1. Each person is to have an equal right to the most extensive total system of equal basic liberties compatible with a similar system of liberty for all.

2. Social and economic inequalities are to be arranged so that they are both (a) to the greatest benefit of the least advantaged and (b) attached to offices and positions open to all under fair conditions of equality of opportunity.

Rawls refers to this conception of justice as 'justice as fairness'.[242] Information

---

[241] Pogge, Thomas W., Realizing Rawls (Ithaca: Cornell University Press, 1989), p 213
[242] Brink, David O., "Rawlsian Constructivism in Moral Theory" in Equality and Liberty, J. Angelo Corett(ed.) (London: Macmillam, 1991), p 196

as the main material of the mass media plays more and more the main source of the economic inequality in our age. Its unjust distribution is much harder to ascertain than the classical tangible goods. Therefore, it has very severe impact on the social equality when there is no just control mechanism of the mass media. The mass media are no more the provider of the entertainment than the main source of the economic profit for some capitalists. With the help of the mass media capitalism has a new face: from the tangible to the intangible. A fare society is a society where no information is hidden from the public, so the masses could also take part in the new source of the wealth.

8. Limited Sympathy Mediation with the Traditional Mass Media

8.1 The Unilaterality of the Traditional Mass Media

8.1.1 The Communication of One to Many: A Condition for Manipulation

As the technological progress of the day sometimes excels our imagination, a fixed definition of the mass media can be easily obsolete, therefore it is better when we let it open to the future. We still do not know whether we have to call Internet (and the World-Wide-Web) as one of the mass media. It still has too small number of people as its "masses".[243] Notwithstanding the quantitative limits, Internet has quite a new feature, which can be very helpful to overcome the structural limit of the traditional mass media. The traditional mass media like book, newspaper, radio, and TV can be marked by their indiscriminate dissemination of information among the masses without much room for the direct reciprocity. Once the information is distributed, it can be hardly retrieved even when it comes out as wrong. As a matter of fact, the responsibility of the mass media has long history. In the 19th century J.S. Mill saw already the power of the mass media, at that time mostly the press, and the difficulty of the controlling the press, freedom of the press.[244] The situation has changed little even if there is the quantitative explosion of the mass media. The unilaterality of the mass media is the main culprit.

This unilaterality of the mass media promotes the poverty of the sense of responsibility for the people both "in" and "out" of the mass media. As nobody in the mass media is ready to take responsibility when something goes wrong

---

[243] There are just about 100 million people who are directly connected with Internet in 1997. About half of them is in the U.S.A., In 2000 it is expectedto be more than 200 millions.
[244] Mill, J.S., "Law of Libel and Liberty of the Press" in John Stwart Mill On Politics and Society, Geraint L. Williams(ed.) (Hassocks, England: The Harvester Press, 1976), p 146, pp148-149

with the disseminated information, the masses do not care about the side effect of the mass media on them so long as it does not hit personally. Not only between the mass media and the masses but also between masses the law of indifference and irresponsibility rules. The main cause of this phenomenon can be nothing but the blocked way of reciprocity among them. One-sided dissemination of information to the masses by the small group of "providers" has such innate structure that cannot be easily mended without the total restructuring of the mass media.

The reciprocity of Internet is still at its early stage. Internet cannot reach so many people at once as radio and TV. But it is almost clear that in the near future Internet will change the concept of the mass media itself. In 1998 man can hit the 320 million Web-sites, which are registered on Internet at the moment, without many problems. When the mass media should mean indiscriminate information dissemination to the public, that could be one feature of the mass media. Not a single newspaper in the world has more than 100 million subscribers, not a single TV station in the world can send 320 million different programs simultaneously. When the quantity alone should be the criterion of the mass media, Internet must be one of the strongest mass media. And when the mass media should disseminate information to the indiscriminate masses, Internet is with this matter also one of the strongest mass media because its non-homogeneous "masses" are scattered in the whole world.[245]

When two people talk to each other face to face, there exists always a latent sense of responsibility for each other as they response to the information from each other personally. Not only the effort to make the information understandable, but also the effort to understand the partner cannot be fully accomplished without the sincere attention to each other, which is mostly the act of will. On the contrary, the indiscriminately disseminated information of the traditional mass media in the air without direct reaction makes the disseminator of the information to have no sense of responsibility as there is no direct human touch. In the person to person conversation, we use not only our head but also our heart to understand the partner. Conversation is not just the exchange of intellectual information but also the dynamic action and reaction of emotion. We have the feeling of the language when it is our mother tongue, but foreign language is just object of understanding, we understand the foreign language only with the head of reason, more or less, as the computer, without the heart of feeling. By the same token, we have difficulty when we want to talk about understanding people with the mass media. The viewers can watch the programs of TV as they are provided, but they have almost no way to respond directly to

---

[245] In 1998, in the U.S.A. there are about 48,7 million people who are directly connected with the Internet. In Europe, about 27,3 million. In Japan, about 5,1 million. In the other countries, 14,6 million.

them, let alone to make them as they really want to. When a viewer does not like a program, all he can do is just turning it off or stowing it away. The situation is not quite different with another traditional mass media. The masses can just stop reading the book or the newspaper when we do not like them. It is hardly possible for them to rewrite them as they like. This can never be the true interaction between the authors and the masses.

There are some new measures of interactivity in a few mass media, for example, the CNN. There are many ways to respond to the news what the CNN broadcasts, for example, by directly phoning, sending email through Internet, and just sending a letter as usual. But non of these ways does guarantee the full participation of the viewer in the making of the broadcasting program. The opinion of the viewer is, at most, just a part of the whole process of the news program and plays always a minor role. A big broadcasting company like the CNN comprises of many people who are partly participating in the whole process of the program making. So it is quite unclear who are in charge of the program, which is provided as a kind of consumer goods to the masses. Everybody can be a part of the production by the CNN, but nobody can be pinpointed as the sole responsible person for that production. Only the abstract entity of the broadcasting company comes forward without any concrete responsibility. It happens, so to speak, "the diffusion of responsibility" somewhere in the mass of production. Like the diffused information, the diffused responsibility promotes the phenomenon of irresponsible anonymity in our postmodern society. As a matter of fact, the phenomenon of the irresponsibility in the anonymity is not peculiar in the mass media, especially in the political arena, it has become even the art of survival. In the thicket of the bureaucracy, it is hardly possibly even to pinpoint the responsible.

But the irresponsibility of the mass media has more impact on the society than any other sub-structure of the society nowadays. Whatever happened in the society must go through the mass media to be known by the masses, which are alleged the basis of the modern, even the postmodern, democratic society. As long as the unilateral relation between the mass media and the masses lasts, there disappears the concrete responsible person. Without the sense of responsibility, the mass media can be easily just a means for certain special interest groups, which are mostly already affluent with the surplus wealth and the too much influence on the society. The information distribution or diffusion through the mass media can be truly for the masses only when it is performed on the principle of social justice. This justice can be achieved only with the sense of the responsibility for the other fellow human beings. As long as there evaporates the sense of responsibility in the mass media, a change both in form and content is needed for the better society where democracy works with the spirit of social justice.

8.1.2 Monopolized Information as Commodity

As Paul Tillich correctly saw, Western technical society has produced methods of adjusting persons to its demands in production and consumption which are less brutal, but in the long run, more effective than totalitarian suppression. They depersonalize not by commanding but by providing; providing, namely, what makes individual creativity superfluous. If one looks around at the methods, which produce conformity, one is astonished that still enough individual creativity is left even to produce these refined methods. One discovers that man's spiritual life has a tremendous power of resistance against a reduction to prescribed patterns of behavior. But one also sees that this resistance is in a great danger of being worn down by the ways in which adjustment is forced upon him in the industrial society. It starts with the education of "adjustment" which produces conformity just by allowing for more spontaneity of the child than any pre-industrial civilization. But the definite frame within which this spontaneity is quietly kept, leads to a spontaneous adjustment which is more dangerous for creative freedom than any openly deterministic influence. At the same time, and throughout his whole life, other powerful means of adjustment are working upon the person in the technological society, the newspapers which choose the facts worth reporting and suggest their interpretation, the radio programs which eliminate non-conformist contents and interpreters, television which replaces the visual imagination by selected pictorial presentation, the movie which for commercial and censorship reasons has to maintain in most of its productions a conscious mediocrity, adjusting itself to the adjusted taste of the masses, the patterns of advertisement which permeate all other means of public communication, and have an inescapable omnipresence. All this means that more people have more occasions to encounter the cultural contents of past and present than in any pre-industrial civilization. But it also means that these contents become cultural 'goods,' sold and bought after they have been deprived of the ultimate concern they represented when originally created. They cease to be a matter of *to be or not to be* for the person. They become matters of entertainment, sensation, sentimentality, learning, weapons of competition or social prestige, and lose in this way the power of mediating a spiritual center to the person. They lose their potential dangers for the conformity, which is needed for the functioning of the technical society. And by losing their dangers they also lose their creative power, and the person without a spiritual center disintegrates.[246]

It is thus not new that man has to pay for the information he gets, but the mass media abuse the masses with information for their own merit, i.e., financial

---

[246] Tillich, Paul, "The Person in a Technological Society", in Social Ethics (Marty, martin E. (Ed.)) (New York: Harper &Row, Publisher, 1968), pp. 134-135

profit. Through the information monopoly the mass media can maximize their profit as any other industry in our age. That is why most of the mass media try to be a sole provider of information. Information in transferable form can be easily found as books, or rather the patented intellectual property. But not like the tangible goods, information is very difficult to be controlled by the law because it is extremely hard to know when the information becomes goods that can be sold and yield profit. In the capitalistic society, every possible thing or labor becomes goods to be sold. The classical definition of goods as the composition of natural resources and human labor can be still applied to the new kinds of products. The mass media need first of all raw information to be processed. This information is processed with the intention of being well sold. Then the end product of information must be attractive enough that any sponsor will willingly give money for that information with the condition of advertisement for his or her products, which is also to be sold well. As a matter of fact, the public is not the first client to receive the information. The public is at the end of this "information process", which just consumes the information and pay for it as much as for the advertisement by buying the advertised products. As of any other products of our society, the masses as consumers have a limited right to choose among the ready-made information, which is produced with the latent egoistic intention of the mass media and the sponsor. The information must be even a "pure" information, i.e., there must be possibly no hint of manipulation of information lest the masses find it not so attractive. The masses do not want to be abused, but they want simultaneously very attractive information for which they pay willingly. Therefore information in the mass media must be very refined. And as usual, refinement induces manipulation.

Most of the mass media pretend to be a "pure" mirror which reflects the true facts of the society, and even try to show themselves as one of the prominent media for the social justice, in that they draw attention of the masses to the problems of the society and suggesting the possible solution. But it is very seldom that the mass media put themselves or the big sponsors under the scrutiny. And as long as the prime object of the mass media is to provide the information which can be very good sold, it is extremely difficult to expect from them a neutral or even a righteous role for the society. The mass media are still providers of information and do their best to sell their information as marketable goods, as any other producer of consumer goods, but with one serious defect. When a consumer product has a failure, a consumer has right to reclaim his money. Even when a consumer finds the product not good which he has purchased, he can try to reclaim his money. On the contrary, the fault information of the mass media can be hardly reimbursed. The masses can normally cancel the subscription of a newspaper or turn off radio and TV, but it does not make the fault or false information good again. The mass media seldom apologize their failure not only because the information itself as goods is quite elusive but also because it is extremely difficult to find the concrete carrier of the responsibility for the false information. In contrast to the normal consumer goods of which responsibility can be easily traced, the information of the mass media is still a commodity without after-sales service. This disappeared responsibility for their product by the mass media is simply wrong, therefore it must be corrected, but as long as the mass media remain as the unilateral media, there is little chance for it. Without the institutionalized and well-practiced reciprocity or interactivity the mass media cannot be well controlled and checked. With the enactment of law many governments in the world try to hinder a company to become a monopolizing one which could eventually damage the society proper. This action must be applied also to the mass media.

Information as the marketable commodity causes one more problem except the commercialism, which is pervasive in the society of the day. It is getting harder for the masses to know what the "good" information is. As any other product in the consume society, there are too many information distributed by too many mass media to be consumed by the masses. There comes naturally fierce competition among them. This competition makes the masses confused. Every one of the mass media claims good quality of its information not only for the masses but also for the society proper. In fact it cannot be purely good for the public interest, as long as it is just a commodity to be sold for the maximum profit. An information with intention does much worse harm for the society because it could manipulate the emotion of the masses arbitrarily for the special interest of some person or group. We have seen already many cases of these unfortunate incidents in the history.

8.1.3 Manipulated Consensus for Special Group-Interest

Around the years of the World War II, there were many cases of control of speech, both for the allied and the German. Both sides used every possible kinds of the mass media to manipulate the consensus of their respective people in the name of patriotism. That was done with the self-justification of common good for the nation, but, in fact, that was for the interest of very small number of politicians and industrialists. The manipulation of the mass media by Adolf Hitler and his royal followers hindered almost perfectly the German to know the truth about the war till the end.

In Germany under the regime of Adolf Hitler, not only newspaper but also movie and radio were all mobilized to propagate the ideology of Hitler and his followers, i.e., the Nazis of NSDAP (Nationalsozialistische Deutsche Arbeiterpartei). Adolf Hitler had used once arms in vain by the futile "Beer Hall Revolt" in November 8. 1923, but he used all possible legal methods to be the Chancellor of Germany. Hitler's party had begun with 12 Reichstag seats in 1928, but in August 1932 it became the major party with 230 seats, which represented 13,732,799 German, 12,923,799, or 1,597 %, more than those of 1928. With once outlawed party Adolf Hitler became the legal Chancellor of the Third Reich on January 30, 1933. He then was the "Führer" of the Germany, which had about 85,000,000 people at that time.[247] In January 1938 he was chosen even as "Man of the Year" by the TIME, a weekly magazine in the U.S.A.[248] A man, who had begun his political career in 1919 as an obscure member of the German Labor Party, became man of the world within 20 years. It is clear that he did something good for many Germans who were then agonized under the shame of loser and high unemployment. Even he purged brutally his "enemies" in the German society, especially Jews, Communist and Socialist, his image as a mystified Führer lived until his death not only in Germany but also in many other lands.[249] The strongly controlled mass media had been a great help for Adolf Hitler who has the great gift as an orator to make it possible. Not only with newspaper and book, but also with radio and movie, especially as in the form of the "Wochenschau", he made a not truly public "public image" of him. This was one of the worst case of personality cults, with that of Stalin, to which the manipulated unilateral mass media contributed greatly.

Those bad cases of the mass media manipulation did not end with the end of the war. With the outbreak of the Cold War, the air of the world was full of the mutual defamation mainly between the U.S.A. and the former U.S.S.R., which was escalated to be another war without arms. The two poles of the Cold War, the U.S.A. and the former U.S.S.R., made every corner of the world to be a potential theater of the Third World War which presumably would result in the annihilation of the whole world. The U.S.A. was the "Imperial and Capitalistic Danger" for the East Bloc, and the former U.S.S.R. was the "Evil Empire" for

---

[247] ...What Adolf Hitler & Co. did to Germany in less than six years was applauded wildly and ecstatically by most Germans. He lifted the nation from post-War defeatism. Under the swastika Germany was unified. His was no ordinary dictatorship, but rather one of great energy and magnificent planning. The "socialist" part of National Socialism might be scoffed at by hard-and-fast Marxists, but the Nazi movement nevertheless had a mass basis. The 1,500 miles of magnificent highways built, schemes for cheap cars and simple workers' benefits, grandiose plans for rebuilding German cities made Germans burst with pride. Germans might eat many substitute foods or wear ersatz clothes but they did eat..., TIME, January 2. 1939 in CD-ROM "TIME Almanic of the 20th Century" (TIME, Inc. magazine Company, 1994)

[248] Ibid..

[249] ...Hitler, in a magnificent piece of propaganda argued that the cause of Nazism was not only the cause of the have-not nations, but of the have-not classes against the oppression of the rich. He justified Nazi oppression as a method of combating that oppression. Apart from that attempted justification, it was a plausible argument--so plausible that the Roosevelt-hating Chicago Tribune equally plausibly editorialized that Hitler "revealed himself once again as a good New Dealer."...,TIME, December 23. 1940 of CD-ROM "TIME Almanic"

many "democratic" countries until the "Fall of the Berlin Wall" in 1989. In most of the underdeveloped countries this situation was used by the rulers to justify their dictatorship. Under such a pressure, the mass media in the world could not play their role as the means for the true mirror of the facts. Even in the U.S.A., which cherished freedom of the press most with their First Amendment, happened "the myth of McCathyism". As long as there was no true reciprocity in the mass media, there could be no guarantee for the "right" consensus during the age of Cold War. The masses, which had no other way to get the information about the "enemies" than the mass media, had to just believe what they had preached. The mass media were greatly to be blamed for the mass hysteria for the nuclear war during the age of Cold War, not just the "bad" politicians. One famous case was the attack of the former North Vietnamese against two U.S. destroyers in the gulf of Tonkin near former North Vietnam. The Congress of the U.S.A. passed the Gulf of Tonkin Resolution on August 7. 1964, expanding the President's authority to commit U.S. troops to regional conflicts. President Lyndon Johnson's commitment to "no wider war" was short-lived. By 1968, over 500,000 U.S. troops were in Vietnam.[250] This attack was faked. The U.S. government wanted to make a cause to be officially involved in the Vietnam War. At that time, the mass media in the U.S.A. did not make much thought about it, and tried to justify the participation in the Vietnam War. The result was disastrous.

A similar case was there by the Persian Gulf War. To make Iraq an evil empire the mass media in the U.S.A. did every possible trick. For the first months of the crisis, the dominant media discourse was overwhelmingly in favor of a military solution, to the benefit of the Bush administration and its corporate supporters. This pronounced bias points to the effects of ownership of the media by corporations like GE which are heavily invested in the military industries, and which have been strongly supporting the conservative and pro-business Republican administrations for the past decade. From the beginning, the media vilified Saddam Hussein as a madman, a Hitler, and worse, and whipped up anti-Arab war fever. Saddam was characteristically described as a 'dictator', a 'military strongman' and a menace to world peace and the American way of life. Mary McGrory described him as a 'beast' *(Washington Post,* 8/8/90) and a 'monster' that 'Bush may have to destroy' *(Newsweek,* 10/20/90; 9/3/90). *The New Republic* doctored a TIME magazine cover story on Saddam to make him appear more like Hitler by shortening his moustache. Cartoonists had a field-day presenting images of the demon Saddam Hussein, and television resorted to cartoon techniques itself as when an NBC 'war game' simulation on August 8. 1990, had a US colonel pretending to be Saddam, staling 'I'll hang a hostage

---

[250] TIME, Inc. Magazine Company, TIME Almanac of the 20th Century (TIME, Inc. Magazine Company, 1994)

every day!' The media eagerly reported all of Saddam's alleged and actual crimes (suddenly focusing on actions and events which had gone unreported when Saddam was a U.S. ally, such as his use of chemical weapons against Kurdish rebels in his own country). There was even speculation on Iraq's plans for future terrorism when no current atrocities were on hand (see *Christian Science Monitor*, 9/21/90).

Saddam Hussein is, of course, a dictator with imperial ambitions who is ruthless, repressive and inclined towards military solutions and actions. Yet his vilification was so extreme that it ruled out diplomatic solutions in advance and reduced any possible Iraqi initiative to resolve the crisis diplomatically to mere propaganda and deception. Week after week, report after report, Saddam was described in purely negative terms with commentators stressing his brutality, irrationality and duplicity. It is significant, however, that the media characteristically describe similar foreign tyrants who are sympathetic to U.S. interests merely as 'military leaders' or 'presidents' and regularly portray them in positive or neutral frames - this was the case with repressive Vietnamese leaders whom the U.S. supported, as well as the Shah of Iran, Chile's Pinochet, the Philippines' Marcos, and even Panama's Noriega, until he fell out of favour with US policy makers. Saddam, by contrast, is constantly demonized as the absolutely evil 'foreign other'. In this way, the frames of popular culture entertainment, which are structured by a Manichean opposition between good and evil, are deployed in the discourse on Saddam Hussein as the absolute villain, the evil demon who is so threatening and violent that he must be destroyed and eradicated.[251]

Under such an environment talking against the war with Saddam regarded as anti-patriotic. This manipulation of consensus by the mass media is bad mainly for the masses in the end because the masses must pay for it all.

It is said that the masses have also responsibility for the sensationalism of the mass media, in that the masses pay their attention to a matter only when it is sensational, or there is just pervasive indifference. It is not totally wrong but there is much room for controversy. At least in the moral perspective there is no justification for the sensationalism of the mass media because gratifying the lustful and bad expectation of the masses cannot be regarded as good. Examples were the cases of the *New York Sun*, the first yellow paper in the U.S.A., and *New York Morning Herald*:

When the first "penny press" was established by Benjamin Day on September 3. 1833, he recognized that, if he was to expand circulation, he would have to appeal to the semiliterate, non-newspaper reader. And this meant emphasis upon

---

[251] Kellner, Douglas, "Television, the Crisis of Democracy and the Persian Gulf War", in Media, Crisis and Democracy : Mass Communication and the Disruption of Social Order (Raboy, Marc and Dagenais, Bernard (Ed.)) (London: Sage Publications, 1992), p 53

editorial opinion; his focus was on local happenings and violence. Six months after the *New York Sun* was founded, it reached a circulation of 8,000, nearly twice that of its nearest rival. Once the *Sun*'s new readers had the habit of reading newspapers, the *Sun* began to offer more significant information. Simultaneously, the recently franchised laboring class showed more interest in the operations of government. Day's format was similar to that of other penny papers founded during the 1830s. James Gordon Bennett's *New York Morning Herald* concentrated on crime news. During the 1830s, a total of 35 penny papers were founded in New York. None survived except the *Sun* and the *Herald*. Nevertheless, in other cities penny papers succeeded with similar formats and news policies - great deal of local news, human interest stories, and substantial doses of entertainment. During the 1850s, however, the trend was away from this kind of sensationalism. The *New York Tribune,* founded in 1841 by Horace Greeley, typified this trend. The *Tribune* sold for a penny, but rather than make unabashed appeals to emotionalism, the *Tribune* reported facts and serious discussions of the issues of the day. It could rival its competitors when it came to sensational crime stories, but this was not its main appeal. The *Tribune* was read by all classes-farmers, the workingman, educators, and politicians. Greeley had raised the press of the masses from the vulgar level of sensationalism to a force for stimulating thought. More important, the *Tribune* was a financial success. Greeley's assistant, Charles Dana, eventually took over *the New York Sun.* By this time, even the *Sun* and *Herald* were offering more substantial material. The increasing literacy and interest of their readers required it.[252]

These cases show that it might be possible to make the mass media "good" when there is enough good will from the side of "the provider" of information, but we cannot hide the fact that in the U.S.A. of the day, not only the sensationalism but also the intention of the manipulation of the masses still lingers on, sometimes even fiercer than before, especially in TV.

Even after the "Fall of the Berlin Wall" the world has become not yet a mutually understandable place. There are still many cases of the manipulation of consensus. Many people in the Western countries see in some of the Islamic countries the next potential "Evil Empire". Many people in the East Asian countries see in some of the Western countries the conspiracy of the capitalistic empiricism to disrupt, and even to conquer the East Asian economic system which once was cherished as the "Confucian model of capitalism". The masses still have not many alternatives to get the information about the other countries except the mass media, which are still tainted with the regional interest. Under such a situation the masses have to be manipulated by the pre-fabricated consensus. This manipulated consensus not only hinders correct mutual

---

[252] Lange, L. David and others, Mass Media and Violence (Washington: U.S. Government Printing Office, 1969), p 19

understanding between different countries, but also distort the basic sense of mutual understanding: sympathy for each other among people as person.

8.2 The Distorted Sympathy: The Abuse of the Unilateral Mass Media

8.2.1 Manipulated Sympathy for the Biased Group-Interest

Many international sports events are regarded to be a good chance for the national unity, which most politicians cherish regardless of their understanding of the sprit of sports. The Olympian Games was hold originally to prevent the rivalry among the πολις in ancient Greece. Nevertheless, after the revival of this peaceful quadrennial sports event in the modern age, it has become a theater both for the national pride show and the commercialism. The IOC (International Olympic Committee), the only "legal" organization having the right to hold this international event, "sells" the right for the broadcasting of the Olympic Games to the mass media. The mass media "use" this event to attract possibly many viewers which can be contributed to the higher audience rating, and sponsors, and, in the end, higher profits. Even though not a few people aware of these "facts", many still enjoy the Olympic Games and feel sympathy with their national players. Especially when a player of their nation wins a gold medal against a player who happens to be a man from the "enemy" countries, there comes often a phenomenon of mass hysteria nation wide. It amounts to wining a war. The situation is not much different with other international sports events.

Many people say that the international sports events function as a way for the catharsis, i.e., they could prevent people from really fighting with each other. But the Olympic Games in Berlin in 1936 never prevented Adolf Hitler and his followers to begin one of the worst wars in the history. The 22nd modern Olympiad in Moscow, former U.S.S.R. in 1980 and the 23rd one in Los Angeles, U.S.A. in 1984 showed extremely well how ugly the Olympic Games could be by the political rivalry. The politicians are not alone to be blamed for such ugliness. It is quite understandable that the masses are happy when their national players win the game. The problem is the mass media especially when the sport reporters become the vanguard of the pseudo-patriotism. Their frantic and biased comments about the games promote not seldom much animosity against the players and people of the other countries, especially of the "enemy" countries. Instead of the original spirit of the Olympiad, reconciliation and mutual understanding, the latent and not seldom obvious animosity against others is promoted in the mass media in the disguise of the national unity and the "true" patriotism. The masses feel natural sympathy for their national players, but the mass media, with the tacit backing of the politicians, manipulate them for their own merit. The wining players become suddenly a national hero and are rewarded mostly with much money. The mass media and the advertisement sponsors use him for their commercial profit. The masses pay for them all in the end. In this way the masses are manipulated by the mass media both emotionally and commercially.

A true patriotism must be cherished because man cannot truly love the other countries when he cannot love his country first, but a fanatic pseudo-patriotism hurts not only the other countries but also one's own country in the end in the globalized world of the day. The patriotism must be based on the proud society where social justice and freedom flourish, never on the politically manipulated hatred against the "enemy". To our sorry there are still many cases of such manipulations of the natural sympathy of the masses. Under such a situation a true intercultural understanding can never be accomplished. At the dawn of our century, the masses were manipulated by the closely controlled mass media. Nowadays, in the Information Age, the masses can be much easily manipulated because they suffer under the loss of orientation in the mass of the mass media, besides the still existing control of the mass media by the politicians and the capitalists. In such a situation we need more refined endeavor to do for the open mass media.

8.2.2 Closed Sympathy as the Result of the Disintegration of Society

It is natural that man tends to have sympathy with what is familiar to him. A child feels more comfort in the bosom of his or her own mother than any other women. A family unity is still cherished in almost all societies in the world. But too stringent dichotomy of "I" and "you", or of "we" and "they', can be as harmful as the loss of identity. As much as a family as the extended ego cannot be sustained by itself in the society, a country as the extended and manifested ethnic group cannot survive by itself in the globalized world of the day. Sympathy just for certain closed group might be a necessary condition for survival in the past when the autarchy played an important role, but the interdependence of the world of the day does not allow such an outdated method to be applied for the sympathy diffusion in the society anymore.

As any other old habit, the closed sympathy for special group is still a ubiquitous phenomenon. Man lives in the Island of closed circle even though he has a virtual contact with the whole world every day. George Orwell was quite right when he said: "*The peak of the shamelessness would be reached when the half of the mankind watch in the TV how the other half of the mankind starve.*" Much worse thing is having sympathy with the needy but doing nothing for them. The traditional mass media give a good excuse for the viewer to evade the humanitarian responsibility for the needy. The report about the needy comes with any other program parallel in TV as if there is no qualitative difference between them. This report about the needy stays as a virtual affair, which has no direct relation to the reality of the viewers. The viewers stay as an indifferent spectators not because he or she does not have the intention to help the needy but because the mass media as a mediator cut the human relation between the viewer and the reality as the mass media make the reality as virtual as they could. For the virtual reality man can hardly have the real feeling of sympathy, if any, it is mostly just an imaginary picture of sympathy, as he can have it when he watches an excellent film. Such sympathy has lost the contact with the real life world, therefore it cannot be a true sympathy. The true sympathy is always open, which can be interactive in real time and on time.

As Gerfried W. Hunold pointed out, the traditional mass media provide the viewer with many problems, especially with the matter of virtuality of others in the mass media.[253] Even if someone in the mass media provokes some interest of the viewer, he is there just as a virtual being. The problem is the "broken" real contact between him and viewer.

Even the accuracy of the information, which the mass media provide, can never be guaranteed as long as there is no open feedback system of verification, let alone the case of sympathy manipulation. The openness of the mass media should mean not only the simple opening to the masses, but also the creation of the field for the coordinated symbiosis of different cultures and many small sympathies of the closed group.

8.3 Problematic Ethos Mediation Based on the Unilateral Understanding

The early Christians engaged themselves with their Christian missionary work only with the help of the Gospels of Jesus Christ. Many Christians were sometimes persecuted because of their belief. The official empire-wide persecution against the Christian lasted in all about 60 years long.[254] After the Christians had acquired the freedom of belief in 313, and furthermore had become the sole imperial religion in 392, the situation changed drastically. Other existing religions were dismissed as superstition by the Christians. The Christians could successively purge the heathen, the Jews and the heretic with the help of imperial force until 565 under Justinian.[255] Against the "enemy" of God violence could be allowed even if it were quite non-Christian according to the Gospels of Jesus Christ. After the Holy War against the "enemies" of God, i.e., Islam, from 1095 to 1291, there was inner-Christian conflict between Catholic and Protestant until the 30 Year War, which ended in 1648 with the

---

[253] Hunold, Gerfried W., "Ethik der Information, Prolegomena zu einer Kultur medialer Öffentlichkeit" in Moral in einer Kultur der Massenmedien (Werner Wolbert (Hrsg.)) (Freiburg, Schweiz: Universitätverlag Freiburg Schweiz,1994), pp. 45-48
[254] Kttje, R., Moeller B.(Hrsg.), Ökumenische Kirchen Geschichte 1, Alte Kirche und Ostkirche (München: Chr. Kaiser Verlag, 1989), pp 84-90
[255] Ibid, pp.155-164

"Westfälische Friede".[256] During the era of colonialism the forced Christianizing of the American continent succeeded even though it resulted in severe demolition of the native cultures in the old New World.

As the Second Council of Vatican acknowledged, there could be some true belief besides the Christianism:

"The Catholic Church rejects nothing that is true and holy in these religions. She regards with sincere reverence those ways of conduct and of life, those precepts and teachings which, though differing in many aspects from the ones she holds and sets forth, nonetheless often reflect a ray of that Truth which enlightens all men. Indeed, she proclaims, and ever must proclaim Christ 'the way, the truth, and the life' (John 14:6), in whom men may find the fullness of religious life, in whom God has reconciled all things to Himself."[257]

There must be other much more important reasons for the sometimes quite drastic method of the Christianizing. One of them could be the closed sympathy. As slave were never man in the eyes of Aristotle, the people in Africa and in the New World could not be the same man as the European Christian for themselves. Such a prejudice plays still great role for many racists regardless of their racial differences. For a long time after the legislation of the civil right law in the U.S.A., even reporters of the public mass media called the black people Negro with the sense of latent contempt. For some white people in the U.S.A. black people are still not human beings as themselves even if there is no plausible reason for their prejudice.[258] Quite a few people in the U.S.A. live as Christian believing in God who loves man more than any other creatures in the world.

---

[256] Fleischmann, Sabine, Daten der Welt Geschite (Niederhausen, Deutschland: Bassermann, 1992), p 136

[257] Pope Paul VI, NOSTRA AETATE, Oct. 28, 1965 from the official website of Vatican www.vatican.va

[258] As a matter of fact, African-Americans in the U.S.A. were treated as any other white slaves at the beginning. But it changed with time as the history shows :

"And then there were the slaves. In 1619 the Virginia settler John Rolfe made a diary note of a dark moment in American history. "About the last of August," he wrote, "came in a dutch man of warre that sold us twenty Negars." In Virginia alone, the slave population grew from about 2,000 in 1670 to 50,000 on the eve of the American Revolution. Most of the slaves sailed from West Africa, chained together in dank, fetid holds for transatlantic journeys that often lasted three months or more. The conditions were unspeakable, the mortality rate horrifying: on some ships more than half the slaves died during the passage.

Initially, blacks worked alongside whites in the tobacco fields of Virginia and the Carolinas, but by 1650 field hands were invariably men and women of color. One reason: because of what science now knows is the sickle-cell trait, blacks were often less susceptible than whites to the depredations of malaria. More important, a terrible distinction had been made, first informally but then in legislation: white servants were considered persons despite their temporary state of servitude; blacks were mere property that could be bought and sold.

-- TIME, Dec. 02, 1993,   Special Issue: The New Face Of America in CD-ROM "TIME Almanic"

They cherish what the Bible tells them and love their family, relatives and friends "truly". However, there could be no Christian love for all, when they love just people whom they want to love, as much as there could be no true friendship between man and slave for Aristotle. A perfect "closed" Christian love can be there only for them. It is totally wrong that Christian love must be a closed, i.e., limited one. The love of God is not only for the Jews and the Christians but also for all gentiles in the world.[259]

The true Christian love is there when the dream of Rev. Dr. Martin Luther King is fulfilled:

"When we let freedom ring, when we let it ring from every village and every hamlet, from every state and every city, we will be able to speed up that day when all of God's children, black men and white men, Jews and Gentiles, Protestants and Catholics, will be able to join hands and sing in the words of the old Negro spiritual, 'Free at last! free at last! thank God Almighty, we are free at last!'"[260]

As we can see in many cases, the closed sympathy brings about discrimination, which is from the beginning man-made, never from God.[261] It would be very disappointing when the globalization should just mean the multi-nationalization of industry and commerce. The conscious of man must be globalized in every respect. When a crisis happens at one corner of the world, the whole world has to suffer sooner or later nowadays. When the economy in the U.S.A. was not good during the 1970s and the 1980s, there were many incidents of Japanese bashing movement. Not only the unemployed workers from Detroit but many mass media saw the scapegoat of the economic problem in the consumer goods from Japan. Many Japanese cars were demolished as the symbol of the hatred against Japan. For the first time after the World War II the "Japs" became the public enemy again. In reality, the Big Three of Detroit had made unprecedented profits during the whole 1980s, but that fact was not much publicized by the

---

[259] Ro. 3: 27-31 Where is boasting then? It is excluded. By what law? of works? Nay: but by the law of faith. Therefore we conclude that a man is justified by faith without the deeds of the law. Is he the God of the Jews only? is he not also of the Gentiles? Yes, of the Gentiles also: Seeing it is one God, which shall justify the circumcision by faith, and uncircumcision through faith. Do we then make void the law through faith? God forbid: yea, we establish the law.

[260] From his address to the crowd before the Lincoln Memorial in Washington D.C. at August 28. 1963.

[261] Some may still claim that God will save only a distinctive race. But it is hardly acceptable not only because it is religiously false but also the natural scientific evidences, which is rational, show us that all human beings must have a common ancestor. When God must have created just one couple of man and woman, Adam and Eve, they must be our common ancestor who had to be fruitful, and multiply, and replenish the earth, and subdue it: and have dominion over the fish of the sea, and over the fowl of the air, and over every living thing that moveth upon the earth. (Ge. 1:28)

mass media.

The mass media have not changed much after that. As the Asian financial crisis broke up in 1997, not seldom was the reaction of the mass media of the West a kind of "Schadenfreude". Not until the fact was found that the bad influence of the crisis could harm the economy of the West that the mass media of the West changed their attitude against the crisis and began to talk about helping the Asian countries. Until then, there were mainly tremendous amounts of criticism against the Confucian model of capitalism, which was famous for the governmental interference of economy and cronyism. The mass media of Asia were not much better. They talked about mostly the conspiracy of the Western financial power in the disguise of the IMF(International Monetary Fund) and the World Bank. As most of the Asian governments, the mass media concerned more on the face-saving and the scapegoat-seeking than on the rational analysis of the fact. The word of mutual understanding was never heard during this period from both sides of the World. The masses in this situation could neither have clear idea about the matter nor avoid the manipulation of the mass media not to have a false picture of the other party. This manipulation of the public opinion by the mass media was the typical method of the incompetent politicians who want to shift the responsibility onto other's shoulder. When the mass media dance with such politicians, mutual understanding is a too far cry for the masses. When the information about the other party cannot flow without being distorted by someone with bad intention in the mass media, such mass media can never be helpful for the intercultural understanding, let alone the ethos mediation.

9. Sympathy Diffusion through the Interactive Mass Media

9.1 Interactivity: The New Dimension of Mass Media

9.1.1 Multi-Reciprocity: The Condition of Just Communication

The most typical feature of the interactive mass media is its multi-reciprocity. Not only the personal but also the collective reciprocity can be supported by the interactive mass media. Two examples can be seen in Internet as the forms of "chatting" and "multi-visual conference". The Internet has begun basically with the interconnected computer system through the existing communication line, mostly telephone cable around the world. It is true that the traditional telephone cannot be one of the mass media as long as it connects just very limited numbers of people at once. A computer alone cannot be one of the mass media either, no matter if it can build the great data base of tremendous information, as long as it cannot disseminate them in indiscriminate way among the masses. Only the

Internet as the amalgam of computer and telephone becomes a new kind of mass media accepted by almost all elements of the society.

One of the serious problems which the unilateral mass media could easily cause is the deafness of the mass media to the masses who are, in the end, their counterpart and wanted consumer. In the whole history of the mass media the interactivity of the communication was never cherished as today. It amounts to be one of the essential pillars of the most potent political system of the day: democracy. In the past there was very limited scope of interactivity among the concerned people. Even in the circle of a family there was a center of communication which was mostly the family-father. The other members of the family had to circle around him, never directly confronting him. It was rather a unilateral communication that prevailed in those days. The situation of the old society was not quite different from that of the family.

Since the French Revolution in 1789 and under the great influence of the philosophy of French Enlightenment, especially of Charles Montesquieu (1689-1755), the political system of modern democracy has never been in serious danger even though there were many attacks against it. The democratic society needs not only the prudent representatives but also the public opinion that can control them well. This is the only check against the government as Bentham described:

"Public Opinion may be considered as a system of law, emanating from the body of the people. If there be no individually assignable form of words in and by which it stands expressed, it is but upon a par in this particular with that rule of action which, emanating as it does from lawyers, official and professional, and not sanctioned by the Legislative authority otherwise than by tacit sufferance, is in England designated by the appellation of Common Law. To the pernicious exercise of the power of government it is the only check; to the beneficial, an indispensable supplement. Able rulers lead it; prudent rulers lead or follow it; foolish rulers disregard it. Even at the present stage in the career of civilization, its dictates coincide, on most points, with those of the greatest happiness principle; on some, however, it still deviates from them: but, as its deviations have all along been less and less numerous, and less wide, sooner or later they will cease to be discernible; aberration will vanish, coincidence will be complete."[262]

The longevity of the democracy has many reasons. One of them is the interactivity between the representative government and the public through the public opinion. The origin of the "interactivity" is not clear. It is used more widely with the technological progress of our century, but it might have a much longer history than its etymological origin. An example in the world of mass media can be found in the interactive TV, which must give the industry more

---

[262] Bentham, Jeremy, op. cit., p 35

merit than to the viewers.[263] As a matter of fact, in nature there is the more pervasive relation of action and reaction. This relation happens always with the time interval, and sometimes in different space. Interactivity happens regardless of the spatiotemporal difference. This has a great meaning for the change of the sociopolitical paradigm in relation to the mass media.

After the Declaration of the Independence of the U.S.A., there has always been increasing expectation from the bottom of the society which voicing not only its opinion but also its demand for social justice. The brilliant progress of the civil right movement has contributed a great deal for the modern democracy in the U.S.A. This kind of achievement has become a model for the rest of the world. As well known, the Declaration of the Independence of the U.S.A. had had a great impact on the French Revolution. Most newly liberated countries after the World War II had just two alternatives for their political and economic system to adopt, either democracy with capitalism or totalitarianism with communism. Until the late 1950s there was no clear sign to discern the merit of the democracy with capitalism. During the 1960s there were various social experiments in the U.S.A. especially with many civic movements for more liberal and just society. As the result of this dynamic social change, there came very great amount of social flexibility in the U.S.A., which contributed for the mature democracy. On the contrary, in most of the communistic countries, restriction and control were the everyday phenomena. With the matter of consensus building the communistic countries had had great efficiency, but that never contributed to building a content society. There had been not only the economic inefficiency but also the social rigidity, which resulted in the resentment of the people in the end. It is true that such resentment had become partly the basis of the modern social ethics especially after the French Revolution.[264] Nevertheless, it can never have a positive function of love with the matter of social justice. Resentment begets just another resentment in the end. The prosperity and the social equality in the U.S.A. are still far from the ideal society where nobody must feel sorry, but such a free society with such a variety of cultures and races has no match in the world yet. To build a society of this much freedom and social justice has been not a matter of course. The civil right movement in the 1950s and the 1960s claimed many sacrifices which were not entirely in vain. It contributed much for the reciprocal communication among the multiple races and cultures. To listen to the other voices and to understand what they should mean to are always the beginning of the true communication. To talk just to persuade others what one believes to be true has never succeeded.

---

[263] Gangloff, Tilmann P., "Die Aktivität hält sich in Grenzen, Interaktives Fernsehen: Vorteile vor allem für die Industrie", in Liebe, Tod und Lottozahlen. Fernsehen in Deutschland: Wer macht es? Was bringt es? Wie Wirkt es?, Tilmann P. Gangloff, Stephan Abarbanell (Hrsg.) (Hamburg: Gemeinschaftswerk der Evang. Publ., Abt. Verl., 1994), p 433

[264] Scheler, M., Vom Umsturz der Werte (Bern: Franke Verlag, 1972), p 70

With the perspective of other, man sees the world in a new way to which he is not always accustomed, but by which he is not seldom enlightened.

It is not extraordinary that Internet has begun and still growing fast in the U.S.A. where the spirit of mutual understanding among the different races and cultures is the necessary condition for the social integration.[265] We may see more interactive mass media beside the Internet and the interactive TV in the near future, but the basic concept of the reciprocity of such mass media will never change. In Internet everybody can tell and listen his or her opinion about almost everything.[266] It amounts to be an ideal field of democratic discussion. In such an environment the passivity of the masses in the traditional mass media cannot exist because man has to be always active when he wants to be in Internet. The active masses cannot tolerate the unilateral mass media, which dictate what the masses must see and hear. In this environment a biased prejudice cannot play a big role. In Internet the traditional human conditions like age, sex, race are hidden behind a virtual identity. This identity cannot be a fake one, it is just a mask for the sociality in Internet as that of the old masquerade. In such a situation a person can be a true person (persona) which etymologically means a voice through the mask. Man can voice his true opinion not seldom when he is sure of his anonymity. Behind a mask man feels a kind of security. Some may talk about the identity crisis in the age of Internet, but this crisis can be mastered with the "flexible self".[267] An identity of a person cannot be a static one as long as it constitutes itself in the dynamic relation with its environment, mostly the society itself. Internet helps this identity building as it removes, or at least, makes an ἐποχή on the incidental but influential human conditions like age, sex and race. The merit of the newly earned identity in Internet could be applied to the whole interactive mass media in the future, which come always with the condition of the sense of duty.

---

[265] In 1998 more than 90 % of web-sites are from the U.S.A.

[266] At the moment most of the communication in Internet is made by writing and reading. Audiovisual communication is just at its beginning. The biggest hindrance for this kind of communication is the small capacity of the copper telephone cable, which is already overloaded with databits. On the one hand, the method of writing and reading may be better for the democratic discussion, mostly because of the anonymity of "authors". Behind the invisible identity in Internet one can freely express his opinion and the other can also freely refute it without the fear of physical confrontation. On the other hand, anonymity gives also a chance to be irresponsible, but in Internet where a single opinion can seldom dominate, such a danger is not big enough to harm the democratic communication on the whole.

[267] Turkle, Sherry, Leben im Netz, Identität in Zeit des Internet (Reinbek bei Hamburg: Rowolt Verlag GmbH, 1998), P 425

9.1.2 Open Information as the Basic Terms of Open Society

In Internet we witness the incessant "updating" of various information day by day. Man has to do the updating, or the information will be easily obsolete in the rapid changing world of the day. As long as information is open to the masses there is no other way to survive in Internet than providing new and "correct" information. Problem is not only the quality but also the quantity of the information. It is assumed that there are about 320 million Web-sites in Internet in 1998. They are just too much to be searched by any existing "search engine".[268] The most powerful search engine can only cover about 34 % of the 320 million Web-sites.[269] Many Web-sites with tentatively "important" information remain anonymous even they are all open to the masses. This is the typical drawback of the new interactive mass media of the day.

Before, the masses itself has been open to the influence of the mass media even if it has had to stay anonymous. The masses does not turn around the information, which the mass media provide, any more, but the information itself turns around the masses to be caught. This could be another Copernican turnover in the history of the mass media. Internet alone cannot substitute all the existing mass media but it is almost certain that it influences all the mass media in the future to adopt its form. As we have seen above, the form of open and indiscriminate information has been already in the traditional mass media, but it lacks always the system of verification by the masses. This unverifiablity exists in Internet too mostly because of the anonymity. Nevertheless this anonymity in Internet can be helpful for the democratic and open communication because people behind a mask open themselves more willingly. This openness of the participants is the foremost condition for the democratic and interactive communication.

Open and reciprocal information alone cannot guarantee the ideal communication, but it is necessary condition of the ideal mass media for the ethos mediation. In Internet everybody can visit everybody's home page and give some opinion if it is necessary. Everybody can have a communication with anybody in real time and on time if he or she keeps certain rules that are grossly required at the moment. He can also communicate with others as a participant of news-group with time interval. Various spatiotemporal modes of information transfer make people much easier to access to the information of Internet. Spatiotemporal limits in the past can be here lightly eliminated by the flexibility of information which can be stored and called anytime and anywhere. In this way information can be truly open to the masses. With the anonymous FTP man

---

[268] Like the "Yahoo" which searchs the asked information in the whole Internet with a few key words.
[269] According to the research of NEC (Nippon Electric Company) in the first quarter of 1998

can his own information open to the masses in Internet. This information can be hit, or visited, by anyone who wants to get it. As above mentioned, there are about 320 million Web-sites, which has URL with anonymous FTP, at the moment, therefore it is sometimes very hard for a man to find the proper information what he really wants.[270] That is why man needs a powerful search engine in Internet, which may come soon. As the index or register of a book, more powerful search engine can definitely help people to find the needed information with very small amount of searching time. The form of information is not only text but also audio-visual files. At the moment, this form of information has very limited usage because of the technical limit, but with the help of the optical fiber cable and the "Interactive TV", or "Internet TV", we may get more convenient access to the information in Internet.

It is still unclear what this mode of information can bring about concretely. Anyway, the merit of the open information for the ethos mediation is clear. In the Middle Ages, the information about the world was shared with very limited circle of rulers and scholars. This situation could be even helpful in sustaining the sociopolitical system of the Middle Ages for a while. However, this could not last for so long. As the sociopolitical change after the Renaissance has shown, only a flexible sociopolitical system which based on the general consensus can guarantee not only economically more affluent but also socially more civilized life of the members of the society. The main ideas of the civilized society, i.e., liberty, equality and fraternity could take their concrete shape only after the diffusion of information, i.e., after all members of the society have free access to the information which they want to. It is true that with the diffusion of information many concepts have become rather obscure, even relative, as the authoritative interpretation of information has disappeared after the spirit of democracy was hailed by the masses. The danger of arbitrary interpretation is sometimes much harmful than the monopoly of information. Relativism is still a very difficult matter not only in the philosophical discussion but also in everyday life. Notwithstanding such a latent flaw of the open information, this is sine qua non for the true democratic society. Closed countries with the closed information management have never succeeded to have an affluent society, let alone a civilized one. The mass media as the main engine of freedom of speech and the press, which is the essence of democracy, must be media only for the open information, lest they become a means for the modern authoritative monopoly of closed information which prevents the civilized society to be functioned well.

---

[270] URL (Uniform Resource Locator) is the web-address. FTP (File Transmit Protocol) tells other computers in Internet what the tagged information is. This make the information in Internet possible to be transmitted and received.

9.1.3 The Democratic Structure of Reciprocal Communication

In Internet, everyone can have principally just one web-site. Of course, it is possible that one man opens many web-sites with different URLs, but that is totally nonsense because man can load into one web-site almost every possible information what he wants to. Even a giant commercial broadcasting company like CNN has just one web-site as any private person in Internet. Everybody is a broadcasting center in Internet as long as he or she has a computer and a web-site in Internet, which cost not much money in comparison to the building of a broadcasting company. Even though there are quantitative and qualitative differences of information, mostly stemming from the technological matters which costs not little, the basic spirit of Internet as a democratic medium still survives because the rash technological development itself makes it for the private person possible to have a computer and an Internet access which are reasonable for their financial condition.[271] The information of the various web-sites of Internet comes to the user indiscriminately like that of other mass media. The information on the screen of a computer-monitor, which has became more than the terminal of Internet, comes to the user with almost the same format regardless the source of information. How the information comes to the user depends more on the web-browser which make the web-searching comfortable. Netscape Navigator, which was originally called Mosaic and the Internet Explorer of Microsoft, dominate the browser market at the moment. These two web-browser are competing with each other to be the sole browser of Internet. Some people even guess that the winner will dominate the future of Internet, but it is going to be more like the difference of TV sending systems of the day, i.e., PAL in Europe and Near East and NTSC in the U.S.A. and most of the Asian countries. And quite different from these TV signal sending systems, different browser of Internet does not require different hardware. The compatibility of hardware and software eliminate the wall between different systems and promote the unhindered communication between netizens (citizens of Internet).

As Internet and WWW of CERN have begun as a kind of information networking among students and scientists, there has been no commercial intention for them. Therefore, there has been no need for the hierarchical structure of Internet. A more loose organization for Internet exists. There are so to speak the backbone super-computers which are under the control of the NSF(National Science Foundation) in the U.S.A. The NSF provides web addresses and controls them. There are ISOC (Internet Society), FARNET (The Federation of American Research Network) and CIX (The Commercial Internet

---

[271] A acceptable computer for Internet access costing less than 1,000 $ sells well in the U.S.A. in early 1998. This trend will influence the world market of computer, and in the end the number of netizen of Internet..

Exchange) which are all functioning as a loose controlling body of Internet. They are all in the U.S.A., therefore some people is talking about the domination or control of Internet by the U.S.A. Such an anxiety can be amplified by the fact that the standard language in Internet is English and more than 90 % of websites are from the U.S.A., but it cannot be interpreted as the cultural domination of Internet by the U.S.A. Internet has begun as a network of computer which was already a machine operated by software in English. Most of the computer operating system and computer hardware system come from the U.S.A. Therefore there must have been already the cultural domination of the U.S.A. before the coming of Internet when it must be there. Without the TCP/IP, which has begun by the ARPANet, the communication of Internet is impossible, it is already ubiquitous in the whole world. We cannot now change such protocols for both technical and financial reasons.[272] When some people think that the dominance of one language and technology in Internet offends the national sentiment, they can try a translation system which makes the Internet communication more convenient, as every participant can use his or her mother tongue. Cultural isolationism does more hurt than good for the globalized world. As the Latin of the Roman Empire enhanced a great leap for the civilization of the world, a common language can do also a good contribution for the progress in the future. The Dark Ages has begun not when Latin still was a common language for the people in the Empire but when it was a privileged language for the small army of rulers and the learned. A sound nationalism has nothing to do with a common language which can make it easy for the people in the world to communicate with each other. A rapid spread of Christianism could be hardly achieved without common languages of old Greek and Latin.

Another seemingly tentative problem may be the somewhat anarchic structure of Internet when we are about to use it as a model for the whole interactive mass media in the future. Even if there are some backbone super-computers and organizations for the loose control of Internet, the original spirit of Internet as the non-governmental and non-commercial institution of the masses still survives. Newly emerging and fast growing commercialism in Internet could endanger this spirit, but nobody can dominate in this world of open information just because of the sheer size and the diversity of Internet users. The traditional division of form and content functions here rather positive and cooperative. The hardware of computer as form cannot stand alone without software as contents for it. Their interdependence does not hurt both of them, on the contrary, shows just how the more rigidly configured hardware can never dictate what the software must do. Software comes in the end from the creativity of man. The rigidity of form cannot control the flexibility of contents.

---

[272] TCP/IP (Transmission Control Protocol / Internet Protocol) is a way of calling another computer in Internet.

This fact makes certainly favorable condition for the mutual understanding, especially ethos mediation. When given conditions of hardware and some features of software, for example, program language and its usage, cannot influence much of the transferable contents, as it is so in Internet, there would be minimal distortion of the information to be transferred. This unbiased information could serve as a medium for the mutual understanding.[273] The thoroughly commercialized mass media with a hierarchical organization must necessarily manipulate information processing for certain intention even if some members of that process do always "correctly".

9.2 The Open Mass Media as the Appropriate Medium for Mutual Undertanding

9.2.1 Formal Prerequisites

9.2.1.1 The Institutionalization of Interactivity

In the early age of the radio broadcasting in the U.S.A., commercial broadcasting industry which had the network-dominated and advertising-supported system won the fight against the broadcasting reformer who intended to make the radio public medium.[274] At that time, to build a broadcasting company or institute it was needed not only the tremendous amounts of money but also legal approval from the government which saw both the strength and the danger of the airwaves. The capitalist in the U.S.A. succeeded in dominating the air with the commercial broadcasting industry with the help of the politicians who wanted to have a compensation from the capitalists. As a matter of fact, after the World War I, capitalism was made even a part of the constitution in the U.S.A., therefore it was almost impossible to question the capitalist basis of the political economy in the U.S.A.[275] The decent broadcasting reform movement of the civic movement, labor organization and church in the 1930s failed and made a way to the commercialization of TV in the 1940s and the 1950s in the U.S.A.[276] We still can see the full aftermath of the commercialization of radio

---

[273] Here the information as a medium functions just as the material to be processed. Man needs another kind of medium which do this job of information processing. For this medium belong not only teacher, "specialist" but also fellow in the classical meaning. Refer to: Faulstich, Werner, Medientheorien: Einführung und Überblick (Göttingen: Vandenhoeck und Ruprecht, 1991) pp. 7-17
[274] McChesney, Robert W., Telecommunications, Mass Media, and Democracy, The Battle for the Control of U.S. Broadcasting, 1928-1935 (Oxford: Oxford University Press, 1993), pp. 252-253
[275] Ibid., pp-262-263
[276] Ibid., p 260

and TV in the U.S.A. Even though there are some public non-profit oriented broadcasting institutes, mostly commercialized broadcasting industry still dominates the air. The coincidence of two World Wars, the Great Depression and the Cold War had unintentionally helped to make a paved way for the commercialization of the mass media in the U.S.A. But, most of all, the lack of feedback system might have been one of the basic reasons for the commercialization of the mass media. If all ordinary citizens of the U.S.A. in the 1930s had had the chance to access to the information of the policy making process directly, and had found out what was going on with the capitalist and the politician in relation to "their" mass media, the results would have been totally different. Two main characters of capitalistic society, commercialism and competition hindered the diffusion of information which was regarded as marketable goods by the profit oriented capitalists who would rather change everything in the society into commodity. The vulgar pop culture of the mass media in the U.S.A. would have been much civilized if it had not been such greed of capitalist. This tragic example of the U.S.A. should be never repeated. Therefore we need a more concrete way of information diffusion and of checking the mass media.

Not just in the forms of letter, phone-call and email, there must be an institutionalized way of interactivity between the mass media and the masses. Only this could guarantee the open mass media with the measure of reciprocal policing among the mass media. Technically it needs a new data processing system that understands every single opinion of the masses. The existing method of opinion poll could be the basis of this new way of interactive system, but never be the ideal one. With the help of the computer armed with AI (Artificial Intelligence) man can analyze and process the opinions of the masses as normal computer data. To prevent the manipulation of this process man needs a quasi-governmental but independent institute. When an ideal democracy is to begin to form its shape, it needs possibly the greatest participation of the masses. In the past it was impossible, first of all, because of the technical difficulty to collect the opinions of the masses and put them into a process of consensus building. In the Information Age of the day it is theoretically possible to make almost all opinions of the masses to be considered. The problem is, as usual, financial and technical. As the interactive mass media must stay as a democratic and independent media for all people, the influences of money must be possibly well prevented. Cost-down is needed here too. However, a technology which can be helpful with this matter is not yet ripe, therefore we have to wait a little bit until it is ripe enough. But we cannot wait long when we know that we can at least try a new way of consensus building, and furthermore, of promoting the communication of the masses. If the existing unilateral mass media have to necessarily have an intention of profit, they must not play a major role here.

The existing public opinion poll is not an ideal method for the democratic consensus building. Opinions not based on enough dialogue among the concerned people cannot reflect the rational consensus of a society. Before there comes a consensus into being, therefore, there must be through and democratic discussion about any matter, or there is just a more or less emotionally tainted mass of views, which can be easily influenced by the so called opinion leaders mostly engaged in the mass media. Every single opinion must be respected as much as a vote in the balloting box. And every single opinion of the masses must be processed as a piece of data, which in the end to be considered in consensus building. In such an environment a demagogue cannot yield much influence as before. Everybody has just one opinion as any other in the interactive society. In this society even the opinion of experts must be regarded as one of many and cross-examined in the system of the democratic consensus building.

To build an electronic system for such an interactive system, it takes quite a few time and money. Here is an example. A written opinion with the size of a DIN4 paper needs about 7,000 bytes of storage space for a normal computer of the day.[277] A spoken opinion in the size of one minute speech with 8 bit monosound system takes about 1,300,000 bytes of hard disk. The actual data transfer rate with a standard modem is about 56,000 bps (bit per second), which means about 4,000 to 5,000 bytes per second. When we want to just gather the opinions of 1,000,000 people with the form of above mentioned data, we need a hard disk with the space of about 130 giga-bytes. To transfer these data, it takes about 7 minutes with 1,000,000 telephone lines which are simultaneously occupied. To send the data we need 1,000,000 PCs, and to process the gathered data, we need many supercomputers like Cray. For a country like China with 1,300 million people, it will take tremendous time and money to build such a system. Even in the U.S.A. in 1998 where only 30 % of the U.S. households own PC it will not be an easy job. That is why we still need the much refined technological progress, with which we can reduce the amount of time and cost. We witness already some progresses, for example, with the optical fiber cable for the faster data transfer, data compressing method for more free storage capacity, and faster PC for the faster data processing. With the Interactive TV we may find a more inexpensive way of building this feedback system of interactivity.

It is clear that technology alone cannot fully guarantee the democratic consensus building. The conscious of every man in the society has to be enlightened enough to be accommodated for the new democratic consensus building. The existing mass media with their character of opinion leader and consensus manipulation cannot be any more a system for the new post-modern

---

[277] A normal computer should mean here a PC with the operating system of Windows 98 of Microsoft, which is used by more than 90% of the PCs in the world, and the CPU of Intel Pentium II 400 MMX or any compatible one. The size of hard disk plays here no role but it must be around 8 giga-byte.

democratic consensus building. It is inevitable that the new and old mass media are on the collision course. To survive in the future, many traditional mass media are briskly adapting themselves in the new environment of interactivity. They are building Internet web-sites, and trying to keep in contact with the masses through the new way of communication, mostly email. But the traditional mass media are closed for the future as long as their basic structure is oriented to the commercialism of maximum profit. The interactive mass media must be open for the future with their flexibility and reciprocity with the masses. The masses and the mass media must find their new relation in the new environment. It must be equal and interactive, never hierarchical and unilateral.

For the intercultural understanding this new mass media is necessary mostly because only it can guarantee the direct multiple cross-checking of the information of the other party. The indirect information about the other party via the traditional mass media can easily distort the true picture of it, and in the end hinder the mutual understanding. A direct access to the data bank of all information about all cultures in the world must be guaranteed first for the mutual understanding. This data bank must be built not by a few scientists, government officers and mass media moguls, but by the masses themselves. For this purpose we need further the diffusion of the small-scaled mass media.

9.2.1.2 The Multiplexing of the Mass Media

It is clear that monopolized mass media in the hands of a few can never be the open mass media in the future. As any other industry in the capitalistic society, rationalized mass media yield more profit, but the manipulated information tainted with the uncontrolled advertisement hurts in the end the society proper. The financial profit for the owner of the mass media can seldom interpreted as the benefit for the masses. The capitalistic greed of some tycoons of the mass media cannot be stopped by the appeal to their conscience. We have to build a new network of the mass media where only the non-commercial "information hub" dominates.

The existing non-commercial hub of the interactive mass media, mostly institutes of the universities around the world, must redraw the map of the mass media of the day. New mass media cannot be thought anymore without the help of computer and its applied technology. The existing network of Internet has been originated from the inter-university computer network.

When the world is connected though the network of computers the main information channels will be the telephone line both through tangible cables and the air. Even if this telephone line is worldwide undergoing the process of privatization, monopoly by a few big companies will be impossible. We may use the existing networks of amateur ham in the world as the basic model of the future telecommunication channel. With the help of the artificial satellite the communication of the future will have less problem of the information transfer. As long as the hubs of these networks are the universities, it will not easy for a few mass media moguls to dominate the world of the new interactive mass media. It can be also assumed that the mass media moguls found many private universities and try to control the flow of information in the networked mass media. But the sheer number of the universities of the world with moderate size of computer powers can provide enough reservoirs to counter such measures from the greedy mass media moguls.

Not only the university but also every individual can build a small independent sender of information as the amateur hams of the day, a small-scaled mass media not in the air but in Internet. In Internet man can already build a home-page which everybody can visit anytime and anywhere when they are connected. The traffic jam in Internet can be mitigated with the new technology like optical fiber cable, parallel computers, and free airwaves. In this environment big information provider may try to act like the big brother of the mass media, but it will be extremely difficult because of the sheer number of the "senders" in the new networked mass media. Nowadays to send a TV program man needs tremendous amounts of money. Not only hardware and software of broadcasting but also the personnel, i.e., producer, broadcasting hosts, actors must be employed. They are all employed just for the production, marketing and transmission of the information they have made. In the end their products must be bought by the masses who are watching them and paying for it by means of the monthly fee or the "enforced" watching of the advertisements they provide. When the "pay per watch" system of the Interactive TV works as the standard of TV program providing, every single program of TV which are now sent lineally must be separately showcased like the tangible goods of show-window, and the masses as buyer can choose his or her program at their will.

In such a situation everybody can provide a single interesting program in the networked mass media and compete with big mass media moguls. As long as the main network servers belong to the non-commercial institutes of the universities, there will be no monopoly of the networked interactive mass media. As a matter of fact, many programs of a TV sender are subcontracted. When the new mass media are established, these subcontractors can also work independently as a small sender.

In this environment censorship is a very important matter. The perennial discrepancy between freedom of speech and the press and the public order must strike the middle way in the interactive mass media. A powerful governmental controlling system may be needed, but it alone cannot control all the transaction in the networked mass media. We need a more diffused way of mutual control which can never be centralized. A diffused control among the multiple mass media could be one of many ways to the democratic mass media.

9.2.1.3 The Reciprocal Control of the Mass Media

Balance and check cannot be the way to be applied only between government and congress. A sound competition is better than a dishonest dealing between interest groups, therefore the competition among the mass media must be continued within the bounds of the democratic fairness. With the method of cutting the spams of junk mails in Internet of the day, we may introduce a way of controlling the unacceptable "senders" in the networked mass media. Not only the pornographic and violent programs but also racially and culturally biased program must be controlled. But a single government cannot do this job well because the networked interactive mass media does not care the national boundaries. Only an international organization like UN can do the job. On the other hand, a grass root control can do much effectively the job of mutual control of the mass media.

As long as computer connects the world of networked mass media, its hardware and software must be standardized when it is to be used without the problem of communicability. We can build this common ground with the concept of interactive control. In the U.S.A. there is already a microchip in TV, which can automatically check programs not suitable for children. This technology can be applied for the networked interactive mass media more easily. When a sender sends a program containing indecent material, it can be automatically censored by hardware and software. Even when the sender manipulates his or her gadgets and software the basic data system cannot be modified, or it is no more usable in the interactive mass media. The standardized interactive mass media make this control possible. A warning system can notify every sender in the interactive mass media the danger. And more, they can do the job of censorship jointly. Its effect will be prompt and direct. As cutting the spams in Internet, the ugly sender must accept the warning and adjust himself. In this way the "pure" interactive mass media must be fairly guaranteed.

Not only the form but also the contents of the mass media must be from the beginning censored by the consensus of all senders, therefore we need another way for the matter of contents. Even though the way of "cutting the spams" can be practically a good way of shutting down the bad sender in the world of interactive mass media, bad guys may build a new sender and do the same thing again. That is why we need another way of controlling the interactive mass media. Public broadcaster can be easily sanctioned nominally by the public opinion because of its publicity. In Internet there are too many small independent private senders. They are too many to be effectively controlled by the governmental censorship department, therefore the self-control of the mass media needs a code of conduct which can be applied like a law in the world of the interactive mass media. Of course, law alone cannot guarantee the desirable environment of the "pure" interactive mass media. We need to organize and categorize the mass media in order to apply the law more effectively. As we can see in Internet of the day, every sender must have an identification code to be a sender which is called domain name. This identification-code functions like an address which can be traced by every receiver anyway. We can add to this identification code the suffix of category. There are already some domain names like ".com", ".org", ".edu" which indicate main purpose of the web-site. We need to make it more elaborate, and furthermore, categorically subdivided. For example, under the domain of ".com" we can add more suffix of ".brod" for broadcasting. A search machine for such names can be also applied for the reference. In this way, like the directories of the computer operating system, the sender of the mass media in Internet can be categorized minutely. This categorized sender can be more easily traced and controlled.

Technical gadgetry alone cannot control the mass media. We need ultimately "enlightened individual" who does his job as a sender correct. As long as the nature of man tends to surrender more easily to the temptation than to the traditionally cherished moral virtues, we have to devise diverse ways of controlling of the senders in Internet. Not only the formal but also substantial control is needed to make the mass media "pure". Two more sources of the problematic mass media of the day are sex and violence besides advertisements. The wrong role model in the mass media of the day is also a great problem, especially for the younger generation.

9.2.2 The Betterment of Contents

9.2.2.1 The Limitation of Sex and Violence for the Just Mass Media

Excessive sex in the mass media is bad not only because it is morally unacceptable, but also because it is a social discrimination against woman on the basis of sexual difference. Excessive sex in the mass media, termed as pornography, is a kind of violence against certain member of the society which has no means of self-defense. Therefore sex and violence in the mass media must be regulated in the spirit of social justice. In the age of interactive mass media, this kind of regulation is needed more than any other time. Because of the total openness of the interactive mass media for all people, it is easily assumed that the pornography can be flourished without any proper safety measure against it. As any other social concepts, the definition of pornography or violence is not an easy matter. A sex scene in TV what could amount to be very shameful and unmoral in China can be shown without much protest from the masses in many countries in Europe. An unbearable violent scene for the European could be harmless for many people in the U.S.A. Nevertheless, we can draw a diffused consensus about it on the basis of common sense. According to the Francis Biddle's Memorial Lecture at the Harvard Law School in April 5.

1984, "Pornography, Civil Rights and Speech,", the full legal definition of pornography, as worded (with some minor variations) in a variety of ordinances, is:

"the graphic sexually explicit subordination of women through pictures and/or words that also includes one or more of the following: (i) women are presented dehumanized as sexual objects, things, or commodities; or (ii) women are presented as sexual objects who enjoy pain or humiliation; or (iii) women are presented as sexual objects who experience sexual pleasure in being raped; or (iv) women are presented as sexual objects tied up or cut up or mutilated or bruised or physically hurt; or (v) women are presented in postures of sexual submission, servility or display; or (vi) women's body parts - including but not limited to vaginas, breasts and buttocks - are exhibited, such that women are reduced to those parts; or (vii) women are presented as whores by nature; or (viii) women are presented being penetrated by objects or animals; or (ix) women are presented in scenarios of degradation, injury, torture, shown as filthy or inferior, bleeding, bruised or hurt in a context that makes these conditions sexual."

In addition, all the ordinances also define *"the use of men, children and transsexuals in the place of women"* as pornography.[278]

In a word a pornography is morally the way of making a person dehumanizing, a means for the lustful purpose of the oppressor. It has therefore always something to do with violence. In the typical Hollywood movie like "Rambo", the "good" or the "winner' has always right to be violent against the "loser" or the "bad". It is rather a self-justice against the tentative "evil" of the society, or even of the world, which could have sometimes a catharsis effect upon not a few viewers who are discontent with their situation regardless of their respective causes. An interesting research was made to find out that the violent scene is not limited in crime, western, and action-adventure style program since long. We could already see many violent scenes in the first slapstick comic film of Charlie Chaplin in 1917.[279] People are amused when they see such scenes, not aware of the violence in the film. The situation has not changed much since then. Violence in programs with a comedy tone and in those with a cartoon format is not much less than that in the crime, western, and action-adventure style programs in TV in the U.S.A. in the 1960s.[280] Nowadays we are witnessing the avalanche of sex and violence in not a few mass media worldwide. We may hope that we can protect ourselves from the unwanted materials in the programs

---

[278] Everywoman Ltd (Ed.), Pornography and Sexual Violence, Evidence of the Links (London: Everywoman Ltd., 1988), pp. 2-3

[279] video file of "chaplin.avi", in TIME, Inc. Magazine Company, TIME Almanac of the 20th Century (TIME, Inc. Magazine Company, 1994)

[280] Lange, L. David, Mass Media and Violence (Washington D.C.: U.S. Government Printing Office, 1969), pp. 328-328

with the interactive TV equipped with the technology of security guard system.[281] But as long as there are enough viewers who willingly pay to see pornography and violence in the mass media, it is impossible to eliminate the pornography and violence from the mass media totally. Enhancing the self-discipline of individual through moral education must be accompanied with the technical measures.

One technological possibility in the interactive mass media may be the reciprocal control with the help of AI (artificial intelligence). With the progress of the computer technology, man can make the machine check out automatically the violent and pornographic materials in the mass media, and prevent them from slipping into the "Infobahn". For the people who are pathologically indulged in such material in the mass media, we may provide a few closed channels, as we are providing substitute for the drug addicts of the day with limited condition. Of course, those channels must be under control of the whole community of Internet. Here happens the clash between freedom of speech or the press and the civic order again, but when such a problem becomes a legal matter, there is not much room for the common sense. Nevertheless, one thing is clear, under the environment of interactivity the mass media have to always respond to the reaction of the masses which sensibility could be expressed directly without the limitation of time and space. The unavoidable direct communication between the masses which are not any more passive viewers but speakers and writers must lead such result with the consensus based on common sense. In such a situation, the definition of pornography and violence may be unavoidably determined by the genuine public opinion not tainted by some opinion leaders.

This work must be accomplished by cooperation of the masses and the mass media. The public confrontations in many phases of the progress of the mass media are helpful as much as harmful in the long run because it splits the masses, and in the end, the society itself. It can be escalated easily not a matter of discussion, but of emotion between warring factions. Everybody can have quite different opinion about the violence in the mass media.[282] But one thing is clear that quantitative and qualitative censorship against the sex and violence in the mass media is necessary. This could be achieved with both the help of the technological progress of the Information Age and the reciprocal policing between the masses and the mass media.

The mass media with possibly minimal contents of sex and violence are

---

[281] Nowadays man can already shut down the door against the unwanted person who send junk email called spam in Internet. And when someone tries to set cookies, which is a way of making possibility of durable contact, man can also cut that out for good with the help of some software.
[282] Larsen, Otto N.(Ed.), Violence and the Mass Media (New York: Harper & Row, 1968), pp 273-293

helpful for the ethos mediation not only because it is more human but also it encourages the fraternal relation between two cultures. Every man has self-respect and wants to be respected by other people. It can be applied to the relation between different cultures. When one culture is to be accepted and adopted well by other culture, there must be cooperation not conflict. Mutual respect is not just a diplomatic gesture but a necessary condition for the true understanding. Enforcing a dominant culture upon the unassuming one is not the true ethos mediation but just a form of violence, therefore it causes always conflict in the long run. As long as sex and violence can be interpreted as a form of inhuman persecution by the strong upon the weak, they must be totally eliminated from the mass media for the ideal ethos mediation.

9.2.2.2 Advertisement Management

When we define advertisement as "calling something to the attention of the public, especially by paid announcements", the modern advertisement has developed just in the last one hundred years. There are actually many signs of the beginning of the old humble advertisements. Signs carved in stone for ancient Greek and Roman merchants 5,000 years ago were simple graphic ads with no words or copy. The forerunner of modern-day billboards informed the mostly illiterate community about a business, its purpose, and its location. During the Middle Ages, a sign in front of the local cobbler might show a boot or shoe; a sign used to indicate the dairy might picture a cow. In time, merchants customized symbols so that their signs were distinct from their competitors' - perhaps the first instance of the now-common use of trademarks and logos in advertising.[283]

Another practice from the same period involved the use of street criers to promote goods and services, much like barkers soliciting business today outside restaurants and businesses or employees offering free samples in supermarkets. Occasionally, the crier might shout his message in rhyme or was accompanied by a musician, giving rise to the first advertising jingles. "Sandwich men" with signs draped over their shoulders, with one in front and one behind, developed also as a method of delivering advertisements during this period as they strolled a town's streets, spreading information and extolling a merchant's offerings. With the invention of movable type and printing in the mid-fifteenth century, advertising went in new directions. As literacy rates increased, printed handbills became popular, and signs began to include copy as well as visuals. By the early seventeenth century, the first examples of newspaper advertising appeared in

---

[283] Kelvin L. Keenan, "Advertising" in Handbook on Mass Media in the United States: The Industry and Its Audiences, Erwin K. Thomas and Brown H. Carpenter (Ed.) (Westport, CT: Greenwood Press, 1994), p3

England, and in 1704 the *Boston Newsletter* was the first American paper to carry advertisements.[284]

Today, without advertisements no one in the mass media can survive. The most prominent sponsors of the mass media exert already great influence upon the present consume oriented society with their products. Their common goal is clear regardless of the vast difference of their products: more sales and more profits. Not only the traditional mass media like book, newspaper, magazine, radio, and TV, but also the new mass media like Internet is already full of advertisements. Most of the time consumed by downloading a web-site in Internet is caused by the banners, small graphical ads on web-sites. As a matter of fact, the whole economic system of the postmodern society cannot be sustained without advertisements. They have become a necessary evil, therefore we have to conceive a rational way of controlling them, not the way to kill them once and for all. It is true that an advertisement is bad when it is used with bad tricks for the intended aim of higher profit. Commercialism itself cannot be blamed today because it is one of the pillars of capitalism which has become the world system, but it cannot be driven without any control by the masses because it will in the end result in an ambivalence of the society which could destroy the society itself when there is no control.

It is difficult to provide any single, concise description of the modern advertising business. Unlike other industries, advertising involves people and operations, which not only are diverse but also in many cases represent extremes and opposites in terms of their backgrounds, skills, and purposes. In a sense, advertising is a management-oriented profession guided by discipline and organized decision making. In the other, it is an art form without boundaries or formality. Advertising products often consist of amorphous ideas and images, and yet advertising entails precise quantification in budgetary and evaluative decision making.[285] Therefore, it is needed a cooperative advertisement management with the interactive mass media. Advertisement must be more a way of information providing than a seduction to stimulate the impulse of consume. Direct and interactive communication between producer and consumer will change the way of advertisement. Legal censorship about advertisement may have a short effect until all concerned parties have a way of direct and interactive communication.

9.2.2.3 Sympathetic Role Model as Preferred Mediator

Many people love "Stars", mostly singers and actors in the mass media, even though they have never met them, let alone "know" them. It is not just a

---

[284] Ibid., p4
[285] Ibid., p7

phenomenon of projection of their loving image on them. The "Stars" are beautiful, young, healthy, and more, very rich. People do not care much about the moral character of the "Stars". The "Stars" represent the sunny side of the life in this world. Ironically many people want to have a life of "Stars" of bad moral character than that of saint with good moral character. A better example for this phenomenon cannot be given than the case of Lady Diana of England and Mother Teresa in Calcutta. These two celebrities of mass media have died one after the other with little interval of time. They are representative characters in their own life respectively. Lady Diana was beautiful, healthy, and rich even if she was not so young. She was shown in the mass media as a compassionate helper for the needy in the mass media. She died as she was driven to the house of her new very rich Egyptian friend after she had had a supper with him at a very luxurious hotel in Paris. She already had committed adultery many times before she divorced her ex-husband, Prince Charles of Wales. She had even manipulated the mass media for her own merit. But nobody cared about "the facts" of her much. Literally, the whole Western world cried when she died. Many may still want a life like her, maybe even including her dramatic death. Even the relative conservative magazine in the U.S.A., TIME could not keep itself from printing her story many times, and it marked the most popular issues of TIME at the newsstand twice, occupying the first and the second place in its history.[286] The story about Mother Teresa could not get even the tenth place.

Mother Teresa was not so cosmetically beautiful and bodily healthy as Lady Diana, let alone materially rich. She lived under a very poor condition, in a ghetto, all through her life, but she was very beautiful in her heart, healthy in her mind and rich in her love. She was almost the living saint of the day. Everybody revered her regardless of their religious difference, but few wanted to live a life like hers. What most of the people presumably want is not always good for their society proper. When everybody must live like Lady Diana, the world will be a tedious place to live in. She might be an interesting person but cannot be an ideal role model, especially for the younger generation when we look into her private life. The Western mass media made her demigoddess and used her for their commercial profit. And she used the mass media for her image makeup. They lived a symbiotic life for themselves but failed in the end to be responsible to the society.

Much worse are the "pop stars" in the mass media of the day. As public figures they have a responsibility for the masses as long as they live on the popularity of the masses, but they are seldom exemplary especially for the younger generation. They do their job just for money and fame which has never

---

[286] 1,183,758 copies for the issue with the cover story of "Princess Diana 'Commemorate'" in September 15. 1997. 802,838 copies for the issue with the cover story of "Death of Princess Diana" in September 8. 1997. The least popular issue was the story about "the Black Cultural Renaissance in the U.S.A.." with just 100,827 sold copies in October 10. 1994.

been the good way of life in the history. The confusion culminates when they identify the role of some "good" movie stars with that of the private life of them. The culture of cult has long history that it might not fade away soon. Mostly personality cult flourishes when there lacks information about the object of it. The open mass media must be helpful in unveiling the true "stars" as private person, but not for the satisfaction of the curiosity of some viewers but for the mutual understanding between "stars" and the masses. Personality cult does hurt the society proper because it promotes distrust among the people of the society in the ends.

Problem is that we cannot have other more influential figures than " pop stars" at the moment as role model in the mass media. Sometimes these pop stars behave even as moral preachers. They hold the concert for the starving people in Africa. They are "educating" the masses about the danger of AIDS. They are singing about the love and peace. They are showing the masses how to live as a 'right' man in the movie. These behaviors of "pop stars" appeal to the masses often much more than those of the intellectuals and leaders of the society. There is no wrong as long as the pop stars live as they preach, but the fact shows us not seldom quite the contrary. Nevertheless, we cannot replace them with the traditional moral preachers, not only because the latter is seldom morally better than the former nowadays, but also they do not simply appeal to the masses anymore, especially to the younger generation. Not a few intellectuals tend to reside in their own nest of knowledge, and ignore more or less the "ignorant" masses. And religious diversity of the day perplexes the masses not knowing what the "real" truth must be.

Despite all these problems, man needs a role model as before. We may need new stars who do not lead an irreconcilable life both in public and in private. The interactive mass media do not allow any more a hidden life of a public figure. That is why we are going to have much fewer heroes as before. Man is simply not perfect but he wants a perfect role model as much as his religious yearning leads to God. A new star as a role model has to be a "perfect" man, but that does not mean he has to be a saint, he has to be a sympathetic role model. A sympathetic role model is an interactive role model who can communicate with the masses with possibly the least problems. A sympathetic role model does not preach but discuss about the concerned matter with everybody else in the society. A sympathetic role model does not "show" before the masses, but he "does" something good for the society together with the masses. A sympathetic role model is not a leader of any kind, but a coworker. He can be a singer, actor, pastor, politician, and anybody else in the society because occupation does not matter. He can show his "bad" side, and just therefore he can be more acceptable for the masses. In our post-modern society of the Information Age, we may not need any more a martyr for the truth who leads a quite afloat life. A secularized world itself is not good, but a radical change of it does more harm than good for the masses. In fact radical change is technically not possible. When we cannot change the world in a day, we have to find a way to change it slowly and steadily. Not only the various national interests of many countries in the world but also the tangling conversation among many religions does hurt the multicultural understanding. In such a situation more sympathetic role model who is ready to communicate with anyone in the world can have more appeal to the masses.

Still, every possible form of open and latent indoctrination by the pop stars cannot be overestimated, and its danger lingers on. These pop stars of the mass media are mostly blamed for the "vulgar Western culture", which many Asians only see in them. A role model who is also sympathetic for the Asian cannot be fabricated. He can be there only through the open communication among the concerned people. Such a role model should not be any more a leader but a coworker among masses.

9.3 Interactive Ethos Mediation in the Information Age

The technological progress is still an on going process, therefore it is quite uncertain what will come in the end as its result. We even cannot anticipate if the technological progress itself will ever keep go on, but one thing is clear that the interactive mass media will change our society enormously. For a long time after the invention of computer many people did not quite understand what man with that machine can do. It has taken about 30 years before man begins to "work" with computer after the invention of it. Only after the invention of PC by Steve Jobs of Apple Computer in the early 1980s, people have begun to use computer as a helpful machine for "normal" life, not only for the scientists. After the invention of WWW by Tim Berners-Lee in CERN in 1989, it has taken not much years to provoke the attention of the people in the world to Internet. As PC, Internet changes rapidly the way of life of many people. The flow of information in Internet takes never a rest as much as the financial market of the world is always open. Everyday new domain names are logged on in Internet as the main way to know the other people in the world. The wall between people of the world melts down as it is getting smaller day by day. The vanishing barrier of time and space makes people in the world more ready to understand each other.

With Internet cultural isolation cannot be any more possible as long as man has to have contact with other cultures just for the survival of everyday life. This environment of Internet directly applied to the interactive mass media, as long as the technological progress can keep steps with the expectation of people. The ethos mediation by the masses with the interactive mass media alone can no more guarantee a fully mutual understanding than the small army of intellectuals in the past. Before the intercultural understanding can begin there must be an internal consensus building of the national identity. The cosmopolitanism has great danger of uniform understanding of the different cultures of the world. The coexistence of various cultures must be guaranteed lest there breaks a cultural war between different parts of the world.

The interactive ethos mediation is possible only when the communication is free from every possible kind of biases. The technological progress makes the world much smaller even though many of the masses are not ready for this new environment, therefore we need an active participation in the interactive communication which eventually leads to the mutual understanding among different cultures. The cultural isolationism based on the latent egoistic national interest does hurt this effort. A big influence of dominating foreign culture never conquers and totally annihilates other cultures however the latter is minor and insignificant. All cultures are interactive, i.e., they exert influences upon each other in every possible way. The Diaspora of the Jews is a good example. Even in a nation there are diverse sub-cultures as many as the dialects. A unified culture is a ghost like the demised communism, therefore the diversity of culture in a symbiotic environment is more appropriate to the reality of the world. Nationalistic cultural jingoism begets only prejudice against other cultures which leads not seldom to war.

Internet shows us the possibility of multicultural understanding with the interactive communication. Even if we use English as the main tool for the conversation in Internet, we should not fear of the "Americanization" of Internet, let alone of the whole mass media. Some people in many countries talk about cultural "Pan-Americanization" of the world after the political and economic domination of the world by the U.S.A., but such rallying word is more or less a total nonsense. The world is too big and diverse to be controlled by a country with one culture. More democratic and open conversation through the interactive mass media is a way of dismantling these kinds of prejudices.

Interactive ethos mediation is a pre-condition for the mutual understanding not the result of the latter. Mutual learning and understanding to each other culture, therefore, need an active participation of concerned parties. The technical difficulties stemming from the spatial-temporal distance can be overcome by the interactive mass media, but it will be of no use when there is no good will to communicate with each other.

10. The Initiation of Modern Confucian Society with Sympathy

10.1 Mutual Understanding under the Environment of Open Information

10.1.1 Intersubjective Understanding: Escape from the Special Group-Interest to the "Enlightened Self-Interest"

Before we can have an intercultural understanding among different societies, we need an intersubjective understanding among different individuals. Philosophically it is still a big problem how to be sure that other subjects have the same idea as mine. Even if the skepticism of the English Empiricism made the situation worse, the truth is clear that a skeptic has to eat and drink today to be a skeptic tomorrow again. A sound sleep does also good for a skeptic. Even a stringent skeptic cannot ignore this kind of "common sense" in the life world. This is the starting point where everybody can begin to communicate with each other with not many disputes.

As a matter of fact, mutual understanding presupposes always pre-knowledge about the counterparts. Knowledge alone cannot make people understand each other fully. We need a hermeneutic method when our experiences tell us that misunderstanding is much more probable than mutual understanding. Therefore man must do the art of avoiding the misunderstanding and promoting the communication.[287] As long as there are still many prejudices and stereotyped images of "others", a true communication cannot come into being so easily as we might hope.

In the modern Confucian society the intersubjective understanding is much less a simple problem because of the social intermingle of tradition and "new" cultures from the West. Since the "Opening to the West (開 港)" the clash between the traditional collectivism and the new individualism has created the awkward blend of group egoism. The traditional rivalry among family clans still lingers on. Most of all, the hierarchical social structure hinders the modern egalitarian spirit to be diffused. Invisible class system hinders the social mobility which could motivate people to exert their ability to the most in maximizing the social productivity. The non-communicability between the "leaders" and the "masses" sometimes results in a social disorder which has been witnessed by the people of the world not seldom. Individuality is sanctioned easily as an asocial idea even if it symbolizes the not reducible dignity of a person in the modern democratic society. The Confucian mentality which sees individual just as a part of the whole harmonious society cannot easily accept the egalitarian interactivity between individuals. There is only a unilateral understanding between "master"

---

[287] De Jong, Johan Marie, "Revolution in Marxismus und Christentum" in Zur Ethik der Revolution (Stuttgart: Kreuz-Verlag, 1970), p45

and "subject". If the "masters" of the society were true to the idea of the Ideal Man of Virtue (君子), there would be no problem, but actually there never has been a true Ideal Man of Virtue (君子) in the whole history of the Confucian society. To set an unattainable goal has driven people to be hypocritical, i.e., people in the Confucian society has been urged to be an Ideal Man of Virtue (君子) even if everybody already tacitly knew that it was impossible even for the direct followers of Confucius. This has resulted in double moral in the Confucian society. Even if the "leaders" already have known that they are not "perfect", they behave as if they were the ideal leader in the Confucian tradition, and the "masses" tend to follow them blindly because it is quite easier just to follow the pre-set path than to make one's own way against all odds. This blind following of the "masses" stops abruptly when the "leaders" are made known that they are not enough to be the true "leaders" of the society. Then, according to the idea of Mencius, they search a new leadership though the incumbent "leaders' resist it. This leads to social clash which is not seldom devastating for the masses.

In the modern democratic society, choosing a new leader is not so dramatic as before, but the traditional mentality of the "leaders" dies hard, as shown in Japan and China. The vast majority of "ignorant" masses should follow the "wise" leaders blindly, then everything will go well. But as the recent financial crisis has shown very well, the leaders not only make failure but also make themselves corrupt with the insatiable greed for material affluence as any other "ordinary" people in the society. Some government officers in Japan show their remorse with committing suicide when their wicked behaviors have been caught by the public, but that does not justify the moral of the leaders. In the tradition of Confucianism committing suicide is amount to the severest sin against parents called "the lack of filial duty" (不孝). Confucian society alone is not notorious for political corruption, but the "Confucian Puritanism" for the "leaders" expected by the "masses" is so strong that the "leaders" must behave hypocritical as if they were "pure" from all "seven emotions", which are strongly despised by the Confucian scholar-politicians themselves. To prevent this hypocrisy man needs to be true to the nature of man. To be true to the nature of man, mutual understanding between the "leaders" and the "masses" is needed. The idea of leaders as representative of the masses must be accepted as it is. For this purpose the active participation of the "masses" is necessary. When the "leaders" make failure, the "masses" should have communication with the "leaders", and the latter must seek wisdom from the "masses". The Confucian idea of the Ideal Man of Virtue (君子) does not fit any more to the modern society. It has been used rather as an excuse for the dictatorship of the "leaders". Everybody as individual with all his weaknesses, who needs therefore help from other, has to accept others as much individual as himself. Social harmony with the superficial hierarchical structure should be replaced by the mutual understanding and active participation. Periodic election alone cannot hinder political blunder of the "leaders". Only the continuous communication between all elements of the modern Confucian society will promote a new brave Confucian society. The old saying of Confucius: "speaking well and showing a smiling face has nothing to do with Jen (仁)"[288] should be interpreted not stopping communication with each other, but being faithful for each other in communicating. For many people in the modern Confucian society, silence is still cherished as an important virtue of the Ideal Man of Virtue (君子). This persistent prejudice about communication must yield to the idea of modern communication oriented society. Intersubjective understanding begins only with communication, not with the old teaching of sage.

10.1.2 Intercultural Understanding in the Globalized World

The West was a sudden shock for the traditional Confucian society in the 19th century. The aftermath of that shock still lingers today. Before the Asian countries could begin to understand the West, they have had to learn and model after the West in almost all aspect of the society. This "catch up" is still an ongoing process. There are quite a few success stories in the realm of applied technologies. Many kinds of consumer goods with quality are produced in the Asian countries and exported to the whole world. Nevertheless, modern democracy and capitalism are not so easy to be cultivated on the soil of Confucian tradition. Originally, the specter of the communism was in Europe.[289] Nevertheless, it devastated many Southeast Asian countries totally and they are still suffering under the quagmire of the aftermath of that specter. Modern democracy has been until recent just an annoyance for the Confucian educated political leaders. There are still many prisoners of conscience who are trying to practice the idea of democracy in Asia. Capitalism has been interpreted rather as a refined justification for the egoistic greed with no bound than an efficient economic system. The Asian countries have had just no time to look into the "root" of those Western cultures which has changed wholly the way of life for almost all Asians. Most of the Asian countries are just trying to "catch up" the visible affluence of the West, therefore understanding the West is still a far cry for them even if the understanding of the true Western culture is most needed especially now when there are the pervasive phenomena of loss of orientation in

---

[288] The Analects of Confucius (論語), chapter 1, 學而, 巧言令色鮮矣仁; Legge, James, Confucius, p 139

[289] Ein Gespenst geht um in Europa - das Gespenst des Kommunismus. Alle Mächte des alten Europa haben sich zu einer heiligen Hetzjagd gegen dies Gespenst verbündet, der Papst und der Zar, Metternich und Guizot, französische Radikale und deutsche Polizisten. – from the Manifest der Kommunistischen Partei by Karl Marx, Friedrich Engels in Internet, www.hss.cmu.edu

the whole Asian countries after the "Asian value" has failed.

It is well known that the European civilization owes much to the Judeo-Christianism. As a matter of fact, Jesus Christ was a Jew. But there were big misunderstanding between the European and the Jews from the early age. Even though they believe in the same God, their attitude for each other has never been of brothers and sisters for a long time. That shows well the difficulty of mutual understanding among cultures however they might be closely interwoven. The Jews still believe in the old conviction of their prophets. The Jewish prophets took their firm stand on two fundamental ideas: firstly, that there was a Covenant between God and His people Israel, and, secondly, that this Covenant bound the Israelites to a just relationship of one to the other. It will be recalled that the patriarchs, individually, had entered into the Covenant with God that they would worship Him alone and that He would protect them. This personal Covenant was broadened in the period of Moses, as a consequence of the Exodus from Egypt, so that the entire population of Israel became God's chosen people to recognize and serve Him as the only God in the world. This Covenant, it should be noted carefully, was voluntary on both sides. God elected Israel in His love and grace, and Israel freely undertook to carry out the will of God.[290] This very God loves not only the Jews but also the whole people in the world after the rise of the Christianism because the Evangelism is, as we well know, the good news of the liberation of all human beings in Jesus Christ.[291] But there has been standing misunderstanding about the meaning of the people whom God loves. For the Jews they are still the only people whom God truly loves, but for many Christians the Jews were the collective murderers of Jesus Christ, the only son of God. This misunderstanding has lasted about 2,000 years. Nowadays few believe that such a discrepancy about God's love could exist any more. In 1979 Jürgen Moltmann and Pinchas Lapide could write a book together, in which they put forward the basic difference between Judaism and Christianism in the fundamental theological dimension, and the result was the mutual appreciation of the two Covenants and the realization that they had validity independent from each other.[292] Many theologians in the South America believed Jesus Christ had identified himself with the poor, the humble, the oppressed, the sick, the weak, and sinners.[293] But, to tell the truth, Jesus Christ identified himself with all human beings because they are all sinners without a single exception. Misunderstanding begets always discrimination even among the people with the same origin of the cultural tradition.

---

[290] Orlinsky, Harry M., Ancient Israel (London: Cornell University Press, 1971), p 127

[291] Fragoso, Antonio, Evangelium und Soziale Revolution (Berlin: Bruckhardhaus Verlag, 1971), p 12

[292] Bernhard-Cohn, Emil, Von Kanaan nach Israel (München: Deutscher Taschenbuch Verlag GmbH & Co. KG, 1986), p 126

[293] Ibid., p 18

It is thus easy to assume that intercultural understanding among the people with quite different cultural origin and history may much harder. Nevertheless, as the modern technological progress makes the world much smaller everyday, it is inevitable that we are forced to understand each other. Especially for the Asians who try to "catch up" the West, knowing the West is still a matter of survival. Mastering at least one of the Western languages, mostly English, in school is almost a national duty, and understanding the Western culture is sine qua non for all Asian countries. Not only the Chinese but also even the North Koreans learn the language of the "enemy", English, very intensively. To survive the new world order, there is no other way for them at the moment even if opening the door wide to the Western culture is still a very precarious matter for most of the Asian countries. Not only the first unfortunate experience with the West in the 19th century, but also the apparent "vulgarity" of the popular culture of the West in the eyes of the Asians make them hesitate what and how to do with this matter.

In such a situation, it is more needed for the Asians to find out the "essence" of the Western culture. With the matter of evangelization of Asia many not favorable things were happened mostly by the lack of mutual understanding. Christianism is still one of the essences of the Western culture even if there was certain unfortunate past with religious matter, both in and out. Without consideration for the Christian idea of brotherly love, it is hard to understand the making of the modern Western society, which is as democratic and civic as possible at the moment. Freedom, equality and fraternity were not hallowing rallying words just for the French in the 18th century. The pursuit of happiness was declared not just for the people of the U.S.A. As long as most of the Asian countries are trying to "catch up" the West, and to be politically democratic and economically capitalistic, there is no better way than going back to the root of the West.

Neither indoctrination nor enculturation but mutual understanding is possible only when the concerned parties are ready to communicate with each other in the democratic forum of dialogue not monologue, let alone preach. The modern technology of interactive communication makes it possible for people in the world to understand each other truly. To be understood in Internet, man has to adjust himself to the unwritten law of communication, i.e., not only TCP/IP (Transmission Control Protocol/ Internet Protocol) but also hardware and software must be compatible with all members of Internet. In this cyberspace of communication the cultural differences among the netizen play minor role. Nowadays, to be understood and to understand with each other, everybody has to master not only English but also new idea which expressed with this language. With the technological progress an automatic translation system with the help of AI (Artificial Intelligence) will remove the language barrier. Until then, as the old Latin was for the Middle Ages, English will be for the Information Age of the day. This could be interpreted as another forced "Opening to the West (開港)" by the U.S.A., and some people in Asia is talking about the "Americanization" of Asia, but this is just the xenophobia which has driven some nationalistic Asian countries into the delayed "opening" and awkward development into the modern democratic country with not a few problems. To be understood by others, man needs to understand the others first. The repetition of the failure in the 19th century, which most of the Asian countries had made, can be avoided only when they are ready to understand first and correctly the new West.

10.2 Sympathy for the Accommodative Society

10.2.1 The Symbiosis of the Monadic Identities

The key interpreters of China on whom Leibniz relied were all missionaries, primarily of the Jesuit order. They were Frs. Matteo Ricci, Nichola Longobardi, Antoine de Sainte-Marie, Claudio Filippo Grimaldi, and Joachim Bouvet, of whom only the last two were contemporary to Leibniz. Much of the 16th century was marked by the failures of the Portuguese from their position at Macao and the Spaniards from the Philippines to establish a missionary and trade base on the Chinese mainland. When the first penetrations were made, the effort was dominated by Italian Jesuits who entered by way of the Jesuit bases in India and Macao.[294] Leibniz' understanding of China, therefore, had to be first influenced by these Italian Jesuits. However, his own understanding of Chinese philosophy, i.e., Confucianism, made him one of the prominent philosophers in Europe with the matter of intercultural understanding. It is true that Leibniz saw in the Chinese philosophy a natural theology quite different from that of Christianism.[295] We may need further study to find out how much influence of the Chinese philosophy had been there upon the philosophy of Leibniz. He took an example form the Foe, who was a founder of a great religious sect, by the explanation of the predetermined harmony (vorherbestimmte Harmonie) of God.[296] In his other book "Discourse on the Natural Theology of the Chinese", he cites seven Chinese texts : *Book of Changes (周易), Book of History (書經), Book of Odes (詩經), Analects (論語), Doctrine of the Mean (中庸), Compendium (性理大全書)* and *Comprehensive Mirror*. The *Compendium* — more fully, the *Great Compendium of Natural and Moral Philosophy (性理大全書 (Hsing-li ta-ch'uan shu))* — is cited most often by Leibniz. It

---
[294] Mungello David E., Leibniz and Confucianism, The Search for Accord (Honolulu: The University of Hawaii, 1977), p18
[295] A title of one of his book: "The Discourse on the Natural Theology in China" shows the fact well.
[296] Leibnitz, Gottfried Wilhelm, Theodicee (Berlin: Akademie Verlag GmbH, 1996), P 68

represents an anthology drawn from the Neo-Confucian school associated with the Sung dynasty (960-1280) philosophers Ch'eng I (I-ch'uan (伊川), 1033-1108) and Chu His (朱熹) (1130-1200) and symbolizes the Ch'eng-Chu (程朱) school of the *Hsing-li (性理)* (natural and moral, or more literally, human nature and principle) philosophy, from which the complete *Compendium* title derives. The work was compiled in 1415 under the direction of Hu Kuang (胡廣) (1370-1418) at the order of the Yung-lo Emperor(regime. 1402-1424).[297] Leibniz even tried to interpret the Book of Changes (易經) with his new binary system, but he never understood fully the meaning of the 64 hexagrams. For his eyes they were just a kind of superstition, but with the Book of Changes (易經) quite a few Confucians tried to explain not only the law of nature but also the vicissitude of human life. It was used to give rational explanation for all human affairs in everyday life. The school of the *Hsing-li* (性理) could not allow supernatural force or being to be the main cause of the human affairs, but tradition has won always in Confucianism.

The school of the *Hsing-li (性理)* had great influence to Korea during the Yi dynasty (1392-1910) and became the state ideology until the beginning of the colonial era by Japan. Its radical rationalism gave not much room for other "superstitious" thoughts. Buddhism was officially sanctioned in Korea under the Yi Dynasty. That was why Korea had the vacuum which could be easily filled with a new religion like Christianism. Japan had accepted also this so called Neo-Confucianism almost as a sole state ideology since the Tokugawa clan unified Japan as one country, but their religion of Shintoism survived and flourished parallel with it, and this religion has given the Japanese their distinctive identity. Despite the differences of applied Confucianism in each country, the rulers and their subjects were to be in a symbiotic relation in the spirit of Confucian harmonious society. The rulers were responsible for the well being of their subjects as much as the latter had to loyal to the former blindly. The hierarchical social structure was never meant to give the rulers rationale for oppressing the subjects in the spirit of Confucius, but in reality there were always inauspicious situations for both of them in the history of Confucian society.

Long after the "Opening to the West (開港)" the situation has never drastically changed even if the expectation of the "ordinary people (百姓)" for the equality was turned to the verge of explosion. Even if the material condition of the Confucian society could afford more or less some needs of the people, true civic freedom based on the equality in every respect has never been realized. Nevertheless, it is impossible to persuade a man to give up that idea, once he has found his identity as a not reducible person, i.e., an individual with human

---

[297] Mungello David E., Leibniz and Confucianism, The Search for Accord (Honolulu: The University of Hawaii, 1977)p 72

dignity, not only because it is a correct view, but also it pleases him who wants to be as free as he can be.

Freedom alone cannot guarantee the harmonious society as long as man has to live together with others. Man has to have his own realm which cannot be shared with others. The egoistic desire of man which is disguised as the individual freedom, must be ascertained and be sanctioned when we want to have a harmonious society where every member feels no sorry, or rather the least sorry. The pre-established harmony thanks to the God's Providence or the Will of Heaven (天 命) alone cannot guarantee the desired harmony in our secular society. The sense of responsibility for others in the society should be learned and practiced. As long as man cannot give up his own interest for that of others, there should be a way of coexistence of people in a given society.

The survival of a species does not wholly depend on the "struggle for existence" as Darwin had depicted in his book.[298] But it needs not seldom the cooperative relation among very different species, i.e., symbiosis. We may easily find many examples of symbiosis in nature: ants and aphids, hermit crabs and sea anemones, bees and flowers, and so on. There are even some examples of organic symbiosis which results in structural change of the organism itself. In certain cases, one of the organisms becomes a structural part of the organization of its partner (for example, the cytoplasmic inclusions of protists, Coelen-terata, Turbellaria and other zoochlorellae, zooxanthellae, kappa-particles [in *Paramecium*], and so forth). Finally, the ultimate stage of the synthesis of organisms includes associations that are bound so completely that it is possible to relate them to the various stages of the formation of a new complex organism, the life of which is regulated by a single physiological mechanism and facilitated by newly arising organs (for example, lichens). The revelation of a series of successive stages of transition from loose associations, the components of which are bound by community relations, to increasingly profound and closely connected associations and, later, to a union of biological systems into an organism with physiological bonds between the symbionts is the basis for (proposing) evolution by means of symbiosis (symbiogenesis).[299]

As we can see in the relation between ants and aphids, each involved symbiont has worked out special adaptations for such a relationship.[300] This kind of adaptation can be found not seldom in the human society too even if it does not function well as that of nature. A national country cannot exist on the meager patriotism of the people when there are little material benefits for them. An individual who has found his identity in the material condition of the world

---

[298] Darwin, Charles, The Origin of Species (1859), chapter III
[299] Khakhina, Liya Nikolaevna, Concepts of Symbiogenesis, A Historical and Critical Study of the Research of Russian Botanists, Stephanie Merkel, Robert Coalson (tr.) (New Haven: Yale University Press, 1992), p 11
[300] Ibid., p 10

cannot rely just on the "pre-established harmony between all substances" of Leibniz:

"*Diese Principia haben mir das Mittel an die Hand gegeben / wodurch man die Vereinigung oder Übereinstimmung der Seele mit dem Körper natürlicher Weise erklären kann. Die Seele folget ihren eigenen Gesetzen / und der Körper ebener gestalt denen seinigen; und beide treffen zusammen kraft der Harmonie / welche unter allen Substanzen voraus festgestellet ist /allermaßen sie durchgängig gewisse Abrisse von einerlei Welt-Gebäude sind.*"[301]

Even if there can be hardly found examples of the "pre-established harmony between all human beings", it is clear that we need a kind of symbiotic relation to which we have to adapt ourselves for the bare survival. This interdependence cannot be sustained without the mutual adaptation. This mutual adaptation presupposes the identity of man which is very individual enough for the existential decision for the survival. In the modern society every individual is a singular monad in his own.[302]

The harmony between man in the modern Confucian society cannot be given from heaven for nothing, let alone from the predestined (greater) harmony alone. It must be made by the efforts of all members of the society. Relying neither on the pre-established (greater) harmony, nor on the pre-fixed hierarchical structure. Making a harmonious society together is only for the people of enlightened self-interest. Saintly giving up oneself, and furthermore, sacrificing oneself for other is hardly acceptable for the modern Confucian society even if this is quite modernized by the Western culture which is very strongly characterized by Christianism. Disintegrated monadic individual from the traditional Confucian ethos of self-sacrifice for family or king, which still cannot find its substitute should see the chance in the Christian fraternal love expressed as sympathy for others. This is not a self-sacrificing love but the spirit of symbiotic "live together" of monadic individuals. Sharing with others without the loss of one's identity is more plausible for the people in the modern Confucian society where

---

[301] Leibniz, Gottfried Wilhelm, Monadologie (Frankfurt a. M.: Insel Verlag, 1996), p 61

[302] Ibid., p 9 Leibniz's monad presupposes the total harmony between the kingdom of God's Grace and that of nature, but the word itself has more or less neutral meaning as he himself explained: "*Das Worte Monade oder Monas, hat bekannter maßen seinen Ursprung aus dem Griechischen, und bedeutet eigentlich Eines. Man hat das Wort behalten, weil man vornehme Gelehrte zu Vorgänger hat, die die Kunst-Wörter der Kürze wegen behalten und mit einer teutschen Endigung nach der Gewohnheit der Engelländer und Franzosen gleichsam naturalisieren. Wenn man die Worte Serenaden, Cantaten, Elemente und dergleichen unzählige mehr in der teutschen Sprache beibehält, ohngeachtet es frembde Wörter sind: so habe ich geglaubet, daß es nicht inconvenient gehandelt sei, wenn ich mich um der Kürze willen des Worts, Monade, und anderer dergleichen Kunst-Wörter bediente. Viele Dinge scheinen Anfangs ungereimet, weil sie noch nicht gewöhnlich sind; ich halte aber davon, daß das ungewöhnliche, wenn es eine vernünftige Ursache zum Grunde hat, nicht für ungereimt könne gehalten werden.*"

pragmatic rationalism is cherished.

10.2.2 The Harmonious Society as the Extended Confucian Family

It is quite natural that man loves whom he can and wants to love. We cannot force a man to love his enemies as long as he cannot help hating them in his true mind. We may love our enemies with the help of Divine Providence, but not all men are so fortunate to have such help, especially in a very secular society which we have now. We need a little bit mundane way of loving our neighbors in our society. Even the villains of the society tend to love their mother. This natural tendency of man is the basis of the Confucian moral system. When a man can see the filial duty (孝 道) as in the human nature embedded virtue, it can be extended for other family members as the form of brotherly love, for elders in a community as respect, for friend as friendship, and for the king as loyalty. This gradual extension of the filial duty (孝 道) is characteristic for the Confucianism which is well clarified in the Great Teaching (大 學):

"Man has to first be a self- disciplined before he becomes a father of family. Man has to be a good father before he becomes a king. Man has to be a good king before he becomes the Emperor of the world."[303]

Even if the modern Confucian society has lost much of its traditional Confucian character, the filial duty (孝 道) still prevails. The traditional family unity plays still great role in the modern Confucian society, especially among the Diaspora of Chinese in the whole world. In the Southeast Asian countries the Chinese could make their tremendous fortune with their extended family clans. This community as an extended Confucian family which is consisted not seldom of traditional 9 degrees of family kinship, promotes nepotism and tends to be cliquish. This hinders the progress and harmony of the modern Confucian society which is to be exposed to the world inevitably. The fierce protectionism of many Asian countries is destined to be obsolete as the globalization proceeds incessantly. There is a great danger of the global aphasia to the country which stick to the idea of isolationism. We can see a good example of this national neurological disorder in North Korea.

The "Opening to the West (開 港)" was really a great shock then to most of the Asian countries. Nevertheless, seclusion must have been much worse for the national interest for them. Only very shrewd Japan could successfully overcome the dangerous aftermath of the "Opening to the West (開 港)". Even this Japan still needs more widen door to the world to be a truly globalized nation. The ethos of a society as an extended family still prevails not only in Japan but also in other Asian countries, but this should be adaptable to the changing

---

[303] The Great Teaching, chapter 1, 經 文, ...修 身 以 後 齊 家 齊 家 以 後 國 治 國 治 以 後 天 下 平..; Legge, James, Confucius, p 359

environment, or it will be just another kind of seclusion. Formal flexibility can hardly win over the substantial one, therefore the concept of the Confucian family must be changed not only in its form but also in its meaning. Not the hierarchical formal structure of family but the identity building function of family should survive the changing environment.

The Confucian society is to be an extended Confucian family as a place of symbiotic cooperation where the interactive communication prevails, not a military camp where only the superior has the right to tell what to do. Every member of family must have his or her tentative function which should be not pre-destined but flexible one. The ethos of the new extended Confucian family could prevent the solitary individual in the modern society who could seldom find his or her place and peace in the society. In the inner circle of family man can find his place and his identity. Modern individualism harnessed by the social sanction alone could not guarantee the quality of life which demands not only the material affluence but also the mutual emotional gratitude. That is why the virtue of the traditional Confucian family should be still cherished. A Confucian family with the mechanism of consensus building through the interactive communication should be flexible enough to survive the harsh condition of the day because not adaptable virtue of tradition just hinders the progress of society in the changing environment.

10.3 "Symbiotic Society" with the Interactive Communication of Masses

10.3.1 Communicable Identity Building as the Prerequisite for Mutual Understanding

Man is not an island, he has to live with others. To live together means to have communication with others. To be able to communicate with others, man has to learn to express oneself and to understand what others express themselves. It is clear that the identity of a man has two sides: inside and outside, which was expressed respectively as "I" and "me" by George Herbert Mead.[304] When there is too great discrepancy between "I" and "me", it will cause problem as it used to happen between "superego" and "ego" of Sigmund Freud. Before man learn to be able to communicate with others, man has to learn first to communicate with himself. It is quite natural to assume that man understands others better when he understands himself good. After the "death of God" man has problem to find his identity by himself. Neither the biochemical explanation, nor the neurobiological explanation about man can give enough clues to know what man is.

A communicable identity means an identity ready to build a consensus with

---

[304] Refer to his book: Geist, Identitaet und Gesellschaft, Frankfurt, 1968

other. How much the Rawlsian "overlapping consensus" can be build is not yet quite clear but it is already there as long as man has to live together. In the traditional Confucian society, the identity of man was predestined, so there was no room for the building of "individual" identity. Adapting oneself to the given paradigm with reference to the examples of the good old sages was the only "given" way of identity building. This pre-formed identity could be relatively well functioned in the pre-fixed society of hierarchical structure. With the beginning of the new era after the "Opening to the West (開 港)" this has become just an obsolete image of oneself. Before, when the social mobility between different classes was neither needed nor possible, it was enough to be able to have a free way for the peer to peer communication. In the modern democratic society where every possible interest group tries to get the most from the given environment, misunderstanding and enhancing hostility stemming from the lack of communication hurt social integration most. An identity must be communicable with each other from the beginning. Socialization is just a way of adaptation, therefore it could not prevent the social delinquency. Uniformity can never guarantee a true harmonious society, as we witnessed the frenzy of fascism in the 1930s and the 1940s in Europe.

Only an identity built on the basis of self-determination can be responsible for the communication which is to be an interactive one for the democratic society building. It is not easy to eradicate the traditional idea of the Ideal Man of Virtue (君 子) who knows everything, makes no failure, and therefore needs not a single piece of advice from others. Accepting others as oneself is difficult, but accepting oneself as others is much more difficult for the Confucian minded Ideal Man of Virtue (君 子). The "elite" of the modern Confucian society find their identities still in the old idea of this perfect man. That leads not seldom to the dictatorship of oligarchy. This small army of "elite" does their job well when other variables in the society are favorable for them, i.e., when there are no unexpected, or at least manageable changes. In reality, in the Information Age with the rash globalization there is no expected change. The mobilization of total idea from all members of society is needed to survive the new Information Age. Depending on the "elite" was a necessary measure in the period of "Spring and Autumn Warring States (春 秋 戰 國 , 722-221 BC)" in Chinese history when Confucius and all other learned of the period "Hundred Philosophers (諸 子 百 家, 551-233 BC) " tried to find the best way for the ideal society, while the common people waited for the Son of Heaven who must be the Ideal Man of Virtue (君 子) in vain with all their agonies for a long time.

This idea of "elitism" has to be replaced by one of the modern democratic ideas, i.e., freedom (more than liberty), equality and fraternity. Everybody has his own identity which is to be respected as any other. Before Christian God there is no difference among people as creatures. This idea of fraternity must be applied to the identity building even if it is foreign to the Confucian society when all the modern Confucian countries will survive the new brave age. How this could be practiced is quite a matter of discussion, and therefore man needs all the more the democratic communication to find a social consensus about that matter.

10.3.2 The Open Consensus Built for the Just Mutual Understanding

Democracy should not mean a simple dictatorship of the majority. There must be always a willing consent from the minority. That is why we need open consensus which is based on the open communication. Democracy as the modern political system is both new and foreign for most of the Asians in the Confucian society, therefore there are many misuses and even abuses of it. The Confucian aristocracy of the learned does not allow any participation of the masses. Even if Mencius himself stressed the importance of the ordinary people, he never meant that the latter should decide the important political affair.[305] Therefore, it is a little bit exaggerated when we are to talk about Confucian democratic tradition. It is easy to understand that the oppressed ordinary people in the traditional Confucian society try to find their just place in the modern democracy. As a matter of fact, the modern Western democracy is more or less the result of the interest conflict among the elements of the society. Whenever there was a clash of interest among people in the society, it was more conflict than conversation what came first. After the bitter experiences of social disorder, all concerned parties learned to make compromise. Here persuasion played an important role which could not be regarded as true communication for the democratic consensus building.

A communication is, first of all, for mutual understanding, not for persuasion. A persuasion, let alone a compromise, does not guarantee the open consensus which is the opposite to the forced consensus, and which is the basis of the democratic world of globalization. Many different opinions can be parallel coexist in the society of open consensus. Understanding, and furthermore, accepting others, which have quite different opinion about the society, world, and even God from one's own, should not mean compromise. A compromise comes into being when the concerned parties give up some of their interest tentatively. We see many political or commercial compromises which are nominally based on the mutual understanding, but in reality, it cannot be established unless the concerned parties are ready to give up some of their interest which can come up anytime as a new theme for the negotiation. It can never be a mutual understanding but just a postponed interest conflict because persuasion is another case of forced consensus. Man must give up at least part of

---

[305] The Book of Mencius, chapter 14, 盡心章句下 民爲貴 ... ; Legge, James, Mencius , p 483

his old opinion or belief to be persuaded. This old opinion which is often branded as prejudice stemmed from the ignorance, cannot be discarded as wrong before it is scrutinized and verified in the light of the ever lasting truth, but in the postmodern society where almost all established truths are open to the discussion, man cannot easily identify the truth. Especially the cosmological truth about the universe is totally open to the future. Every new astronomical discovery forces man to correct the "old truths" about the universe. The new quantum-physical knowledge does have the same effect. Every new found particle and its relation to others, i.e., forces, force us to rethink about the nature of matter, and furthermore of the world in which we live. Nowadays, the law of uncertainty is applied not exclusively to the realm of quantum physics, but to the life world of man.

Notwithstanding the brilliant progress of the neurobiological understanding of the human nature, man still does not know who he himself is. The consciousness and the self-consciousness of man, in which all human knowledge, feeling, and will reside, are not just a bundle of billions of human brain cells. To make the problem more complicated, the human consciousness is private. As long as the consciousness stays in the realm of private, man cannot understand it because man can understand only what is objectified. The etymological meaning of person betrays the secret of the human nature.

Persona, the etymological root of person, means mask, through which comes the voice of the concerned man. We can begin to understand the other person only with the voice coming through the mask. Everybody behaves more or less in the same way, but that does not mean that everybody must have the same consciousness. All men are different from each other, not only because the combinations of their genes are unique, but also their peculiar consciousness is never reducible. Nobody has met the same man as oneself in every respect. Men must be respected not because they are the same but because they are different. By the same token, man must first try to understand others because others are not the same as himself. Apology is good to make oneself to be understood by others, but asking first is better to understand others. As mentioned above, man can understand only the objectified matter, and to make oneself an object is much harder to see others as object. Man can know and understand better about himself by knowing and understanding from others what others know and understand about him.

It is clear that man can communicate with each other because man has similarity in many respects. Not just the physiological but the psychological similarity between men cannot be denied. On the basis of this similarity, man can begin to approach other man to communicate and to understand, which might be extremely difficult job, for example, with chimpanzee, which has 95 % of the human genes.

All men are same only on some conditions. Men are same as the creature of

God. All men are equal before the law, in that all are subject to punishment unless they observe it. But without predication, all men are yet different, therefore we still need a consensus which must be not coerced one. As John Rawls once said, an overlapping consensus, therefore, is not merely a consensus on accepting certain authorities, or on complying with certain institutional arrangements, founded on a convergence of self- or group interests. All those who affirm the political conception start from within their own comprehensive view and draw on the religious, philosophical, and moral grounds it provides.[306] And this overlapping consensus consists of all the reasonable opposing religious, philosophical, and moral doctrines likely to persist over generations and to gain a sizable body of adherents in a more or less just constitutional regime, a regime in which the criterion of justice is that political conception itself.[307] Even though there are many controversies about the essence of justice, it is still correct that each person is to have an equal right to the most extensive total system of equal basic liberties compatible with a similar system of liberty for all.[308] To be treated as a person is not a result of compromise but a natural right, or at least, rationally considered to be right. The concept of overlapping consensus may be the starting point of open consensus. To ascertain how much is overlapped, people have to approach to each other open, without the influence of outer coercion, i.e., people have to make a voluntary move to each other. As well known, the will enhances the sense of responsibility in the end. When people can approach to each other with the sense of responsibility, it could be the ideal condition for the mutual understanding.

10.4 The Harmonious Society without the Confucian Hierarchy

Leonard Shihlien Hsü talked about the Confucian philosophy of democracy in his book.[309] But it is, once again, very difficult to accept that Confucianism has an ethos of democracy, especially that of modern democracy. The people of the Confucian society were more or less the followers of the good rulers at best, according to the teaching of Confucius himself. In the history of all Confucian countries in East Asia, there has never been a civic revolution against the rulers. Every protest against the rulers was regarded as revolt. Only the learned and the royal subjects could lead revolution against the corrupt king or Emperor, with the justification of Mencius. In spite of the intellectual tendency towards egalitarianism during the late Ming dynasty in China, Confucian society was

---

[306] Rawls, John, Political Liberalism (New York, NY: Columbia University Press, 1993), p 147
[307] Ibid., p15
[308] Rawls, John, A Theory of Justice (Cambridge, MA: Harvard Press, 1971), p302
[309] Hsü, Leonard Shihlien, The Political Philosophy of Confucianism (London: Curzon Press,1932), p174

still based on a moral code both hierarchical and differential.[310] Therefore, It cannot be denied that the traditional Confucian society has had a kind of oligarchic political system, which had the Emperor at the center and the learned around him, who were simultaneously scholars and professional politicians. Almost all pupils of Confucius and Mencius were the ambitious scholars who had the aim to be a highly ranked politician. Even Confucius and Mencius did their best to be a political celebrity in any land which would accept them. They never tried to build a new ideal society by themselves, like Plato in ancient Greece. They just tried to make the already established sociopolitical entity better meaning the revival of the ideal old society that is minutely depicted in the Book of Book (書 經). There is no room for the individual creativity in this situation. Every new idea must be stifled in the hierarchical structure of the whole society. Change means revolt unless it aims the old institution of the ideal Confucian society where the small group of the learned help the rulers to be a philosopher-king.

That is why the sociopolitical change in the traditional Confucian society has been extremely difficult. When something does not go well, man has to just refer to the old way described in the sacred books of Confucianism. This paradigm had survived well until the traditional Confucian society had to open itself to the more powerful West, because both the well organized sociopolitical system and the Confucian education were aimed to indoctrinate the idea of Confucianism, which was the amalgam of political ideology and moral theory.

The individualism which came with the "Opening to the West (開 港)" forced the ordinary people to rethink about their social identity. Until then, the identity of a person could not be thought without the hierarchically structured Confucian society. Every possible ideal relation, which a person might have in his life, was from the beginning predetermined. Every relation of oneself to all sociopolitical elements was explained by Confucius and Mencius too minutely.

In the traditional Confucian society, an individual did not exist, but functioned just as a part of the organic society. In this society, responsibility meant more of less conformity to the given paradigm of hierarchical sociopolitical structure. There was no room for the sovereign determination by the freedom of will. This was the most important hindrance for the social development. As the modern secular society shows, any prefabricated social system cannot be sustained without the voluntary consent of the individual. A good example is the fall of the communistic system. Without the true consent of the people, for the coercion of the consent from the people, most of the communistic countries needed a vast bureaucracy which eventually has had to collapse under its overweight. The rulers of the traditional Confucian society had to see the same destiny. The idea

---

[310] Yang, Hohn D., Confucianism and Christianity (Hong Kong: Hong Kong University Press, 1983), p 72

of the Confucian harmonious society was good in itself. The philosopher-king as the Ideal Man of Virtue (君 子) stays at the center of the society like the North Pole, and everyone else around him keeps his position like the stars in the sky, and then there is an everlasting harmony in the society as in the universe. But the North Pole is not the center of the universe, but just one of millions and billions stars of the universe. And the universe is not in a static state but in an incessant vicissitude. A harmony does not mean anymore an eternal repetition of the old "perfect" system, but an approach to the equilibrium in motion, as the new understanding of the universe tells us very well. After the Big Bang, the materialized energy gathers to be a star. This star explodes when it cannot emit energy anymore, and becomes material for other stars in the universe. Not a single star stays in a spatiotempoally fixed point in the universe. Even the black hole which is in a situation where no time flows, attracts other materials in the universe with its great gravity and becomes heavier. By the same token, a man in the modern secular society cannot stay where he is now as the society changes continuously. The fixed harmonious society of the traditional Confucian thought is obsolete. It even hinders the harmony of the modern secular society. The system must be changed as man changes, but man cannot be sure of his change without the right criterion. That is why we still have to refer to the old, even obsolete, system when we want to find the new system. We have to learn from the failures of the past to know the right way in the future. The Confucian hierarchical sociopolitical system was wrong because it could not care much to induce the voluntary consent of the individual on the basis of the freedom of will. However, it had its merit because it saw the society as a big family where nobody must be ignored as a human being on the basis of humanism.

11. Epilogue : Love in Jen and Jen in Love

Confucian Jen (仁) is Confucian Jen (仁), and Christian love is Christian love. We cannot say that the Jen (仁) is in its essence the love, or vice versa. Nevertheless, we may find in them an overlapping consensus of Rawls as far as they have sympathy as their common beginning moment, which develops fully in their respective ways. When there is a common ground, communication between them can beginn. By means of communication man can begin to understand mutually. Communicability does not have to mean the identity lost, on the contrary, an identity manifests itself more distinctively when it is situated under foreign environments. As Christian love can find its identity more clearly in the Confucian society, Jen (仁) could find itself distinctively in the Christian society.

At the end of the second article of the "DECLARATION ON THE

RELATION OF THE CHURCH TO NON-CHRISTIAN RELIGIONS (*NOSTRA AETATE*)" proclaimed by His Holiness Pope Paul VI on October 28, 1965, the catholic church urges her sons to be friendly to other religions :
The Church, therefore, exhorts her sons, that through dialogue and collaboration with the followers of other religions, carried out with prudence and love and in witness to the Christian faith and life, they recognize, preserve and promote the good things, spiritual and moral, as well as the socio-cultural values found among these men.[311]

There is overdue need of communication between religions.

Even though there is no mention about Confucianism in this declaration, it is clearly mentioned that through inter-religious, and furthermore, through intercultural dialogue we have to learn to treat others as brothers and sisters created in the image of God. Both relations of man to God and to his fellow human beings are overlapping in himself, as the Scripture says: "*He who does not love does not know God*" (1 John 4:8), or we cannot truly call on God, the Father of all.[312] The communication between God and fellow human beings can be facilitated only by the loving man as a mediator of them. In the end, love itself mediates them, but in reality man is the only mediator of love between God and himself.

It is clear that Christianism is needed for the modern Confucian society to understand the globalized world because the latter lacks still such ideas as fraternal love and individual freedom. The God of Christianism guarantees His believer the promised land, and they can live in this harmonious land as brothers and sisters, but it is absurd to presume that God had had no concern for the people who never knew Him, let alone those who believed not in Him until Christianism was introduced to them. There have existed already many gods who cared for the well-being of "gentiles". There have been non-theological moral theories too which served for the harmony of society. As long as they are for the well-being and harmony of man, they cannot be refuted just as superstitious or even false ideas. When we look into them, we may find a common ground from which we can begin to understand each other.

It is extremely difficult to introduce, and to diffuse a foreign culture or norm in a society where there is already a very strong social paradigm which is based on the very long tradition of highly sophisticated religion or philosophy. Christianity has been the sole state religion in the West for more than 1,600 years, and it still has great influence on about one fourth of the world population. Confucianism has been the single sociopolitical system in all East and Southeast Asian countries for more than 2,000 years. It still has a tacit influence on about one fourth of the world population. There was Tang Dynasty in the history of

---

[311] from the website of http://www.vatican.va in the Internet
[312] Ibid.

China when Buddhism was the state religion, but the sociopolitical system was never changed. It was always Confucian. Japan's state religion is said to be Buddhism, but her society itself is strongly Confucian. In other Asian countries, the situation is not quite different. Even in Indonesia where Islam is the state religion, political culture and family structure are very Confucian.

Confucianism has its own religious ritual and priest. In a family father is the priest, and in a nation the supreme political leader is the priest even if there is neither well organized professional priesthood, nor great temples. That is why many think that Confucianism is not religion. But Confucianism is more than a religion. It is a comprehensive cultural phenomenon in East and Southeast Asian countries as much as Christianity is for the West. We may talk about the cultural clash between these two great religions as some scholars insist. Such a cultural clash happens when there is not enough communication between them. When man understands others through sympathetic communication, he may find not seldom that the other party has even something helpful for himself.

In this way, it can be shown that Christianity can be rather complementary for the modern Confucian society. Too stringent hierarchical formality in society hinders flexibility, which has helped Confucianism to survive for a long time. The family oriented teaching of Confucius is abused as the excuse for cronyism, which hinders the sound socioeconomic development. In a rapidly changing and globalizing world, social rigidity and cronyism function anything but positive. Even if the modern Confucian society needs change, totally discarding the traditional culture to adopt new one is just nonsense. As Confucius interpreted traditional teachings in a new light for his contemporary, the modern Confucian society must reexamine the tradition and restructure itself with the help of foreign culture.

Confucianism is human with its spirit of Jen (仁). Nobody must be excluded from the social net of care, but that does not directly mean the fraternity of all mankind. Father is father, and son is son. Children must do the filial duty (孝道) for their parents, and the latter must be affectionate to the former. Man and wife have to show their respect to each other. There must be faith between friends. Subjects must loyal to their King, and the latter must protect the former. All these are various faces of Confucian humanism manifested in the hierarchically structured society, which is principally based on the good nature of man. Confucius did not want to talk about God or death, not because he did not believe such things, but because he had to concentrate himself first on living human beings in this world. He just made a phenomenological ἐποχή on the matters of God and death. Without the idea of individual freedom, a human society could stand in the old ideal Confucian society, but once the never reducible identity of individual is found and cherished, and its dignity as a person on the basis of freedom given by God, a open society cannot stand only with its well-framed structure any more. It needs the voluntary participation of individuals with freedom. In the new Age of Information the reciprocal open relation between society and individual is not only for political stability but also for the bare survival of all human beings because individual creativity, which can be optimized only in an open society, is the main engine of the socioeconomic progress of the day. Modern Confucian society must be able to survive without great dependence on the traditional hierarchical sociopolitical structure. For this purpose, it is needed to reinterpret the Confucian humanism in the light of Christian love.

We may say that we have seen the Christian humanism in Confucianism, and vice versa, with the postulation of universality of humanism, regardless of cultural differences. Christian love bases on Christian God, but there is no God in Confucianism. When there is no matching partner, there is great difficulty for intercultural understanding. That is why we need a mediator. A mediator is neutral as far as it can find the overlapping consensus from both parties. Nevertheless, absolute neutrality cannot be guaranteed as long as this mediator should come from a distinct environment, be an individual who has his own personal history as a not reducible person. That is why we may need a cyberspace for this mediation, which cannot be seen but exist "there".[313] In this space we can tentatively agree with each other that we might have a common ground for the mutual understanding. It is not finding what is hidden there, but working together to make it visible and believable. It is different from persuasion because it is cooperation, not one-sided exhortation. Two parties do not stand against each other, but look into the space, which they believe it is there, and try to find out what they can understand from it. It does not matter here whether they have different interpretation about what they see. They have seen the same thing in this space, and this is the beginning of communication and mutual understanding. In this way neither party is the object to be observed,

---

[313] This word of cyberspace was first used by William Gibson, a science-fiction writer, in his book, *Neuromancer*(1984). He saw the players in the video arcades on Vancouver, Canada who were hunched over their glowing screens, as he was wandering past that block. He could see in the physical intensity of their postures how *rapt* the kids were. those kids clearly *believed* in the space the games projected. That image haunted Gibson. He didn't know much about computers – he wrote his breakthrough novel, *Neuromancer,* on an ancient manual typewriter-but as near as he could tell, everybody who worked much with the machines eventually came to accept, almost as an article of faith, the reality of that imaginary realm. He said that they developed a belief that there's some kind of *actual space* behind the screen, some place that they couldn't see but they knew it was there. Gibson called that place "cyberspace." In the years since, there have been other names given to that shadowy space where our computer data reside: the Net, the Web, the Cloud, the Information Superhighway. But Gibson's coinage may prove the most enduring. In 1989 it had been borrowed to describe not some science-fiction fantasy but today's increasingly interconnected computer systems – especially the millions of computers jacked into the Internet. - Main sources from the Web Site of www.internetvally.com

but they are just two independent subjects, which can preserve their identities all through this cooperation.

What can Christianity learn from Confucianism? Confucianism is not just the obsolete residue of past. Readiness to accommodate foreign culture, flexibility and perseverance for compromise are the well-known characters of Confucianism. Not forced but open consensus from mutual acceptance is the key factor for peaceful coexistence in the future when the traditional international boundary cannot exist any more and the individual creativity plays the major role. Regional egoism in the name of false nationalism or fake religious piety does not guarantee any more the interest of people in the globalized world. It creates just a new kind of isolationism, which should mean underdevelopment in the end. In the past, when someone was right, it meant his opponent was wrong. In this situation, the truth is either this or that, there could be no compromise. At best there could be the forced consensus, which was not true consensus because it was either from the force of the stronger over the weaker, or from the manipulation of the ignorant by the learned. In the new democratic society where not uniformity but individuality is cherished, the truth may have multiform. It is clear there must be one truth, but as long as we cannot persuade everyone about it, we can make a phenomenological ἐποχή until we have a favorable spatiotemporal environment for the open consensus of the truth in the future.

We have seen many cases of forced consensus, which was formed just from a false ideology in the disguise of the absolute truth, in the history. When one truthful party should annihilate the other party, which has also dignity and freedom, the former cannot be any more the defender of absolute truth. Not the forced consensus but the coexistence of differences is the true democracy. Only when a society can accommodate the differences of individuals, it can be a society with future in the age of information.

There may be the danger of relativism. But we can avoid this when we look into the essence through the thicket of accidents. That is why we need the phenomenological reduction. As a matter of fact, all people live in this world already with an attitude of phenomenological ἐποχή. We may take a simple example of paper on which we write something. What is a paper? It is out of wood pulp. The wood pulp is out of many vegetable cells. A cell is composed of the elements, which are of 103 sorts. An element is composed of some neutrons, protons, and electrons, which are called particles. A particle is composed of quarks, which are some units of energy in a certain spatiotemporal moment. We still do not know of what a quark is composed, but one thing is clear that a quark is a unit of energy, which has no concrete form. In the end, every matter in our world is just the condensation of energy, but we cannot say that a paper is just the lump of formless energy. We can touch the paper, and write on it something, and send it as a letter of important information. A paper is both a concrete matter and a formless energy. We do not know what the truth of a paper is, not only because we cannot define what it is with our limited language, but also because we do really not know what it is. To define what a paper is as difficult as to define what God is. Nevertheless, we are using it as a paper with not many problems in our world because we have made a latent phenomenological ἐποχή about it. We can use a paper with the phenomenological ἐποχή without the danger of negating its existence, even though we do not know what it is.

We can use the same phenomenological ἐποχή about Christian love and Confucian Jen (仁). Even if we cannot have universal definitions about these two concepts, we can use them as describing the essence of these two religions respectively, as we can use the paper even if we cannot define what it is. We can see as much phenomena of sympathy in Christian love as in Confucian Jen (仁). We cannot know whether these phenomena of sympathy are same or quite different in both religions. All we know is that they are there. Like the cyberspace, they are in some place that we cannot see but we know they are there. In this way we can begin to communicate with each other about sympathy, and furthermore, about Christian love and Confucian Jen (仁). When we have to define first exactly what they are before we begin to talk about them, we will never have the chance for it.

For this purpose the interactive mass media are the ideal medium. With this open medium we may begin to have the open communication of the intercultural understanding. We need communication nowadays all the more because we have to fight against our selves even if we are in the nominally "civilized" world. As Freud once told to a reporter, mankind has never been so far removed from either barbarism or animals as it might like to think.[314] We have to tame this inner "barbarian" if we want to live in a truly civilized world with others. If others must be hell for my ostensibly peaceful life, the problem is mostly not others but "I", which still cannot be so civilized to accept others as fellow human beings. The philosophical intellectualism has many flaws but intellectual enlightenment can be the only rational method which is found by mankind. Not only the enlightened self-interest but also the enlightened rationalism might be employed still well for the better mutual understanding between different cultures.

---

[314] TIME,1930s Highlights, MEDICINE, Intellectual Provocateur, June 26, 1939 in TIME Almanac of the 20th Century (TIME, Inc. Magazine Company, 1994)

Bibliography

- Bibles

Ellinger, K., Rudolph, W. (ed.), Biblia Hebraica Stuttgartensia (Stuttgart, Germany: Deutsche Bibelgesellschaft, 1990)
Nestle-Aland, Novum Testamentum, Graece et Latine (Stuttgart, Germany: Deutsche Bibelgesellschaft, 1991)
Timnathserah Inc., Online Bible (Ver. 7.05/ Win32) (Winterbourne, Canada: Timnathserah Inc., 1998), downloaded from the website of www.OnlineBible.org and installed under Microsoft Windows 98, last updated in April 16. 1998

- Chinese Classics

Han, Sang-Gab (tr.), The Book of Mencius & The Great Learning (Seoul, Korea: Sam-Seong Publishing Co., Ltd., 1986)
Lee, Ga-Won (tr. & ed.), The Book of Mencius (Seoul, Korea: Hong-Shin-Sa, 1994)
Legge, James (tr. & ed.), Confucius : Confucian Analects, The Great Learning & The Doctrine of the Mean (New York: Dover Publications, Inc., 1971)
Legge, James (tr. & ed.), The Works of Mencius (New York: Dover Publications, Inc., 1970)
Mordhashi, Tetsuji, Great Chinese-Japanese Dictionary, Bk. 4 (Tokyo, Japan: Taishukan Publishing Co. Ltd., 1984)
Moritz, Ralf, Konfuzius: Gespräche(Lun-yu) (Stuttgart: Philipp Reclam jun., 1998)
Ritsema, Rudolf (tr.), I Ching : The Classic Chinese Oracle of Change, The Divinatory Texts with Concordance (Shaftesbury, Dorset, GB: Element Books Ltd., 1994)
Ryu, Jung-Gi (tr. & ed.), The Four Books and the Three Classics: The Great Leaning, The Doctrine of the Mean, The Analects of Confucius, The Book of Mencius, The Book of Odes, The Canon of History, I Ching: The Book of Change (Seoul, Korea: Myung Moon Dang, 1994)

- Books and Articles

Aristotle, Metaphysica, W.D. Ross(tr.) (New York: Random House,1982)
Aristotle, Nichomachean Ethics, (Tr. David Ross) (Oxford: Oxford University Press,1980)
Barth, Karl, "Von der Göttlichkeit und Menschlichkeit Gottes", in Die

Theologie des 20. Jahrhunderts, Karl-Josef Kuschel(ed.) (München:R. Piper GmbH & Co. KG, 1986)
Bentham, Jeremy, "Constitutional Code", vol. I, in The Collected Works of Jeremy Bentham, J.R. Dinwiddy(ed.) (Oxford: Clarendon Press, 1984)
Bernhard-Cohn, Emil, Von Kanaan nach Israel (München: Deutscher Taschenbuch Verlag GmbH & Co. KG, 1986)
Bloch, Ernst, Naturrecht und menschliche Würde (Frankfurt a. M. : Suhrkamp, 1985)
Brink, David O., "Rawlsian Constructivism in Moral Theory" in Equality and Liberty, J. Angelo Corett(ed.) (London: Macmillam, 1991)
Ching, Julia, Konfuzianismus und Christentum, Detlef Köhn (tr.) (Mainz: Matthias-Grünewald-Verlag, 1989)
Darwin, Charles, The Origin of Species, 1859
De Jong, Johan Marie, "Revolution in Marxismus und Christentum" in Zur Ethik der Revolution (Stuttgart: Kreuz-Verlag, 1970)
Descartes, Rene, Discourse on Method and meditations, Laurence J. Laufleur(tr.) (New York: The Bobbs-Merrill Company, Inc.,1960)
Everywoman Ltd. (ed.), Pornography and Sexual Violence, Evidence of the Links (London: Everywoman Ltd., 1988)
Faulstich, Werner, Medientheorien: Einführung und Überblick (Göttingen: Vandenhoeck und Ruprecht, 1991)
Feng, You-Lan, A Short History of Chinese Philosophy, I. J. Chung(tr.) (Seoul, Korea: Hyung-Sul Publishing, 1981)
Fleischmann, Sabine, Daten der Welt Geschite (Niederhausen, Deutschland: Bassermann, 1992)
Fragoso, Antonio, Evangelium und Soziale Revolution (Berlin: Bruckhardhaus Verlag, 1971)
Gangloff, Tilmann P., "Die Aktivität hält sich in Grenzen, Interaktives Fernsehen: Vorteile vor allem für die Industrie", in Liebe, Tod und Lottozahlen. Fernsehen in Deutschland: Wer macht es? Was bringt es? Wie Wirkt es?, Tilmann P. Gangloff, Stephan Abarbanell (Hrsg.) (Hamburg: Gemeinschaftswerk der Evang. Publ., Abt. Verl., 1994)
Giles, Herbert A., Confucianism and its Rivals (London: Williams and Norgate, 1915)
Habermas, Jürgen, Moral Consciousness and Communicative Action (Cambridge: MIT Press, 1990)
Hadrat Mirza Tahir Ahmad (Pub.), The Holy Quran (Surrey, U.K.: Islam International Publications Ltd., 1992)
Hesse, Hermann, Demian Die Geschichte von Emil Sinclairs Jugend (Frankfurt a. M.: Suhrkamp Verlag, 1997)
Hessen, J., Lehrbuch der Philosophie, 2 bd., Wertlehre (München: Ernst Reinhardt Verlag, 1969)

Hoobler, Thomas and Dorothy, Confucianism(New York: Facts On File, 1993)
Hsü, Leonard Shihlien, The Political Philosophy of Confucianism (London: Curzon Press,1932)
Hunold, Gerfried W., "Ethik der Information, Prolegomena zu einer Kultur medialer Öffentlichkeit", in Moral in einer Kultur der Massenmedien, Werner Wolbert (Hrsg.) (Freiburg , Schweiz: Universitätverlag Freiburg Schweiz,1994)
Hunold, Gerfried W., "Identität", in Grundbegriffe der christlichen Ethik, Jean-Pierre Wils, Dietmar Mieth(ed.) (Paderborn: Ferdinand Schöningh, 1992)
Husserl, Edmund, Die Crisis der europäischen Wissenschaft und die transzendentale Phänomenologie (Hamburg: Felix Meiner Verlag, 1977)
Husserl, Edmund, Die Phänomenologische Methode, Ausgewählte Text I, Klaus Held(ed.) (Stuttgart: Philipp Reclam Jun, 1985)
Husserl, Edmund, Phänomenologie der Lebenswelt, Ausgewählte Texte II, Klaus Held(ed.) (Stuttgart: Philipp Reclam Jun, 1985)
Jens, Walter, Über die Notwendigkeit einer verfremdenden Betrachtung biblischer Texte, in "Die Theologie des 20. Jahrhunderts", Karl-Josef Kuschel, (Hrsg.) (München: Piper, 1986)
Josephus, Flavius, Geschichte des Judaeischen Krieges, Heinrich Clementz(tr.) (Leipzig: Verlag Philipp Reclam jun. Leipzig,1990)
Keenan, Kelvin L., "Advertising", in, Handbook on Mass Media in the United States: The Industry and Its Audiences, Erwin K. Thomas, Brown H. Carpenter (Ed.) (Westport, CT: Greenwood Press, 1994)
Kellner, Douglas, "Television, the Crisis of Democracy and the Persian Gulf War", in Media, Crisis and Democracy : Mass Communication and the Disruption of Social Order, Marc Raboy, Bernard Dagenais (ed.) (London: Sage Publications, 1992)
Küng, Hans, Ching, Julia, Christentum und Chinesische Religion (München: R. Piper GmbH & Co. KG, 1988)
Küng, Hans, Julia Ching, Christentum und Chinesische Religion (München: R. Piper GmbH & Co. KG, 1988)
Khakhina, Liya Nikolaevna ,Concepts of Symbiogenesis, A Historical and Critical Study of the Research of Russian Botanists (New haven: Yale University Press, 1992)
Kierkegaard, S., The Sickness unto Death, Alastair Hannay(tr.) (London: Penguin Books, 1989)
Kttje, R., Moeller B.(Hrsg.), Ökumenische Kirchen Geschichte 1, Alte Kirche und Ostkirche (München: Chr. Kaiser Verlag, 1989)
Kunst, Arnold, "Use and Misuse of Dharma" in The Concept of Duty in South Asia, Wendy Doniger O'flaherty, J.Duncan M. Derrett(ed.) (India: Vikas Publishing House Pvt Ltd.,1978)
Lange, L. David and others, Mass Media and Violence (Washington: U.S. Government Printing Office, 1969)

Larsen, Otto N. (ed.), Violence and the Mass Media (New York: Harper & Row, 1968)
Leibnitz, Gottfried Wilhelm, Theodicee (Berlin: Akademie Verlag GmbH, 1996)
Leibniz, Gottfried Wilhelm, Monadologie (Frankfurt a.M.: Insel Verlag, 1996)
Marx, K., Das Kapital, Kritik der Politischen Ökonomie, Band III: Der Gesamtprozeß der Kapitalistischen Production (Frankfurt a.M.: Verlag Ullstein GmBH, 1971)
McChesney, Robert W., Telecommunications, Mass Media, and Democracy, The Battle for the Control of U.S. Broadcasting, 1928-1935 (Oxford: Oxford University Press, 1993)
Müller, P., Kierkegaard's Works of Love, Christian Ethics and the Maieutic Ideal, Stephan & Jan Evans (tr.) (Denmark: C.A. Reitzel, 1993)
Moore, George Edward, Principia Ethica (Cambridge: Cambridge University Press, 1980)
Mungello, David E., Leibniz and Confucianism, The Search for Accord (Honolulu: The University of Hawaii, 1977)
Nietzsche, Friedrich, Also Sprach Zarathustra, (tr. Thomas Common) in Internet
Ooms, Herman, "Neo-Confucianism and the Formation of Early Tokugawa Ideology: Contours of a Problem", in Confucianism and Tokugawa Culture, Nosco, Peter(Ed.) (Princeton ,New Jersey: Princeton University Press, 1984)
Orlinsky, Harry M., Ancient Israel (London: Cornell University Press, 1971)
Plato, The Republic, Ch. VIII, (tr. Benjamin Jowett, M.A.) (New York: P.F. Collier & Son, The Colonial Press,1901)
Pogge, Thomas W., Realizing Rawls (Ithaca: Cornell University Press, 1989)
Pope Paul VI, NOSTRA AETATE, Oct. 28, 1965
Putnam, Hilary, Reason, Truth and History (Cambridge: Cambridge University Press, 1981)
Rawls, John, A Theory of Justice (Cambridge, MA: Harvard Press, 1971)
Rawls, John, Political Liberalism (New York, NY: Columbia University Press, 1993)
Sahakian, William S., Ethics: An Introduction to the Theories and Problems (New York: Barens & Noble Books, 1974)
Scheler, Max, Der Formalismus in der Ethik und die Materiale Wertethik (Bern: Franke verlag, 1974)
Scheler, Max, Die Stellung des Menschen im Kosmos (Bern: Franke Verlag, 1975)
Scheler, Max, Vom Umsturz der Werte (Bern: Franke Verlag, 1972)
Scheler, Max, Wesen und Formen der Sympathie (Bern: A. Franke AG Verlag, 1973)
Schopenhauer, Arthur, The Basis of Morality (London: Swan Sonnenschein, 1903)

Schweitzer, Albert, Kultur und Ethik (München: C.H. Beck'sche Verlads Buchhandlung, 1955)
Solomon, Robert C. (ed.), Phenomenology and Existentialism (New York: Harper & Row, Publishers, 1972)
St. Augustine, de civitate dei, from the Christian Classics Ethereal Library server at Wheaton College in Internet, last modified Sep. 16. 1996
St. Thomas Aquinas, Summa Theologica, Fathers of the English Dominican Province(tr.) in Internet
Tang, Yi-Jie, Confucianism, Buddhism, Daoism, Christianity and Chinese Culture (Peking: The University of Peking, 1991)
Tillich, Paul, The Person in a Technological Society, in Social Ethics (Marty, martin E. (Ed.)) (New York: Harper &Row, Publisher, 1968)
Tu, Wei-Ming, "Yi T'oegye's Perception of Human Nature: A preliminary Inquiry into the Four-Seven Debate in Korean Neo-Confucianism", in The Rise of Neo-Confucianism in Korea, De Bary, Wm. Theodore (ed.), (New York: Colombia University Press, 1985)
Turkle, Sherry, Leben im Netz, Identität in Zeit des Internet (Reinbek bei Hamburg: Rowolt Verlag GmbH, 1998)
Watt, Paul B., "Jiun Sonja(1718-1804): A Response to Confucianism within the Context of Buddhist Reform", in Confucianism and Tokugawa Culture, Nosco, Peter(Ed.) (Princeton ,New Jersey: Princeton University Press, 1984)
Wils, Jean-Pierre "Person und Subjektivität", in Grundbegriffe der christlichen Ethik, Jean-Pierre Wils, Dietmar Mieth(ed.) (Paderborn: Ferdinand Schöningh, 1992)
Yang, Hohn D., Confucianism and Christianity (Hong Kong: Hong Komg University Press, 1983)
Youn, Sa-Soon, "Yi T'oegye's Identification of 'To Be' and 'Ought': Yi T'oegye's Theory of Value" in The Rise of Neo-Confucianism in Korea, De Bary, Wm. Theodore (ed.), (New York: Colombia University Press, 1985)

- **Magazines and Newspapers**

Die Zeit, Feb. 19., p. 25
Weltbild, N. 14, 4. Juli 1997, (Augsburg: Weltbild GmbH, 1997), p 29
TIME, October 10. 1994, the whole copy
TIME, February 23. 1998, p 31
TIME, May 5. 1997, p 42
TIME, September 8. 1997, the whole copy
TIME, Special Issue, The New Age of Discovery, Winter 1997/98, p 99
TIME, March 9. 1998, p 40

- **Web-Sites**

abbey.apana.org.au : Website for many Catolic documents in electronic text format, edited by Australian community of St. Michael's Depot. For example, some official Catholic documents like "The Cathechism of the Council of Trent", "The Cathechism of Pope St. Pius X."
ccel.wheaton.edu : Website for the Christian Classic Ethereal Library where many classic Christian books, both for Catholic and Protestant, in electronic text format mostly from public domain, prepared by Harry Plantinga, a computer scientiest at the Wheaton College, Wheaton, Il, U.S.A. For example works of St. Thomas Aquinas, St. Athanasius, St. Augustine, St. Bernard of Clairvaux, John Bunyan, St. Teresa of Avila, John Wesley, and so on.
eng.hss.cmu.edu/marx : Many Marx's works in electronic text format, including complete "the Capital" and some joint work with Engels in the website of Humanity and Social Sciences Computing at the Carnegie Mellon University, PA, U.S.A.
mars.superlink.net/user/fsu/index.html : Many URL(Uniform Resource Locator)s for the themes of Chinese philosophy, prepared by Francisco S. Su. Information of not only Confucianism but also Taoism and other Chinese teachers can be well traced.
web.mit/edu/athena.mit.edu/activity/c/csa/www/documents/readme.htm : Some of Early Church Documents (ca. 96 - 150 AD) which are mostly epistles of the early Church Fathers like Clement, banabas, Hermas, Polycarp, Ignatius, and so on, prepared by John Brubaker & Gary Bogart.
www.bris.ac.uk/Depts/philosophy/VL/etext.html : many URLs for general philosophicla themes, maintained by Daniel Brickley at the University of Bristol, GB.
www.emory.law.edu: Website for some information about the Constitution of the U.S.A. and other legal information.
www.geocities/\.com/Athens/7084 : Voluminous documents of "The Early Church Fathers Series", prepared by Dr. Maged Nabih Kamel. From the epistles of the early Church Fathers to the documents of the Seven Ecumenical Councils of the Undivided Church are well arranged in the Microsoft Windows help text format.
www.gtu.edu/library/LibraryRef.html : Information about many different Christian denomination like American Baptist, Presbyterian, Lutheran, Methodist, Eastern Orthodox Christianity, prepared by Graduate Theological Union Library in Berkeley, CA, U.S.A.
www.internetvalley.com : website for very extensive information about the history of Internet, from ARPA of 1958 to WWW in 1991, prepared by Gregory R. Gromov with many help of other reporters of the world.
www.manasch.edu.au/cc/staff/sas/sab/www/index.htm : Many materials relat-

ed to the general Chinese philosophy and Chinese culture are prepared by Steven A. Brown.

www.nasa.org : Official website for voluminous information about the universe and the Earth, prepared by Brian Dunba and Sudha V. Chudamani.

www.OnlineBible.org : Official Website for the OnlineBible. The copyright has Timnathsearch Inc. in Winterbourne, Ontario, Canada. Various translated version of Bible, in English, French, German, Spanish, and other European languages.

www.sunnypress.edu : Website for many useful information about various Confucian schools, prepared by State University of New York, NY, U.S.A.

www.usc.edu/dept/annenberg/thomas/ngerm.html : website for some Nietzsche's collected works in English, for example, "Twilight of the Idoles", "Beyond Good and Evil" and some critical comment on his philosophy.

www.vatican.va : Official website of Vatican where many documents about the official teaching of Catholic church can be found, foremost, the whole documents of the Second Vatican Council.

- CD-ROM

TIME, Inc. Magazine Company, TIME Almanac of the 20th Century (TIME, Inc. Magazine Company, 1994)

Appendix

The Analects of Confucius

Chapter 1 Learning*	Chapter 11 Old senior
Chapter 2 Politics	Chapter 12 Yan-Yuan
Chapter 3 Dancing	Chapter 13 Zi-Lu
Chapter 4 Good city	Chapter 14 Xian
Chapter 5 Gong-Ye-Zhang	Chapter 15 Wei-Ling
Chapter 6 Yong is	Chapter 16 Ji will
Chapter 7 Describe and	Chapter 17 Yang-Huo
Chapter 8 Tai-Bai	Chapter 18 Wei-Zi
Chapter 9 Seldom said	Chapter 19 Zi-Zhang
Chapter 10 In hometown	Chapter 20 Yao

The Book of Mencius

Chapter 1 King LiangHui 1	Chapter 8 Li-Lou 2
Chapter 2 King LiangHui 2	Chapter 9 Mo-Zhang 1
Chapter 3 GongSunChou 1	Chapter 10 Mo-Zhang 2
Chapter 4 GongSunChou 2	Chapter 11 Gao-Zi 1
Chapter 5 TengWen 1	Chapter 12 Gao-Zi 2
Chapter 6 TengWen 2	Chapter 13 True Mind 1**
Chapter 7 Li-Lou 1	Chapter 14 True Mind 2**

* The title of every chapter of "The Analects of Confucius" is the same as the beginning words of it. As a matter of fact there was no official title for each chapter. Refer to the translation of James Legge: Legge, James, Confucius: Confucian Analects, The Great Learning & The Doctrine of the Mean (New York: Dover Publications, Inc., 1970)

**Only chapter 13 and 14 of "Mencius" have no main character. Refer to the translation of James Legge: Legge, James, The Works of Mencius (New York: Dover Publications, Inc., 1970)

* Remarks on the Translation of the Chinese Classics

All quoted texts from the Chinese Classics are translated by the author of this work himself.

FORUM INTERDISZIPLINÄRE ETHIK

Herausgegeben von Gerfried W. Hunold

Band 1 Jean-Pierre Wils: Verletzte Natur. Ethische Prolegomena. 1991.

Band 2 Dorothee Beckmann/Karin Istel/Michael Leipoldt/Hansjörg Reichert (Hrsg.): Humangenetik - Segen für die Menschheit oder unkalkulierbares Risiko? 1991.

Band 3 Peter Kaufmann: Gemüt und Gefühl als Komplement der Vernunft. Eine Auseinandersetzung mit der Tradition und der phänomenologischen Ethik, besonders Max Schelers. 1992.

Band 4 Gerhard Droesser: Freiheitspraxis im Prozeß. Zur geschichtsanthropologischen Grundlegung einer Theologie des Ethischen. 1992.

Band 5 Andrea Redeker: Abweichendes Verhalten und moralischer Fortschritt. Zur Steuerungsfunktion der Normkritik in der theologisch-ethischen Reflexion. 1993.

Band 6 Elke Hümmeler: Erfahrung in der genetischen Beratung. Eine theologisch-ethische Diskussion. 1993.

Band 7 Walter Schaupp: Der ethische Gehalt der Helsinki Deklaration. Eine historisch-systematische Untersuchung der Richtlinien des Weltärztebunds über biomedizinische Forschung am Menschen. 1994.

Band 8 Alfons V. Maurer: Homo Agens. Handlungstheoretische Untersuchungen zum theologisch-ethischen Verständnis des Sittlichen. 1994.

Band 9 Berthold Saup: Zur Freiheit berufen. Zur Dimension des Ethischen im Marchtaler Plan. 1994.

Band 10 Dorothee Beckmann: Hippokratisches Ethos und ärztliche Verantwortung. Zur Genese eines anthropologischen Selbstverständnisses griechischer Heilkunst im Spannungsfeld zwischen ärztlichem Können und moralischer Wahrnehmung. 1995.

Band 11 Gerfried W. Hunold / Dorothee Beckmann (Hrsg.): Grenzbegehungen. Interdisziplinarität als Wissenschaftsethos. 1995.

Band 12 Helga Willinger: Ethische und rechtliche Aspekte der ärztlichen Aufklärungspflicht. 1996.

Band 13 Wilfried Lochbühler: Christliche Umweltethik. Schöpfungstheologische Grundlagen · Philosophisch-ethische Ansätze · Ökologische Marktwirtschaft. 1996.

Band 14 Anton Georg Schuster: Finaler Rettungsschuß. Theologisch-ethische Untersuchung zum finalen Rettungsschuß als lex specialis. 1996.

Band 15 Gerhard Bachleitner: Die mediale Revolution. Anthropologische Überlegungen zu einer Ethik der Kommunikationstechnik. 1997.

Band 16 Gerhard Gansterer: Die *Ehrfurcht vor dem Leben*. Die Rolle des ethischen Schlüsselbegriffs Albert Schweitzers in der theologisch-ökologischen Diskussion. 1997.

Band 17 Elmar Kos: Verständigung oder Vermittlung? Die kommunikative Ambivalenz als Zugangsweg einer theologischen Medienethik. 1997.

Band 18 Manfred Waltl: Eigennutz und Eigenwohl. Ein Beitrag zur Diskussion zwischen Soziobiologie und theologischer Ethik. 1997.

Band 19 Jürgen in der Schmitten: Die Entscheidung zur Herz-Lungen-Wiederbelebung. Studie im deutsch-amerikanischen Vergleich. 1998.

Band 20 Gunter M. Prüller-Jagenteufel: Solidarität – eine Option für die Opfer. Geschichtliche Entwicklung und aktuelle Bedeutung einer christlichen Tugend anhand der katholischen Sozialdokumente. 1998.

Band 21 Michael Pindl: Versöhnung mit dem Leiden. Leidfreiheitsideologie und Gewalt gegen behinderte Menschen aus der Sicht eines im christlich-buddhistischen Dialog gründenden Ethos. 1998.

Band 22 Wolfram Winger: Personalität durch Humanität. Das ethikgeschichtliche Profil christlicher Handlungslehre bei Lactanz. Denkhorizont – Textübersetzung – Interpretation – Wirkungsgeschichte. 1999.

Band 23 Christa Schnabl: Das Moralische im Politischen. Hannah Arendts Theorie des Handelns im Horizont der theologischen Ethik. 1999.

Band 24 Thomas Laubach: Lebensführung. Annäherungen an einen ethischen Grundbegriff. 1999.

Band 25 Manfred Maßhof-Fischer: Ethik und Vorurteil. Moralpsychologische Studien zu den Legitimationsstrategien soziokulturellen Handelns im Konfliktfeld von Mythos und Rationalität. 2000.

Band 26 Simon Kofi Appiah: Africanness – Inculturation – Ethics. In Search of the Subject of an Inculturated Christian Ethic. 2000.

Band 27 Jong Bom Lee: Intercultural Ethos Mediation with the Mass Media. Sympathy as the Means for the Mediation of the Christian Ethos in the Modern Confucian Society. 2001.

David C. Ratke (Hrsg./ed.)

Theologie zu Beginn des 3. Jahrtausends im globalen Kontext – Rückblick und Perspektiven / Theology at the Beginning of the 3rd Millennium in a Global Context – Retrospect and Perspectives

Anläßlich des 60. Geburtstags von Hans Schwarz
On the Occasion of the 60th Birthday of Hans Schwarz

Frankfurt/M., Berlin, Bern, Bruxelles, New York, Wien, 2000. 340 S.
ISBN 3-631-35922-5 · br. DM 89.–*

23 Theologen aus zwölf verschiedenen Ländern und fünf Kontinenten waren zu einem einwöchigen Symposion an der Universität Regensburg und dem Missionskolleg der Evangelisch-Lutherischen Kirche in Bayern in Neuendettelsau versammelt, um über die Aufgabe der Theologie zu Beginn des 3. Jahrtausends nachzudenken. Säkularisation und die Zukunft der Kirche, das Theodizee-Problem, die Spannung zwischen Kontextualität und Katholizität sowie das Verhältnis zwischen Theologie und Naturwissenschaft sind nur einige der Themenbereiche, die hier bearbeitet wurden. Die Themen reflektieren auch die Arbeitsgebiete des Regensburger Systematikers Hans Schwarz, zu dessen 60. Geburtstag dieses Symposion veranstaltet wurde. Eine Bibliographie seiner wissenschaftlichen Veröffentlichungen rundet diesen Band ab, der Kirche und Theologie sowie Kirche und Weltverantwortung an der Schwelle zum 3. Jahrtausend im Rückblick und Ausblick thematisiert.

Papers of 23 theologians from 12 different countries and 5 continents evoke a global context in which the contributors reflect on the challenges for theology and the church at the beginning of the new millennium. The papers, many of them in English, resulted from a week-long symposion at the University of Regensburg honoring Hans Schwarz on his 60th birthday. A bibliography of his works concludes the volume.

Frankfurt/M · Berlin · Bern · Bruxelles · New York · Oxford · Wien
Auslieferung: Verlag Peter Lang AG
Jupiterstr. 15, CH-3000 Bern 15
Telefax (004131) 9402131
*inklusive Mehrwertsteuer
Preisänderungen vorbehalten